PHYSICIANS AND THE LAW

The Intersection of Medicine, Business, and Medical Malpractice

TIMOTHY E. PATERICK, MD, JD, MBA

American Association for PHYSICIAN LEADERSHIP

978-0-9848311-3-5 Print
978-0-9848311-4-2 Ebook
Published by **American Association for Physician Leadership, Inc.**
PO Box 96503 | BMB 97493 | Washington, DC 20090-6503

Website: www.physicianleaders.org

13 8 7 6 5 4 3 2 1

Copyedited, typeset, indexed, and printed in the United States of America

PUBLISHER
Nancy Collins

EDITORIAL ASSISTANT
Jennifer Weiss

DESIGN & LAYOUT
Carter Publishing Studio

COPYEDITOR
Pat George

Table of Contents

For Jamil Tajik, MD—

ultimate friend, scholar, teacher and mentor.

About the Author

Timothy E. Paterick MD, JD, MBA, and Master's in Physician Leadership and Management, is a cardiologist with a passion for preventive health measures, sports medicine, the law, and teaching residents and fellows medicine. While practicing full-time cardiology Paterick has written over one hundred peer reviewed articles in medical literature, has been an invited speaker across the country on medical and legal issues, and has authored three other books: *Invest in Yourself: A Cardiologist's Narrative for Heart Health*, *Health through Hope: Look in People's Eyes*, and *Physician: Time to Invest in Yourself—Work-Life Balance, the Needs of the Patient, and Medical-Legal Risk Management.*

His continued study of medicine, law, business, and leadership/management has led to an understanding of how they intersect and impact practicing physicians.

Dr. Paterick played college basketball at the University of Wisconsin – Madison on scholarship. He then graduated from Rush medical school in Chicago, Illinois. After medical school he trained in internal medicine and cardiology at the Mayo Clinic in Rochester, Minnesota.

Dr. Paterick is a lifelong scholar-athlete. He was named first team All State in high school and to the top 24 high school basketball players in America his senior year in high school. At the University of Wisconsin, he was awarded the Ivy Williamson award for outstanding achievement in athletics and academics. After completing medical education at Rush Medical College and his medical training at the Mayo Clinic, Dr. Paterick completed his law degree at the University of Wisconsin followed by his

MBA at Edgewood College. He also completed a master's degree from UT – Southwestern in Physician Leadership and Management.

Dr. Paterick's passion is teaching medical residents, physician assistants, nurse practitioners and cardiology fellows and young basketball players. Many medical residents and cardiology fellows have achieved high levels of clinical expertise through his teaching and mentorship. Both his sons, having played Division 1 college basketball, exemplify his basketball-teaching prowess. They are highly successful professionals reifying his teaching/mentoring abilities. He attributes any success he has experienced in life to his wife and life-long best friend, Barb. Dr. Paterick can be reached at tpaterick@gmail.com

An Introduction to Medical Malpractice in the United States

Medical malpractice is any act or omission by a physician during treatment of a patient that diverges from accepted norms of practice in the medical community and causes an injury to the patient. Medical malpractice is a specific subset of tort law—a body of law that provides remedies for civil wrongs—that deals with professional negligence. Negligence is defined generally as conduct that falls short of a standard; the most common standard in tort law is the reasonable person standard, which is the standard of reasoned conduct that a person in similar circumstances would do, or not do, in order to protect another person from a foreseeable risk of harm. Physicians practicing in the United States generally carry medical malpractice insurance to protect themselves in case of charges of medical negligence and unintentional injury; it is often a requirement for hospital privileges and employment with a medical practice.

To win monetary reparation for injury related to medical negligence, a patient needs to prove that substandard medical care resulted in injury. The allegation of medical negligence must be filed within a state-prescribed time period called the statute of limitations. If the injured patient successfully establishes that negligence led to injury, the court determines the monetary amount that will be paid to the patient in compensation for the injury. Damages take into account actual economic losses, such as lost income and cost of future medical care, as well as noneconomic losses such as pain and suffering.

One exception to medical liability can arise in the context of those who volunteer assistance to others who are injured or ill. This exception is expressed in the Good Samaritan laws. The Good Samaritan exception is to address the bystander fear of being sued for unintentional injury or death. In the United States, Good Samaritan laws vary from jurisdiction to jurisdiction and specify who is protected from liability. The Good Samaritan statutes do not require the bystander to provide aid to a victim. Vermont and Minnesota specify a reasonable duty to provide assistance to an injured person at the scene of an emergency. Calling 911 for assistance can satisfy assistance.

Although not uniform, the Good Samaritan provisions have some general underpinning supporting rational and reasonable behaviors. The principle of "eminent peril" may affect the scope of the laws.

- When there is no peril and the bystander causes injury, the court may hold the actor accountable.
- Once the bystander renders care, they must not leave the scene unless another rescuer takes over.
- Consent in emergent situations is implied.

Good Samaritan laws generally immunize the responder from legal liability as long as the responder acts in good faith, according to her level of training, and in a rational and reasonable manner.

MEDICAL MALPRACTICE AND THE U.S. COURT SYSTEM

Current medical malpractice law has its origins in 19th century English common law. Common law is developed through decisions of courts and judges, as opposed to law developed through legislative statutes or executive decisions.

In the United States, the framework and rules that govern medical malpractice law are established through decisions of lawsuits filed in state courts. Thus, state laws govern medical malpractice and can vary across jurisdictions.

All states have trial courts, where civil disputes are filed and litigated, trailed by a system of appeals courts, with the final authority resting with the state supreme court. The home residence of the parties involved and the location of the alleged misconduct, which is referred to as the venue, guide the location of the trial court for a case. Cases filed in the wrong court can be dismissed for lack of venue. State trial courts have jurisdiction over medical malpractice cases, meaning they have the legal authority to hear and decide the case.

Legal rules guide venue and jurisdiction in each state. If the malpractice claim involves the federal government acting through a federally funded clinic or a Veteran's Administration facility, then the action is filed in a federal district court. Each state has at least one federal court. Federal courts have jurisdiction when there is complete diversity of state citizenship, or if a federal question is invoked during the alleged negligent conduct.

The United States Constitution affords every citizen the right to a jury trial. A jury trial is a legal proceeding during which a group of individuals chosen from the public are asked to consider the evidence presented during a case and make a judgment about the validly of the alleged negligence. The choice of jurors is guided by court rules and with the participation of the attorney from each side. There can be striking of jurors if there is a question of impartiality. In contrast to a jury trial, a bench trail is one in which a judge or panel of judges makes the ultimate decision. In the United States, physicians can expect a jury trial in all cases of medical malpractice.

Under special circumstances, a medical malpractice case may be filed in a federal court if the question is of a federal nature, the parties live in different states, or there is a federal constitutional issue. U.S. district courts have a judge and a jury panel that hears the case. The substantive law applied by federal courts to resolve legal disputes is derived from the state in which the district court is located. Thus, if a medical malpractice case is tried in federal court, state malpractice law still applies, with federal procedure rules of jurisprudence guiding the litigation process.

THE LEGAL SYSTEM OF THE UNITED STATES

The system of law governing the resolution of civil disputes between parties in the United States is referred to as the adversarial system, where respective advocates for each side in a dispute skillfully present arguments before an impartial jury or judge. The adversarial system is used in common law countries to resolve disputes related to negligent medical conduct.

The aggrieved patient who initiates the lawsuit before the court is called a plaintiff or complainant. The plaintiff is seeking a legal remedy from the court. If the plaintiff is successful, the court enters judgment for the plaintiff and issues a court order for damages. The party against whom the complaint is directed is the defendant. In medical malpractice cases, the defendant is a physician or the professional organization that employs the physician.

In the United States, a medical malpractice lawsuit begins with the filing of a summons, claim form, or complaint, which is called a pleading. The pleading sets forth the alleged negligence committed by the defendant physician with a demand for relief. In some jurisdictions, the legal action begins with physical delivery of documents on the defendant by a process server. These documents are then filed with the court accompanied by an affidavit verifying that they have been given to the defendant physician according to certain rules of legal procedure.

LEGAL ELEMENTS OF MEDICAL MALPRACTICE

In the United States, the patient alleging medical malpractice must prove four elements to successfully claim negligence:

1. The existence of a legal duty to provide care/treatment to the patient.
2. A breach of this duty by failure to adhere to the standard of care of the medical profession.
3. A causal relationship between the breach of duty and the injury to the patient.
4. The existence of damages that flow from the injury allowing the legal system to provide remedy.

The existence of a legal duty comes into play when a professional relationship is established between the patient and the physician. The existence of a relationship between the patient and the physician is critical to establishing a legal duty. The physician is said to owe a duty of reasonable professional medical care to the patient. The physician assumes this duty the minute he or she undertakes the care of the patient. A duty does not exist without an established relationship. Covering call and providing emergency services assumes a duty of reasonable care.

A breach of the standard of care is irrelevant legally unless the injured plaintiff shows a direct relationship between the alleged misconduct and the subsequent injury. The breach of the duty by the physician must be the proximate cause of the injury.

The final element of an accusation of negligence is damages. Absent a showing of damages, a plaintiff cannot maintain a cause of action for medical negligence. Courts determine monetary damages based on an attempt to make the patient whole. Punitive damages are rare in medical malpractice cases and are earmarked for egregious actions.

THE PROCESS OF TRIAL

Because the legal system promotes efficient self-resolution of civil disputes, medical malpractice cases and civil litigation in general seldom come to trial. Several legal processes have been developed to promote self-resolution, the most vital of which is the process of discovery.

Discovery is a lengthy period of information sharing among the parties after the filing of the lawsuit and prior to the trial with the goal of developing a factual understanding between the adversarial parties. The discovery process includes requests for all documents, interrogatories, and depositions. Documents include medical records, clinic notes, and billing information. Interrogatories are forms submitted by attorneys to the opposing party to gather demographic and preliminary information about the other party.

A deposition is a witness testimony that is given under oath, and recorded for use in court at a future date. The rationale is that by requiring disputing parties to exchange facts and underlying information, such as respective expert testimony, the parties can reach mutual understanding and settle the case. Absent settlement, information obtained during discovery is presented during trial.

For most physicians, the deposition is an intense encounter with the legal system. In the United States, the Federal Rules of Civil Procedure and their corresponding state equivalents govern the taking of testimony by deposition. The patient's attorney files notice with the attorney defending the physician that a deposition is needed. All parties agree upon a time and place.

The attorneys and a representative of the insurance company that has issued the malpractice coverage on behalf of the physician typically attend depositions for both parties.

A deposition begins with a court reporter administering the oath that the party being deposed would take if the testimony were taken in court. The attorney who ordered the deposition questions the deposed party, then the attorney for the other party may cross-examine. There may be a redirect followed by a re-cross until all parties have exhausted their questions. A written record of the testimony is available to all parties in the litigation.

Deposition testimony is significant in that it can be used to impeach or contradict the physician's later testimony in open court. Consequently, thorough preparation for deposition is essential, including researching records before delivering testimony. Experienced lawyers conduct a mock deposition to ensure the physician is comfortable with the process. The deposition is a permanent record under oath, so honesty is essential.

At trial, the plaintiff's attorney has the burden of proving every element of the case by presenting information amassed during pretrial discovery. The plaintiff's attorney must convince the jury that more likely than not, the physician was negligent.

The physician's attorney offers defenses to negate the evidence presented by the aggrieved plaintiff. The *more likely than not* legal standard required in medical malpractice litigation is called the preponderance of the evidence standard. The preponderance of the evidence means an impartial jury, after hearing and considering all the evidence discovered by the parties, will find a greater than 50% probability that professional negligence did occur and return a verdict against the physician.

The process of attorney selection in medical malpractice litigation is different for plaintiffs and defendants. In the United States, the patient hires his or her attorney; the attorney collects legal fees only if a monetary damage is awarded to the patient. This practice discourages medical malpractice lawsuits and unscrupulous advocacy on behalf of the patient.

The medical malpractice insurance company appoints defense attorneys on behalf of the physician and pays the legal fees. Physicians may hire, at their own expense, personal counsel for additional insight and guidance.

Many lawsuits are settled out of court, with terms agreed upon by both parties and payment of monies by the insurance company. The insurance company generally allows physicians to have input into the settlement decision, often giving the physician the authority whether to settle or proceed with litigating the claim. Some professional liability policies do not allow for physician input.

The process of legal discovery and negotiations between parties usually occurs over many months to several years and the plaintiff's attorney must fund the proceedings, including court costs, attorney time and work product, and fees for expert testimony. Preparation and prosecution of a medical negligence lawsuit can cost as much as $100,000; this amount reflects the risk the plaintiff's attorney assumes in return for the probability of settlement or a favorable verdict.

The losing party can apply for a new trial or appeal the judgment to the next higher level of court. Appeals courts exist in every state and in the federal system for this purpose. The legal system is very deferential to the finality of a jury trial; successful legal appeals usually concern a specific point of law or procedural issue that may have misapplied during the jury trial.

Monetary payments are typically reported to the National Practitioner Data Bank and to state medical licensing boards and medical societies. This reporting, which is related to ensuring quality of care, may impact physician reputation and ability to practice medicine.

TORT REFORM MOVEMENT

The present state of medical malpractice litigation has led to a tort reform movement such that many states have adopted a variety of administrative and legislative measures to curb the growing volume of malpractice actions. The measures include reducing damage awards, limiting contingency fees, limiting the time between alleged injuries and filing a lawsuit, allowing future damage awards to be paid in installments, and limiting damage awards in general.

Alternatives to the strict tort liability system have been considered, including changing the trial and jury system to less-formal processes involving professional decision makers. The goal of alternative dispute resolution is to reduce costs, expedite the handling of negligence claims, eliminate profligate juries, and screen out cases without merit. Some propose changing to enterprise liability. This eliminates physician liability and shifts responsibility for physician liability to the healthcare organization that employees the physician.

A system that addresses patient injuries in a fair, equitable, timely, and economically just manner is necessary. Even physicians who win a jury verdict lose in terms of personal stress, cognitive friction, and time taken away from work, family, and friends.

SECTION 1

The New Business Model of Medicine

CHAPTER 1

The Chaotic Work World of Physicians

Physicians are immersed in a work environment where daily challenges seem to represent a place of increasing disorder and confusion. The degree of "entropy" in the physician workplace is increasing exponentially. Healthcare systems are in a state of chaos and are dynamic, meaning the behavior at one time influences its behavior in the future. The initial changes have future exponential fluctuations that have created a state of healthcare crisis.

These systems are nonlinear; the metaphor to describe the unruly nature of the physician work world is that in which the flap of a butterfly wing in Brazil can set off a tornado in Texas. The tornado affecting physician work life needs be understood to be rectified. Physicians must slow down and pay attention.

Physicians live in digital time. Their rhythms are rushed, rapid fire, and relentless, with their days carved into bits and bytes. Physicians celebrate breadth rather than depth, quick reactions rather than considered reflections. Physician actions and activities often skim across the surface, lighting for brief moments at multiple destinations. They race from patient to procedure without pausing to consider the impact of their chaotic pace. They are wired up, but melting down physically and emotionally.

Most physicians are just trying to do the best they can in situations where they are seeing too many patients in too little time and attempting to meet RVU goals to maintain their salaries. When demand exceeds capacity, they make expedient choices that get them through the day, but they pay an emotional and physical toll over time. The toll manifests itself in suboptimal clinical decisions that run the risk of negligence, too little sleep, too little exercise, and a regimen of fast food consumed on the run, coffee to fuel up, and sleeping pills to cool down.

Physicians often return home from the fast and furious pace of work feeling exhausted, experiencing their families not as a source of joy, but as another demand in an already overburdened life. Physicians are immersed in smartphones with daily planners and to-do lists, pagers, e-mails, phone messages, and pop-up reminders on the computer—all designed to help them manage their time more efficiently and be more productive for the organization. They take pride in their ability to multitask and work long hours—a skill that the corporate systems clearly view as a badge of honor.

The 24/7 schedules describe a world where work never ends. Physicians have been indoctrinated to believe that words like *obsessed, crazed,* and *overwhelmed* describe their everyday life rather than an insane existence. Physicians, constantly feeling stressed for time, assume they have no choice but to cram as much as possible into every day in order to survive.

CHAOS THEORY

Why are physicians living in a state of chaos? In the book *The Signal and the Noise: Why So Many Predictions Fail—But Some Don't* (Penguin Group, 2012), Nate Silver examines chaos theory across many domains to help explain the impact of small changes in a dynamic system. The application of chaos theory to the healthcare model can give us insight into the reasons healthcare delivery is failing and why physicians are burning out.

Chaos theory applies to systems in which two properties exist: (1) the system is dynamic, meaning the behavior at one point in time influences behavior in the future; and (2) the system is nonlinear, meaning change results in exponential rather than additive relationship—akin to the stock market. The intersection of a dynamic system with exponential change can result in a real mess, such as today's healthcare delivery system.

The most basic tenet of chaos theory is that small changes in initial conditions produce large and unexpected divergence in outcomes. These changes are not random, despite the use of the word "chaos" or a recitation of Murphy's Law. It is a reflection that certain outcomes of "system change" are hard to predict. The problem begins with the inevitable inaccuracies in our assumptions.

An example will clarify. Assume we are adding 5 + 5, but we erroneously key in 6 for the second entry. We have an outcome of 11 rather than 10. We are wrong, but not by much—because addition is a linear function that is forgiving.

However, in dynamic systems such as healthcare, exponential functions extract significant punishment when there are inaccuracies in our assumptions. If instead of calculating 5^5 (3,125), we use 5^6 (15,625), we have missed our end point by 500%! This inaccuracy explodes if the system is dynamic, and this output feeds into the next input algorithm. Thus our small initial mistake results in a growing, larger mistake.

Does Chaos Theory Apply to Humans?

Human beings are the epitome of a dynamic system, with nonlinear behaviors that are highly vulnerable to inaccurate predictions. In scientific studies results frequently cannot be replicated. This reinforces the notion that our predictive models are flawed. Why? Because the smaller the study the less likely the research findings are to be true, the smaller the effects the less likely the research findings are to be true, and the greater the financial benefits, the less likely research findings are to be true.

We must return to the paradigm of considering new insights null and void without compelling evidence. Add to this the fact that with the introduction of the Internet, the world is exploding with new information. The quantity of information is increasing by 2.5 quintillion bytes per day; however, the amount of useful information in this exploding data set is unknown. Most of this information is noise, and the noise is increasing faster than the truth. There are so many hypotheses to test, so much data to mine, but a relatively small amount of meaningful, useful information.

Complex systems like the World Wide Web can reproduce a mistake many times over. It may not fail as many times as a simple system, but when it fails, the result has exponential impact. The fact that this incredible, rapid, and efficient information machine has the potential to spread bad ideas and bad information should cause us to pause and reflect on what information we are putting into our models, because we have so much noise we cannot identify the objective truths we need to create accurate prediction models.

THE POWER TO PREDICT

The illusions of validity and skill are supported by a powerful professional culture. People can maintain an unshakeable faith in any proposition, however absurd, when a community of like-minded believers sustains them. Given the professional culture of the medical community, it is not surprising that a great many individuals in the world believe themselves to be the chosen few who can lead the rest.

The idea that the future is unpredictable is undermined every day by the ease with which we explain the past. As Nassim Taleb points out in *The Black Swan* (Random House, 2007), our tendency to construct and believe coherent narratives of the past makes it difficult for us to accept the limits of our forecasting ability. Everything makes sense in hindsight. The illusion that we understand the past fosters overconfidence in our ability to predict the future.

Because we are influenced by stories, we must remember they represent individual, anecdotal events that may make a significant impression on us, but may not represent the experience of the population. Statistics can help put anecdotal messages into a broader context. Understanding statistics about the risks and benefits of treatment is called *health literacy*—it allows one to grasp the scientific data and make a more considered choice than if using accounts in isolation.

We all are familiar with a well-marketed narrative by the drug companies about the impact of high cholesterol on our health. A common notion is that taking a statin will reduce your risk of a heart attack by 30% over the next 10 years. Why, then, would anyone *not* take a statin? Let's look into the facts.

An existing algorithm allows the calculation of your risk for a heart attack over 10 years. This algorithm considers age, sex, total cholesterol, high-density lipoprotein cholesterol, blood pressure, smoking status, family history, and medications. Let's assume the risk identified is 1%. This means one of 100 people with this risk will have a heart attack over the next 10 years.

So what does it mean that a statin will reduce one's risk of a heart attack by 30% over the next 10 years? Let's become statistically literate. Your 1% risk means you have a one in 100 chance of a heart attack. This implies three of the 300 will have a heart attack. The statin treatment reduces the risk by 30%. The 300 patients with a 1% risk would suggest three heart attacks without statin treatment. Thus, treating all 300 patients would prevent one heart attack (one-third of three). The other two patients would have a heart attack despite taking the statin. The remaining 297 patients would not have a heart attack without the medication, but would incur the expense and the risk of side effects.

Therefore, 300 represents the number of patients needed to treat in order to help one person. This is referred to as the number needed to treat (NNT). The same data can be framed in a positive narrative—a statin will reduce the chances of a heart attack by 30%—or in a negative narrative—it would be necessary to treat 300 patients to help one person.

The amount of money spent on drug advertising is clearly an attempt to ingrain a positive narrative into the public's neuronal networks. Physicians often refuse to use predictive models to obtain better clinical approaches to complex medical problems. Instead, they may hang onto illusions (heuristics) without applying all the available information.

A distinct lack of statistical literacy is applied to clinical scenarios. Bayes' theorem is a mathematical formula for determining conditional probability. That is, it tells us the probability that a hypothesis is true if some event has occurred. This simple formula can lead to major predictive insights that overwhelm the illusion of reflexive thinking, often referred to as automatic type 1 thinking.

In its most basic form, it is an algebraic expression with three known variables and one unknown variable. Let's give it some teeth by looking at a simple model: that of breast cancer among women in their 40s:

- The chance a woman in her 40s will develop breast cancer is 1.4% (14/1,000).
- What is the probability if she has a positive mammogram? A mammogram will be a false positive about 10% of the time.
- If breast cancer is present, the mammogram detects it 75% of the time.

Using these statistics, the physician has an illusion of very sad news. But if you apply Bayes' theorem to these statistics, you come to a different conclusion: The chance that a woman in her 40s with a positive mammogram has breast cancer is 10%. The false positives dominate the calculation because the prevalence is 1.4%. Testing predictive models must be applied to get past unproven narratives and illusions, as the breast cancer example demonstrates.

The business medical models and evolving technology and marketing have overtaken the critical thought necessary to make considered medical decisions. Let's consider a clinical scenario that substantiates the impact of technology on medical decision-making.

A 50-year-old lean, active attorney came to the office for a second opinion. After seeing an advertisement, his wife had given him a computed tomographic scan of his heart for his 49th birthday. The scan showed a high calcium score, and the rollercoaster ride began.

At the initial consultation, the patient reported being fatigued, had muscle aches that prevented any exercise, was unable to sustain an erection, was depressed, and was fearful a stent would "clot off." Without stress testing and in a setting of no symptoms, the attorney underwent an angiogram, and four stents were subsequently placed. He had been working out on an elliptical for 45 minutes five days per week. He was started on a drug regimen including a statin, a beta-blocker, aspirin, and clopidogrel.

This problem of inappropriate use or overuse of medical procedures is rampant as physicians, hospitals, and the device industry all become aligned and incentivized to continue. This example reflects the complexity of too much information without an ability by the consumer to use statistical literacy to make considered decisions; this was a wife responding to an advertisement and a physician practicing in chaos.

WHY ARE PHYSICIANS PRACTICING IN CHAOS?

The models and paradigms that have been forced upon physicians were never adequately tested, and the exponential fluctuations that have occurred in healthcare as a result of these changes have resulted in a healthcare crisis for society. The physician workplace is dynamic and nonlinear. There have been constant perturbations in physicians' work lives during the last 40 years, including managed care models, employee status, and business models of medicine run by corporate teams; changing reimbursement brought on by Obamacare; changing care paradigms with nurse practitioners and physician assistants; electronic medical records; mandated schedules; and RVU expectations, to mention a few.

The newest disruption is the planned introduction of ICD-10 into the reporting world of physicians. This new code set increases the number of reporting codes from about 13,600 to 69,000, and it represents a dramatic increase in reporting detail and granularity. This increasing complexity in coding has the potential to cause an exponential increase in errors and loss of physician time to do the physician work of patient interaction and care.

No true hypothesis testing was performed to identify whether any of these "small" changes with exponential effects would improve patient care. These alterations have led to physicians running on a "hedonic treadmill" (*i.e.*, as physicians do more, expectations increase, and there is no gain in satisfaction), resulting in physician anger, fear, anxiety, resentfulness, depression, exhaustion, and hopelessness.

This constellation of emotional and physical findings does not allow for optimum patient care. We have a crisis in healthcare. Patients are at risk, and ultimately we all become patients. The answer to complex problems is simplification—distillation to essential components that are manageable and predictable.

IDENTIFYING SOLUTIONS

First, physicians must become aware that they are living in chaos. They must jump off the hedonic treadmill and attempt to understand why and how they arrived at this point of frenzy and chaos. This requires understanding that the dynamic medical systems in the new business model of medicine are nonlinear and are running out of control.

Physicians currently are assuming more risk for less financial remuneration. They must be proactive and unite to protect their patients and their own professionalism. Just as the baseball team cannot play without the players, the healthcare system cannot function without physicians. Physicians must work together to negotiate for healthcare models that allow for in-depth medical decision-making that permits considered reflection when building a paradigm of healthcare and when treating patients.

The present-day chaos is killing physicians and patients. The future of our society's health depends on concerted efforts by physicians to ensure patient-centered models. The exponential ramifications of untested changes in the delivery of healthcare must be stopped. We need proactive physicians who blaze the trail to recovery of our healthcare system. Simplification will require fewer players and simpler models that prioritize patient care. We have wandered a long way down a misguided path of medical care with layers of confusing bureaucracy. It is not simple to reverse the course. Physicians must return to a model of interacting with a patient in a fiduciary relationship.

CHAPTER 2

The Healthcare Crisis: Competition Is the Problem and the Solution

When judged by any responsible national or international criteria, the U.S. healthcare system has reached the point of crisis. Serious issues exist regarding access, quality, and costs of our present system. Previous reform efforts have not been successful in addressing these concerns. A true market-driven, comprehensive healthcare system incorporating appropriate elements of competition with respect to pricing and the quality of services, along with the availability of accurate, transparent, data-supported information, would offer a higher probability of success in dealing with the causes of our healthcare crisis than would a government-run, single-payor system.

As the 21st century began, healthcare dropped down significantly in the list of national priorities. The focus increasingly was on the economic uncertainties of a post-1990s dotcom bubble, the horror of 9/11, the threat of global terrorism, and the wars in Iraq and Afghanistan. Despite the lack of public attention, a national healthcare crisis was brewing. The ongoing coronavirus pandemic highlighted how unprepared our healthcare systems were to face adversity.

ANATOMY OF A CRISIS

Medical costs have skyrocketed, making ever-increasing claims on the nation's resources. In 1970, healthcare spending totaled 7% of the gross domestic product (GDP). By 2007, these costs had risen to approximately 15.2% of the GDP, giving the United States the dubious distinction of being firmly at the top of this list for first-world countries. Switzerland, Germany, and France followed at 10%–11%; Canada, Australia, the

Netherlands, and Sweden had spending in the 9% range; costs in Finland, Japan, and the UK measured at 7%–8% of the GDP.

Projections suggest in the absence of comprehensive reform that by 2020, healthcare spending will consume 21% of the GDP. In 2019 it was 17.7%. For workers and employers currently participating in health insurance programs, in some cases health insurance premiums have been rising four times faster than wages. Together with the recent sharp economic downturn, the trend suggests that an increasing number of employers will no longer continue to offer health insurance, and employees retaining their jobs will not be able to afford the rising costs. Consequently, many middle class Americans are "going naked" in insurance industry parlance. Roughly one in three of the 46 million uninsured Americans earn more than $50,000 per year.

Healthcare inflation has become a primary issue in labor negotiations, workers' compensation, and pension programs, and jeopardizes our nation's ability to compete in a global economy. U.S. healthcare costs now exceed $2 trillion per year. An ever-increasing aging population is accelerating the explosion in Medicare and Medicaid costs at the state and federal levels; these costs are overtaking public education as the most expensive line item in virtually every state budget. In spite of a widespread belief for many years that fundamental reform of the healthcare system was necessary, this reform has not occurred.

FACTORS INFLUENCING HEALTHCARE REFORM

Many factors shape and influence the discussions regarding healthcare and its reform. Culture, social customs, personal experiences with the healthcare system, personal and overall economic circumstances, political posturing, existing laws and regulations, and enormously powerful interest groups are all influential factors. In addition, more than 800 different organizations are registered as healthcare lobbyists in Washington, D.C., each with its own uncompromising, often single-issue position(s) on healthcare issues and goals.

Another important factor influencing the debate on healthcare reform is how the issues are framed. Not surprisingly, politicians prefer to identify the primary issue as one of "access," as expressed in numbers of people with or without access. The central themes of their recommendations for reform target providing access to healthcare for the uninsured and dealing with the burdens of rising and high costs for employers, their employees, and especially vulnerable groups such as children and older Americans.

Providing universal access is an important goal, but if not implemented in conjunction with a reform model that provides the fundamental changes needed to sustain quality and control costs, it could seriously exacerbate the existing crisis.

Today's healthcare issues are similar to those faced by the Clinton administration in the early 1990s: rising healthcare costs and increasing numbers of uninsured people. Congressman Newt Gingrich led the opposition to the Clinton-style healthcare reform, stating in a February 1995 issue of *Forbes* magazine, "One of the challenges I have made to doctors is I said, you're either going to Canada or to Wal-Mart. You can go to a nationally controlled bureaucratic structure or you can go to the marketplace. But you are not going to stay in the 'gilded status' where you have all the knowledge and you share none of it."

Gingrich's Canada represents a big government-run system. The Wal-Mart reference symbolized a healthcare system run by private enterprise, based on a competitive market for goods and services. Like many observers of the current healthcare system, Gingrich had concluded that our current hybrid system of both, using a combination of government-funded (Medicare and Medicaid) and employer- and privately funded (insurance) care would not successfully improve value by improving quality and controlling cost.

The conclusion seemed to be that the United States must opt for either a government-run, single-payor system or a market-based private system.

OUTCOMES OF PAST HEALTHCARE REFORM EFFORTS

Health Insurance Evolves

An insurance model is optimal when people face unequal risk, such as the varying potential for illness. Actuarial tables can be constructed and the risk spread by pooling per-capita *contributions* of large numbers of consumers. A percentage of the pool will become ill and have high medical expenses. Most, however, will stay healthy and generate nominal expenses for the system. Insurance thus becomes the intuitively "best" model when it can be marketed efficiently.

In the United States, employer-sponsored healthcare programs have covered a large percentage of the working population since the wage control laws passed during World War II. A legislative tax subsidy was granted under the Internal Revenue Code of 1954. Tax-deduction dollars are disbursed by an employer's allowing employees to be insured (usually full-time employees only). Benefits have always varied substantially from one employer to the next.

Over time, U.S. society has weighed the desirability of completing the New Deal vision of "social" (*e.g.*, healthcare) insurance for all. Toward this end, Medicare and Medicaid were enacted in 1965. More recently, the Bush administration added a subsidized prescription drug benefit. A number of states also guarantee health insurance coverage for children. Nothing further has been done to take the United States toward a Canadian-style, government-run healthcare model, although many believe Obama Care is taking us in that direction.

1993 Clinton Plan

The last effort to craft and successfully legislate comprehensive healthcare reform at the federal level occurred early in the Clinton administration. This unsuccessful effort clearly illustrates a number of the difficulties in the implementation of reform.

The 1993 Clinton-era plan was essentially an effort to reform healthcare insurance, financing, and delivery systems. The attempt at insurance reform specified stable, inclusive risk pools with rules that would require insurance companies to compete to ensure medical care for all, rather than merely to cover those with favorable risk characteristics.

These insurance reform efforts did not help contain costs, but did broaden the insurance marketplace at the state and federal levels through the adoption of the Health Insurance Portability and Accountability Act (HIPAA). The adoption of HIPAA allowed employees insured under an employer's group plan to change jobs and be covered under the new employer's plan without a prolonged waiting period.

The continuing "political warfare" since the implementation of Obama Care highlights the political complexity of introducing healthcare reform. Ideally, healthcare delivery reform should improve how people receive medical care (*i.e.*, how nurses, physicians, and hospitals function in the delivery of care). Among other problems that led to an early collapse of these proposals, the 1993 Clinton Plan did not understand and significantly evaluate how people receive medical care from providers or institutions. Although well-meaning, the Clinton plan was socially and politically naïve, and no fundamental reform resulted.

Marketplace Reform Efforts

After 2000, American healthcare spending accelerated sharply, as a result of Congressional failure to reduce entitlement spending and the public backlash against private cost control being experienced by patients in managed care programs. In this same time period, health insurance cost sharing began to be implemented in businesses that previously had paid 100% of employee healthcare insurance premiums. Cost sharing increased as more employers experienced dramatic annual cost increases in their plans and began to try slowing these rising annual costs. Significant numbers of employees became unable to afford coverage through the workplace.

Experiencing less choice and less control over medical care and increased personal expense, the employee/consumer has intensified political and public support for consumer-directed healthcare as a guiding principle of healthcare reform. Until the recent economic downturn, a number of Americans have reflected the simplistic belief that private, market-based solutions are preferable to bureaucratic solutions. This model advocates using health reimbursement accounts, health savings accounts, and flexible spending accounts, coupled with high individual deductibles. With the passage of HIPAA in 1996, these programs have been incorporated into a series of federal enactments—most recently the Medicare Modernization Act of 2003.

All healthcare consumers want improved healthcare delivery that is affordable, accessible, and yields good outcomes. This is a top priority for both individuals and for corporate America. In spite of these efforts to introduce market forces into healthcare cost and delivery, sustainable, efficient, and effective reform has not occurred. Market-based elements of competition have been successful in providing higher-quality and lower-cost goods and services in a number of industries in the United States. Healthcare remains an important exception, however.

Several reasons can be cited for the failure of the previous attempts to reform healthcare using market forces. In the absence of transparency and consumer understanding of price–value relationships and quality parameters for healthcare, a true "market" has not been created. In addition, while all those providing healthcare sense that fierce competition exists, Porter and Teisberg, in *Redefining Health Care: Creating Value-Based Competition on Results* (Harvard Business Review Press, 2006), make a compelling case that the current competition in healthcare has been at the wrong level and in the wrong forms, promoting inappropriate goals or objectives, failing to generate needed information, existing in the wrong geographic markets, and providing dysfunctional incentives for payors and providers.

The competitive elements currently operating in the U.S. healthcare system have in some cases become the root causes of performance problems. Redeploying competition into effective healthcare sectors could provide important opportunities for realizing needed reform.

For example, competition currently occurs at the level of health plans, networks, and hospital groups. Shifting the competition to the level of independent healthcare providers identifying and implementing treatment for diseases could reduce errors, spark innovation, drive improvements in quality, and create efficiencies that would reduce costs patient-by-patient and disease-by-disease. This competition is absent today in much of our healthcare system.

A form of pseudo-competition at the level of networks and health plans operates within single, closed groups. Networks compete to sign up healthy subscribers and exclude the sick patients who are costly. By discounting prices to employer providers, they are able to capture large groups of patients who, in order to have their medical care costs reimbursed, are required to obtain their entire healthcare from particular networks that have contracted with their employer.

Health plans build comprehensive services in closed networks and restrict patients to their participating providers. This prevents competition at the level of all available providers, and especially forecloses any competition at the national level. Participants are forced to see the providers available in the network.

Health plan marketing focuses on participant satisfaction surveys and lacks information about provider quality, value, or patient outcomes. Patients have no information about how the care they receive meets national standards or if it is comparable to centers of excellence.

Logical incentives for payors, for example, are to attract healthy subscribers and be able to raise rates for those who are or become unhealthy. Managed care organizations restrict treatments and out-of-network services, shift cost to providers and payors, and inhibit innovation. Without open competition, health plans offer comprehensive services without regard to prevailing medical standards. They may refer patients only within the network (if at all), and are incentivized to spend less time with patients, discharge patients prematurely, and practice "defensive medicine."

Patients too easily become prisoners of healthcare systems that are not encouraged through true competition to create the greatest value at the level of disease treatment and outcomes. As a result, an important driver for our present and past reform efforts—cost reduction—has become too narrow an objective. Service provider groups in the healthcare system are able to reduce their own costs simply by transferring them to someone else in the same plan. Total costs are not reduced, and may even increase.

Shifting costs among payors and providers, restricting patients with illnesses from obtaining referrals to centers of excellence, and providing information that does not inform choice with respect to achieving better outcomes does not replicate the competitive elements found in private enterprises where competition serves to enhance value by improving quality and reducing cost.

POTENTIAL SUCCESS OF FUTURE HEALTHCARE REFORM

Government-Run, Single-Payor System

The basic model utilized in the majority of developed countries in the world is a government-run, single-payor system, with various modifications within the system and options for private care outside of the system.

The greatest advantages of this type of healthcare system are that there is universal coverage, it encourages more preventive care, it allocates a fixed amount in the national budget to healthcare, and in general, savings are realized in the total administrative costs of the system. Several disadvantages of such a government-run system have prevented its adoption in the United States to date. Americans worry about enforced rationing of healthcare services; excessive government intrusion into medical decision-making; lack of competition to maintain and improve the quality of medical services; lack of cost controls; blunting of innovation in healthcare technology, financing, and delivery; and excessive waiting periods for "needed" services.

Based on the size and diversity of the U.S. population and what serious students of U.S. healthcare reform observe in other systems around the world, the potential for a government-run, single-payor system to successfully provide desired, realistic clinical outcomes, safety, and services to patients, while also controlling costs, appears problematic.

If true healthcare reform does not occur using effective, market-based strategies, there is a strong probability that the United States could go down the road with some form of governmental-run, single-payor system that could erode hard-won quality achievements and continue to be more costly than necessary.

Competitive Marketplace System

For a competitive, marketplace type of system to work in healthcare as successfully as it has in a number of U.S. economic sectors, broad and fundamental changes will need to occur in the healthcare marketplace. The work of Porter and Teisberg provides an important model for these changes. Ultimately, everyone at some level should be a "payor" for the care they receive and be able to make judgments about both the quality and the cost of this care. In this process, the system must mandate that everyone has health coverage, as well as provide subsidies for those unable to make required payments.

Clear and equitable parameters to measure the quality and the price of healthcare services must be developed in order to measure the performance of providers. This healthcare information must be severity indexed, simplified with one price per hospitalization or period of care, and also standardized to enable wide geographic comparisons. Information generated must be accurate, accessible, and readily understood, so that individual patients and employers can make informed decisions when selecting and purchasing healthcare services. Strong incentives must be created to have patients and employer plans utilize this value-based information.

The objectives of value-based healthcare competition will change dramatically from those in the present system. Instead of phantom reductions of the cost of care in single health plans or systems (a frequent problem now because costs often are not reduced, but rather shifted internally), true opportunities will be created to rationalize the cost of U.S. healthcare. True market competition will reward and accelerate innovations that lower the total cost of providing care.

Current forms of competition encourage health plans to compete annually for subscribers solely based on the price of premiums, to enlarge their organizational size primarily to enhance bargaining power, and to trap patients in their networks. Payors and providers compete by shifting costs among one another. This needs to be replaced by a system wherein individual providers compete regarding the quality and price of services they provide with respect to specific diseases and procedures. The geographic market for secondary and tertiary care would thus expand from predominantly a collection of local markets to more efficient regional and national levels.

In shifting from local to regional and national markets, changes are also necessary to provide nondiscriminatory health insurance. These changes would include the removal of network restrictions, elimination of pre-approvals for care out of the network, and prohibition of re-underwriting. Assigned risk pools would also be made available for those who need them.

CONCLUSION

Competition can encourage incentives for both payors and providers to create greater value for healthcare customers versus short-term shifting or cutting of costs. Delivering higher quality per unit of cost should be rewarded. Given the present structure of the U.S. healthcare system, employers must take action to initiate these change processes.

There have been national efforts to encourage large employers and other purchasers of care to seek greater value for their employees, such as those of the Leapfrog Group. Findings suggest, however, that many large employers are not using their purchasing power with health plans and providers to improve the quality of healthcare received by their employees.

Although a significant number of surveyed employers report examining health plan quality data, many seem to attach a low level of importance to it in their subsequent decision-making. Further, provider quality information is even less commonly examined or used by employers to reward provider performance or to influence employees' choices of providers.

Futuristic Thinking Must be Now

If the first rule of systems is that everything is connected to everything else, the second rule is that you can optimize individual pieces only up to a point. If you do not develop a new system, everything you do will be constrained. If you put together a new system, and you do it right, the new system benefits many individual processes as well as the whole. Optimizing only individual processes can merely lead to incremental change; optimizing the system can lead to transformational change.

In healthcare, the new system must put healthcare coverage in the hands of employers with respect to choosing and paying for plans. At a broader level, the new healthcare system seeking transformational change must construct a value- and market-based structure that includes clear, accurate specification and measurement of healthcare "goods and services" in order to define quality, establish pricing, and then "grade" those delivering these goods and services.

This is well-stated in a 2008 *New York Times* Op-Ed, "How to Take American Health Care from Worst to First," by Billy Beane, Newt Gingrich, and John Kerry: "America's healthcare system behaves like a hidebound, tradition-based ball club that chases after aging sluggers and plays by the old rules: we pay too much and get too little in return. To deliver better healthcare, we should learn from successful teams that have adopted baseball's new evidenced-based methods. The best way to start improving quality and lowering costs is to study the stats." The Money Ball approach to professional baseball should be applied to medicine.

The healthcare changes introduced by Obama Care have been at the center of political partisanship. But those who come after Obama would be wise to heed the lessons of his health reform effort. For Democrats, those lessons are relatively straightforward. It is easy to imagine the next Democratic president passing a healthcare bill that does four things: expand Medicaid coverage up to 200% of poverty, boost subsidies in the exchanges, add a public option that can use Medicare or Medicaid's pricing power, and let people above age 50 buy into Medicare.

A bill like that could pass the Senate with 51 votes, it would build on what has worked both in America and elsewhere, and it would be straightforward for the government to administer and voters to understand.

CHAPTER 3

Optimal Medical Outcomes with Limited Liability: Risk Management Principles for Medical Practices at the Intersection of Medicine, Law, and Business

Physicians practice at the intersection of medicine, law, and business. Each discipline creates its own challenges for the practicing physician: to practice efficient, effective medicine; to limit potential liability; and to create a positive financial outcome. Those challenges increase with escalating costs and reduced reimbursements.

In this chapter, the common clinical presentation of chest pain is used to create a paradigm to educate physicians to understand efficient and effective approaches to diagnosis and treatment and how effective communication with patients and meticulous documentation of all medical encounters can limit the potential for liability. Ultimately, given today's reimbursement formulas, physicians must also understand the cost of testing, in relation to its benefits, in an attempt to yield a positive financial outcome

Physicians have always had to be proficient in the three components of their profession: the science of medicine, the art of medicine, and the business of medicine. The intersection of medicine, law, and business creates challenges for the practicing physician—to practice effective medicine, to limit potential liability, and to create a positive financial outcome.

Protocols developed to treat complex emergency conditions need to take into consideration cost-effective pathways that yield good clinical outcomes and positive financial results. In the context of patients with chest pain, this chapter explores ways to limit liability and achieve financial stability as well as good clinical outcomes.

CARDIOVASCULAR DISEASE AND ITS IMPACT ON THE U.S. POPULATION

Cardiovascular disease (CVD) is the leading cause of death in men and women. More than 70 million U.S. residents have one or more types of CVD, and within that subset of patients are 13 million who have coronary heart disease (CHD).

The major issue confronting patients and physicians is the prognosis of CVD, which accounts for more deaths than the next five leading causes of death (Table 1). Key sex differences include late age of onset of CHD in women and differences in the initial symptom complex at presentation of CHD.

TABLE 1. Facts about Cardiovascular Disease

1. Every minute of every day, a U.S. resident has a lethal coronary event.
2. The estimated incidence of myocardial infarction is more than 500,000 new coronary events and 300,000 repeat coronary events annually. More than 350,000 people die annually of coronary heart disease (CHD) before hospitalization. These are typically sudden deaths precipitated by ventricular fibrillation.
3. Statistical data suggest that 50% of men and 65% of women who die suddenly secondary to CHD had no prior symptoms that they recognized.

Recently released statistics from the American Heart Association (AHA) show that 483,000 American women died from heart disease and stroke in 2003, and there appears to be a difference in the approach to heart disease when women and men are compared (Table 2). Using data from 2013-2016, about 8.8 million females alive had CHD. Of these, 3.3 million had a history of myocardial infarction (MI, or heart attack).

Physicians would be prudent to maintain an awareness of the standard of care in medicine that applies to diagnosing and treating chest pain because chest pain: (1) is prevalent; (2) may be life threatening; (3) has a complex differential diagnosis; and (4) is managed most effectively if

TABLE 2. Risk Factors for Coronary Heart Disease

Among identified risk factors for coronary heart disease (CHD), some can be modified through diet, exercise, medication, and smoking cessation, although others, such as heredity, sex, and age, are not modifiable. Some risk factors greatly increase the likelihood of CHD; others are associated with CHD, but their contribution to CHD is yet to be precisely identified. Identification of modifiable risk factors is important; attempts to alter these risk factors is critical when managing patients with CHD or a family history of coronary artery disease or as a primary prevention approach.

1. Smokers have a 2- to 4-fold higher risk of developing CHD than nonsmokers.
2. Abnormal cholesterol levels are a modifiable risk factor. The risk of CHD increases as a person's blood cholesterol rises; this risk increases dramatically when other risk factors are present. Data from epidemiologic studies and clinical trials have shown that for every 1 mg/dL reduction in low-density lipoprotein cholesterol, the relative risk for CHD is reduced by 1%.
3. Hypertension increases the risk of stroke, myocardial infarction, renal failure, and congestive heart failure. American Heart Association (AHA) statistics suggest 33% of adults have hypertension, and of these, 30% do not know they have this treatable risk factor.
4. Physical inactivity is a modifiable risk factor. Moderate to vigorous exercise performed on a regular basis (three times/week) is necessary to overcome the risk associated with physical inactivity. The relative risk of physical inactivity is comparable to that associated with hypertension, hypercholesterolemia, and smoking.
5. Diabetes mellitus is a modifiable risk factor. The risks are greatest in people who have poorly controlled blood glucose levels. AHA statistics suggest that 75% of patients with diabetes die of cardiovascular disease. The prevalence of diabetes appears to be increasing at a 5% annual rate.

recognized immediately and treated within minutes to hours when it represents as acute coronary syndrome (ACS), aortic dissection, or other life-threatening condition. The misdiagnosis of these life-threatening conditions is a frequent cause of expensive malpractice awards.

PRE-HOSPITAL ISSUES THE PHYSICIAN MUST EVALUATE

The latest American College of Cardiology/American Heart Association (ACC/AHA) Guidelines for Unstable Angina caution that patients with symptoms that suggest a possible ACS should not be evaluated over the telephone, but should be referred to a medical center for evaluation by a physician who is accomplished at electrocardiographic (ECG) analysis and treatment of emergency conditions.

All physicians should have protocols for managing telephone calls from patients about chest pain and accessing emergency care. Clear and prompt documentation of telephone encounters is crucial to maintain continuity of care and minimize malpractice risk. Written telephone protocols should guide both medical staff and nonmedical staff, in the physician's office and on the hospital campus, to direct patients with chest pain to immediate care for rapid, timely, and accurate diagnosis and treatment.

When an unanticipated negative outcome occurs, there may be allegations regarding the timeliness of the diagnosis or treatment. In both the physician outpatient office and the campus of the hospital, it is important to demonstrate that the practice plan for handling chest pain over the telephone is well thought out, clearly written, known by the entire office, and respectful of the community standard of care (Table 3). The establishment of chest pain protocols demonstrates that the physician's office has an emergency plan to manage patients who call to report potentially life-threatening conditions.

TABLE 3. Physician's Office Handling of Telephone Communication Regarding Chest Pain

1. Every staff member at the physician's office must know the following:
   - Chest pain may indicate a medical emergency independent of patient age and sex.
   - Patients with chest pain need immediate attention.
   - Protocols detailing how the phone communication should be handled.
2. There should be written materials outlining office protocols for handling a patient with chest pain presenting on the phone.
3. Office personnel should be required to take written tests to identify competence in handling the phone communications.
4. Mock phone calls allow the office staff to practice the protocols and demonstrate proficiency.

Effective treatment of an ACS requires recognition of the diagnosis and rapid access to care that includes defibrillation, administration of thrombolytic, angioplasty and stenting, and emergency coronary artery bypass graft surgery. Early access to emergency care benefits patients with an ACS (Table 4).

Many factors may delay access to emergency care, including patient and family denial, time taken to contact physicians, and limitations in emergency care access systems. However, the goal for all physicians whose

TABLE 4. Benefits of Early Access to Emergency Care

1. Early treatment of myocardial infarction may help limit the progression of disease, prevent the loss of cardiac function, and even prevent death.
2. Early treatment of myocardial infarction results in reduced mortality and infarct size and yields improved left ventricular function.
3. Many patients do not seek immediate medical care, and many delay treatment for more than 12 hours, at which point reperfusion therapy may offer limited benefit.

patients have chest pain is to ensure prompt arrival to the emergency department (ED).

PHYSICIANS EVALUATING CHEST PAIN IN THE ED

In the United States, millions of people present to EDs annually with a primary complaint of chest pain. Approximately 15,000 of these patients have an ACS, but are discharged from the hospital because of problems in diagnosis and management. Problems include failure to: (1) repeat serial cardiac blood markers; (2) repeat ECGs during recurrent chest pain; (3) perform exercise testing: and (4) perform angiography.

Good patient outcomes depend on timely and accurate diagnosis. Failure to diagnose an ACS leads to severe morbidity and mortality, as well as malpractice allegations. Recognizing the diagnosis and providing prompt, accurate treatment are the cornerstones of reducing morbidity and mortality associated with an unrecognized ACS such as: unstable angina and non–ST-elevation and ST-elevation myocardial infarctions.

Professional societies such as the American College of Cardiology (ACC), American Hospital Association (AHA), and American College of Emergency Physicians (ACEP) have developed evidence-based guidelines for unstable angina and suspected myocardial infarction. All hospitals and their physicians should review these guidelines and develop protocols consistent with them.

These guidelines often are used as representative of the standard of care in malpractice cases. To prevent suboptimal outcomes and to reduce liability exposure, it may be prudent for physicians to treat all chest pain as an impending ACS. Ruling out life-threatening conditions is a proven axiom of healthcare risk management.

The history, physical examination, and ECG form the basis of the diagnosis. The history and physical examination generate the differential diagnosis in patients with chest pain and provide the foundation for determining the probability of an ACS, or other life-threatening condition, and the need for further diagnostic testing. It is important to remember that the findings on physical examination are often normal in patients with an ACS. The examination may be more revealing of alternative causes of chest pain such as aortic dissection, pulmonary embolism, cholecystitis, and myocarditis or pericarditis.

The ECG is the most readily available and widely used diagnostic tool for patients presenting with chest pain to the ED. The ECG plays a vital role in the decision-making process and helps to define patients who are candidates for reperfusion therapy. The ability to correctly identify the changes on the ECG representing ischemia and injury is paramount to ensure patient safety and limit the potential for professional liability. The physician evaluating the ECG must also recognize the precise details on the ECG associated with other life-threatening conditions such as pulmonary embolism and cardiac tamponade.

Whenever uncertainty surrounds the clinical circumstance, a cardiologist should be consulted to review the ECG in person or through advanced mobile phone or fax transmission. This should be available via the hospital protocol mechanisms that allow cardiologic interpretation of ECGs. Failure to have a fail-safe system available for cardiologic interpretation of a complex ECG can lead to serious patient harm and considerable liability exposure for the hospital and the treating physician. A normal ECG, however, does not rule out the possibility of acute myocardial infarction or unstable angina, and certain clinical presentations such as myocarditis, pericarditis, and left bundle branch block can make ECG interpretation perplexing.

In addition to ECG analysis, physicians need to fully understand how to use serial cardiac blood markers, repeat ECGs during periods of recurrent chest pain, exercise testing, echocardiography, nuclear imaging, and angiography in the assessment of chest pain. To promote patient safety, each medical facility should have protocols for an observational period that includes careful assessment for further symptoms or signs of an ACS.

THE FIDUCIARY RELATIONSHIP INHERENT IN THE PATIENT-PHYSICIAN RELATIONSHIP

The English word *fiduciary* draws from the Latin word *fiducia* for "confidence" or "trust." The bond of trust between the patient and the physician is vital to the diagnostic and therapeutic process. It forms the foundation of the patient-physician relationship. The evaluation of the patient is the beginning of a complex legal relationship that creates a duty for the physician to the patient. Physicians must act as fiduciaries for the patient, meaning the physician must act in the patient's best interest medically.

This fiduciary relationship creates a host of duties for the physician. Physicians must clearly communicate to both the patient and the patient's family the established diagnoses, discharge medications with benefits and potential adverse effects, medical limitations and restrictions, follow-up instructions, the actions the patient needs to take and in what time frame, and the long-term prognosis. All verbal discussion and communication with the patient should be reinforced in writing and given to the patient. The patient should acknowledge receipt and understanding of the instructions and sign off with a signature.

RISK MANAGEMENT PRINCIPLES

1. The physician's office should have emergency care access instructions and protocols.

Emergency care access instructions vary by community and depend on factors such as the distance to the hospital and the availability of ambulance and paramedic services. The physician and the staff in the physician's office must be fully aware of and comply with community standards when instructing patients how to seek access to emergency care. The established procedures that instruct patients to call 911 for rapid emergency medical transport and ambulance response are not available in all locations. Areas without 911 codes or ambulance services should have alternative protocols that fit the standard of care within the community.

Mock calls to practice these emergency procedures and written materials for review with evidence of testing of the principles would be prudent behavior for all medical offices. These procedures demonstrate a commitment by the physician and staff to emergency medical care.

2. Documentation of protocols, procedures, and communications is mandatory from the perspective of patient safety and risk management.

To ensure continuity of care and to protect the medical staff if care is called into question, telephone communications about patient care must be documented in detail and made part of the patient's permanent medical record. Lack of documentation of the phone communication seriously compromises the physician's defense against malpractice allegations (Table 5). Physicians have been sued for malpractice on the basis of a single telephone communication. The persuasiveness of these arguments loses its appeal when telephone communications are well documented.

TABLE 5. Malpractice Allegations

1. Delay in diagnosis and treatment due to hindered access to emergency care.
2. Failure of the physician to obtain patient's informed refusal of outlined recommendations for emergency care.
3. Aiding and abetting the unlicensed practice of medicine if there is no physician involvement documented in the record.
4. Negligent supervision of allied health professionals.

Documentation of the telephone communication by the physician and/or a member of the physician's staff evaluating the complaint of chest pain should include the time of the call, the name and status of the person handling the phone conversation, the patient's complaint in the patient's own words, questions asked and the answers to these specific questions, the developed differential diagnosis, the action of the physician, the recommendations to the patient, and the rationale for the advice given to the patient.

If the office medical staff handled the telephone communication, the physician must document reviewing the phone record and co-sign the record with date and time. It is important to note the time the patient was advised to seek emergency care and to give the details of the emergency access instructions. If the patient was referred for follow-up to the office of an alternative consultant, the physician should record the rationale for that recommendation.

It is also important to document that the patient understood the instructions and agreed to follow the given medical advice. Patient lack of understanding or agreement should automatically trigger active physician involvement to implement the recommendations or document informed refusal.

There should be documentation of communicating with the ED about the patient in transit with clear discussion of the chief complaint and pertinent medical history and relevant medical material needed for comparison faxed, such as ECGs. The physician should document in the patient's medical record the medical information provided to the ED with date, time, and signature (Table 6).

TABLE 6. Importance of Documentation

Why is accurate and objective documentation of utmost importance for medical care and risk management?
1. It creates a record of care that allows for continuity of care for the patient.
2. It provides a record of the physician's actions and the rationale for these actions. The physician should document as though the patient will read the record, and it should reflect the truth but have language that is vigilant about documenting informed consent conversations with the patient, including discussions about risks, benefits, and alternative therapeutic options.
3. The language should be descriptive and objective because, in malpractice cases, the patient's record plays an integral role in supporting the physician's case that the patient's care and treatment met the standard of care.
4. It is important that the physician's hand-written documentation be logical and legible.
5. Medical record documentation is the strongest defense available to the physician in defending against allegations of negligence because it provides a concrete account of the medical thinking and services provided.

The success of patient follow-up and adherence to discharge instructions is often a reflection of the quality of the hospital staff and the physician's communication of these important details to the patient. All physicians should develop a system to verify whether patient follow-up occurred after discharge. Failed patient follow-up should trigger the system to call the patient to identify why follow-up did not occur and arrange for follow-up care. The conversation with the patient and/or family members should be documented in the patient's permanent medical record with sufficient detail to clearly demonstrate why the patient failed to follow-up.

THE BUSINESS OF MEDICINE

Successful and respected physicians must achieve and maintain the highest skills in the science of medicine and in the art of caring, while maintaining financial stability in their practice. This is no less true of the medical organizations to which many physicians now belong.

Illustrative Examples

The complexity for contemporary physicians attempting to achieve excellent clinical outcomes while minimizing medical liability and sustaining a positive bottom line for their healthcare organizations is illustrated by our experience with Medicare patients in two diagnosis-related groups (DRGs): DRG 122 (circulatory disorders with acute myocardial infarction) and DRG 143 (chest pain). The cost estimates were based on information that was available in our database for two calendar years.

The **DRG 122** cohort comprised the 32 consecutive patients who presented to the ED with myocardial infarction in the calendar years 2015 and 2016, with total organizational costs ranging from $2,029 to $15,085. The mean cost was $6437 (95% confidence interval [CI] $5,307–$7,567). The mean organizational reimbursement for these 32 patients was $5,327 (individual patient data were not available). Consequently, the organization's mean cost exceeded the mean organizational reimbursement by approximately $1,110 per patient.

The **DRG 143** cohort comprised the 51 consecutive patients who presented to the ED with chest pain in the calendar years 2015 and 2016, with total organizational costs ranging from $1,593 to $16,003. The mean cost was $4,313 (95% CI of $3,552–$5,074). The mean organizational reimbursement for these 51 patients was $3,061. Consequently, the organizational mean costs exceeded the mean organizational reimbursement by approximately $1,252 per patient.

Comments

The review of these two DRG categories demonstrates the current difficulties that healthcare organizations encounter while striving to maintain best practices in medical care with excellent clinical outcomes and optimal risk management. While these sustained patient care efforts are crucial for the long-term success of healthcare organizations and cannot be compromised, the viability of the organization depends also on maintaining positive financial results.

In the current reimbursement climate, the results of the study indicate that in my institution, despite our emphasis on best practices for both clinical care and risk management, the organization loses more than $1,500 per patient in each of the two DRG categories reviewed. A limitation to our analysis is the small sample that was available for review. The trend suggests the need for a larger study to further elucidate the magnitude of the problem.

Not only is the current financial loss per patient not consistent with long-term organizational well-being, but also the projected future additional decreases in Medicare reimbursement, if implemented, will exacerbate these losses.

CONCLUSIONS

Patients with chest pain must quickly receive the attention of a physician. The comprehensive history and physical examination, diagnostic testing to rule in and rule out diagnoses from the differential diagnosis, effective communication, conscientious follow-up, and accurate and objective documentation are fundamental aspects of safe and effective patient care and are paramount in avoiding allegations of negligence and mounting a successful defense in medical malpractice litigation.

The goals of a physician practicing in today's medical environment must be: (1) to be cognizant of the disease processes and to have an efficient and effective management strategy that yields good clinical outcomes; (2) to understand the importance of diagnostic capability, communication skills, documentation of all medical encounters with precise details and rationale for the outlined strategies and follow-up to limit potential liability; and (3) to understand cost-effective strategies that allow for good clinical outcomes and positive financial results.

The financial issue is an ever more pressing concern for physicians and healthcare organizations, as described in the paradigm for managing chest pain. The concept of a positive financial outcome is becoming illusory and should raise concern for all of society, as the practice of good medicine is fundamental to the future of society. This requires an intersection of medicine, law, and business that works for patients, physicians, healthcare organizations, and insurers. The current reimbursement model functioning in the real world today has many flaws and needs renovation with contributions from all concerned participants in the healthcare policy of the future.

CHAPTER 4

The Fundamentals of Liability Insurance: Physician and Organization Perspectives

Professional liability insurance is critical to physicians to protect their assets. Current medical practice reveals that most physicians will experience an allegation of negligence during their medical practice lifetime.

Professional liability insurance is a contract between the physician and the insurance company. Physicians must understand the contract to identify the correct policy for their medical practice, to have appropriate coverage for the assumed risks, and to pay premiums that are reasonable within the marketplace.

Prudent physicians should understand their duties and rights, as outlined in the liability contract, and the duties and rights of the insurance company. It is imperative for physicians to understand when the policy affords them a right to defend an allegation of negligence and when they must settle, by the structure of the contract.

Physicians must understand the issues surrounding settlement and judgment reporting to the National Practitioner Data Bank. Finally, physicians need to understand how a physician organization handles professional liability insurance.

Medical liability insurance evolved to provide a practical solution to the economic losses associated with professional work. Insurance methodology is based on "risk pooling" and the statistics of large numbers, the principles that allow insurers to spread risks among large numbers of individuals and to predict losses with reasonable accuracy.

Insurance transfers risk from the individual to the group; thus, it is an effective way to deal with risk and losses when dealing with large groups.

A risk must involve certain elements before it can be insured: It must be pure risk; the loss it entails must be due to chance; the loss must be definite and measurable; the loss must be predictable; the loss cannot be catastrophic; and the loss exposure must be allocated throughout a large group that is randomly selected.

The true worth of insurance lies in its ability to protect the value associated with an individual's earning potential and to provide financial security. Medical professional liability insurance is important to physicians to help protect their assets.

WHY DO PHYSICIANS NEED MEDICAL LIABILITY INSURANCE?

The answer to the question of why physicians need medical liability insurance is straightforward: Most physicians, over the course of their medical careers, will use it. Unfortunately, doctors often must scramble for coverage, as insurance can be extremely costly or unavailable.

PHYSICIANS NEED TO READ AND ANALYZE THE MEDICAL LIABILITY POLICY

A medical professional liability policy is a legal contract between the physician and the insurance company. The contract specifies that the physician will pay the insurance company a premium in exchange for the company's agreement to pay for the costs of the investigation, the defense, and any judgments or settlements. Physicians have little opportunity to bargain with the insurer over the terms of the contract, but they should read and question anything they don't understand regarding the policy before any claims are made.

Generally, the first page of a policy is the declaration page. It provides essential information such as the name of the policyholder, the insured individuals and entities, dates of coverage, the limits of the coverage, any deductibles, the type of policy, and the premiums charged. There are also endorsements, riders, or amendments that outline modifications to the main policy. These may include exclusions for coverage, additional benefits of coverage, and changes in policy terminology as required by law.

The policy may include a certificate of insurance, which is useful when providing proof of insurance to a hospital or state medical board, since the certificate does not contain information such as mailing addresses and premium charges.

Coverage is limited to the physicians or entities listed on the declaration page. The physician's corporation is generally a named insured for no additional premium. The same holds true for any nursing or administrative employees who are automatically covered along with the physician.

Other professionals who work with or are employed by the physician are not covered unless specifically listed as insured on the declaration page; nurse practitioners, physician's assistants, and technicians generally require their own specific policy coverage.

THE EXTENT OF MEDICAL LIABILITY COVERAGE

There are limits to the coverage the professional liability policy provides to the physician. Traditionally, the policy limits are identified as two separate dollar amounts; the first dollar amount identifies the maximum amount the insurer will pay for any one claim, and the second dollar amount refers to the aggregate limit for all claims during the policy period, for example \$300,000/\$600,000 (*i.e.*, \$300,000 for any one individual claim, and a total of \$600,000 aggregate for all claims incurred during the policy period).

The physician must understand the maximum amount the insurer will pay for judgments and settlements, and the insurer's cost of defending the insured. Some policies specify that defense costs are included in the yearly aggregate limit of coverage. In this case, the defense costs are subtracted from the aggregate limit, meaning that the aggregate limit could be used up with defense costs before any amount is paid to settle the case; it is possible that in the event of additional claims, little or no coverage will be available to the insured.

It also is important to understand coverage limits in relationship to one's specialty and locale of practice, as there are significant differences in the frequency of claims and the amount of jury awards based on these variables. It's important to understand these differences in risk in order to accurately calculate appropriate liability coverage.

TWO MAJOR CATEGORIES OF POLICIES

There are two broad categories of professional liability insurance: (1) occurrence and (2) claims-made. Understanding the distinctions between these types of policies is critical for physicians.

Occurrence insurance provides coverage for incidents that happen during the policy period regardless of when the allegation of negligence is filed. This type of policy has significant risk for the insurer, as the risk of a future claim beyond the policy period does not allow for calculation of frequency, or severity of the dollar risk in the future. The response of the insurance industry was to hedge the bet by charging seemingly disproportionately high premiums to handle the risk of increasing claim frequency and the cost of settlements, judgments, and defense attorney fees in the future.

The occurrence policy provides coverage into a future without limits so the judgment must be paid by a single year's premium plus any investment income the insurer earns on the investment. These factors put insurers in the precarious position of going out of business if they charged premiums and received investment returns that did not meet the cost of judgments, settlements, and defenses.

Claims-made insurance accounts for the bulk of policies in effect today. *Claims-made policy coverage is available only when the alleged malpractice and the claim are made against the insured while the policy is in force.* This can leave the physician uninsured for claims made for malpractice occurring before or after the effective policy periods of the claims-made policy. To alleviate this gap in coverage, the physician may negotiate for a "retroactive date" of coverage in the first instance and "tail coverage" in the second.

The retroactive date means that insured physicians can acquire coverage for time periods when they were insured by a different company or did not carry insurance. The retroactive date is one of the few provisions of claims-made policies that can be negotiated. The insurer may offer the retroactive date gratis in order to induce physicians to purchase the policy, or the company may impose a one-time charge for retroactive coverage.

The insurance company often requests a compilation of possible incidents that could result in a claim before deciding on the wisdom of a retroactive date. The policy will have an addendum excluding from coverage any events that occurred during the retroactive period that the physician knew, or should have known, would result in a claim but did not disclose. Thus, it is in the physician's best interest to be transparent and disclose all potential claims. If an insurer has canceled their coverage because of increased claim frequency, medical behavior deemed egregious, or fraud, physicians generally will not be able to obtain coverage from another company.

When physicians retire from the practice of medicine they must obtain an extended reporting period endorsement known as "tail coverage." This has a variable period available from three years to perpetuity. Tail coverage does not alter policy limits, retroactive dates, or the fundamental rule that the claim must have been made subsequent to the effective date, retroactive or not, of the policy.

Tail coverage is expensive, particularly when it is in perpetuity, because this essentially changes the claims-made policy into an occurrence policy with all the attendant risks of predicting future costs into an undefined future period. As a hedge, some insurers offer tail coverage with a deductible that is applied to any defense and/or indemnity costs once a claim is made against the physician—risk sharing between the physician and the insurer.

Typically, no charge is made against a physician who becomes disabled or against the estates of physicians who die. Physicians who are disabled or retired and resume practice would be prudent to purchase a new policy with retroactive coverage.

A standard requirement for coverage is that the physician promptly reports any claims or significant incidents to the insurer. Failure to do so may compromise the insurer's ability to investigate the incident and defend the alleged negligence. Companies may enforce a time period for reporting after which coverage is denied.

Here's an example of a complex scenario that could arise: A claim is made late in the policy coverage dates and the physician does not receive notification—and therefore cannot report the claim—until after the coverage period lapses. In this instance, tail coverage would prevent a coverage issue because the reporting would fall within the provisions of policy coverage. If this becomes a legal issue between the insurer and the physician, the majority of the courts have ruled that despite policy language, physicians have a reasonable period after the claim to report to the insurer, even if the policy period has lapsed.

OTHER POLICY PROVISIONS PHYSICIANS SHOULD STUDY

Deductibles

Medical malpractice insurance deductibles do not deter filing with the insurer, as they may with property and automobile insurance. In medical malpractice insurance, a claim must *always* be filed with the insurer.

Deductibles primarily serve to reduce the insured's premium cost and to defray the insurer's defense and indemnity costs. The insured may elect to pay a deductible cost in exchange for a lower premium. The deductible may be a fixed amount or a percentage share of the total costs.

The deductible can be structured in a couple of ways: (1) only applied to any judgment and settlement payments (indemnity); or (2) a first-dollar offset to defense costs and judgments and settlement. When the deductible is applied to indemnity payments, the physician has no costs until after a judgment or settlement. The physician may be billed periodically and must pay promptly to avoid policy cancellation. If any unsatisfied deductible amount remains after the payment of defense costs, it must then be applied to any judgment or settlement costs. Deductibles usually are applied on a per-claim basis, although exceptions and a limit may be written into the policy.

Because high deductibles may make a physician reluctant to settle a case, some policies may impose compulsory settlements on the insured. Insurance companies may impose deductibles on a physician as a condition of issuing the policy. This occurs when there is a history of recurrent small claims brought against the physician, or when the physician's practice tends to generate such claims. Typically, these deductibles apply on a first-dollar cost basis for defense costs. In addition to involuntary deductibles, premium surcharges may be imposed as a result of individual risk factors or the performance of high-risk procedures.

Insuring Agreement

The insuring agreement specifies the conditions under which the insurer will provide coverage and the items it will cover under the policy. This section explains what the insurance company considers to be valid claims against the physician, the extent of the obligation to defend the physician, and a detailed explanation of when a claim is covered.

Physicians must read this section with due diligence to understand and appreciate the precise situations in which they must notify the insurer of a claim. This is also a time to identify any potential limitations in the policy from the physician's perspective so adjustments can be introduced or alternative coverage sought.

Exclusions

Standard exclusions appear in every policy; those that are specific to a particular individual or practice specialty are appended as endorsements. Standard exclusions include that defense and indemnification coverage is available only for acts rendered in the course of a professional service. Policies universally exclude indemnification for intentional or criminal acts, sexual misconduct, defamation, fraud, unlawful discrimination, antitrust violations, false imprisonment, and drug trafficking. There are policies that will cover defense costs associated with these claims, except criminal charges, up to a specified limit.

Most policies make exclusion for any contractual agreements a physician undertakes in agreeing to a managed care organization's hold-harmless clauses. These agreements may create an obligation for the physician to indemnify the managed care organization not only for the physician's acts, but also for the managed care organizations acts.

Because liability insurers are not likely to include coverage for a managed care organization in the physician's policy, the physician must have the managed care organization remove the hold-harmless clause or refuse to sign the contract. Physician gatekeeper duties associated with a managed care organization may not be covered absent a written addendum to the policy. When in doubt, the physician should discuss the issue with the insurance company and obtain a policy endorsement authorizing such activity.

Some insurers include practice exclusions within their policies such as voiding coverage for the use of non-Food and Drug Administration–approved drugs, chelation therapy, or weight loss drugs, to name a few. There may be restrictions on procedures such as bariatric surgery and obstetrical procedures performed by general practitioners. Coverage may be voided for procedures the physician has not been credentialed to perform.

Additional Benefits

Policies usually include a section listing additional benefits the insurer automatically provides beyond the defense, settlement, and judgment costs. These may include the insurer's administrative costs and costs incurred in the course of the physician's defense such as travel, lodging, and lost time from practice to attend legal proceedings.

DUTIES INHERENT IN THE MEDICAL PROFESSIONAL LIABILITY INSURANCE CONTRACT

Duties and Rights of the Physician

The physician's basic contractual obligation is the payment of premiums in a timely manner. Delayed payment can lead to a notice to cancel from the insurer. The insurer typically sends a 10-day notice, commonly required by state law, indicating that the payment must be made by a specific date to avoid cancellation. Physicians who ignore payment dates may end up without indemnification, have difficulty obtaining further medical liability coverage, and face financial jeopardy if claims lead to judgments that are not covered.

Also, the physician has a duty to inform the insurer of any change in the practice's business model, including practice location, additional partners, or specialty practice, as these may require a change in premiums and/or an endorsement to the policy. The policy may also require the physician to notify the insurance company of any disciplinary actions taken by the state medical board or a healthcare facility. Coverage is often excluded for any incidents that occur while the physician's license was restricted or revoked.

In the event of an allegation of negligence, the physician is obligated to provide the insurer with all pertinent information as defined in the policy. The policy will define what incidents constitute a valid claim. It is essential that the physician provide all information promptly, before any relevant evidence is lost or destroyed. The physician is obligated to cooperate in the insurance company's investigation, to participate in discussions with attorneys, and to attend depositions and other legal proceedings.

The physician is required to assert his or her rights against any third party who may be liable to the physician for any damages related to the claim. When the company asserts its right of subrogation, damages collected must be returned to the insurer. The physician should never contact the patient, plaintiff, or opposing attorney and should not make any payments or incur any expenses without consulting with the insurance company.

The policy states the rules regarding settlement. A settlement is a legally binding agreement between the plaintiff and the physician whereby the plaintiff accepts a financial payment in exchange for agreeing to dismiss or not to pursue legal action.

Most physician-owned insurance companies will not settle without a physician's consent. Commercial carriers may include a clause that compels the physician to settle when the company deems it expedient. *Settlements must be reported to the National Practitioner Data Bank.*

Duties and Rights of the Insurance Company

The primary duties of the insurance company are to provide the physician with an investigation and defense of the claim and to provide indemnification in the event of a settlement or judgment. Generally, these duties remain even if the insurer becomes insolvent or declares bankruptcy. Although insurance companies are free to decline renewal of a policy because of adverse experience with a physician, the circumstances under which they may cancel a policy are typically listed in the policy. These circumstances include fraud or misrepresentation when obtaining the policy; the physician's commission of a criminal act; and activities such as patient abuse, molestation, and egregious or intentional acts of negligence.

Insurers usually reserve the right to inspect a physician's practice, including the physical premises, books, and records. These inspections are performed in the context of determining suitability for offering or renewing insurance coverage. Under federal law, insurers are required to report all settlements and judgments to the National Practitioner Data Bank. State laws vary, but some impose an obligation upon the insurer to report payments to the state licensing authority.

STATE GUARANTY ASSOCIATIONS

Each state has a state guaranty association (SGA) that protects the interests of physicians if the insurance company becomes nonoperational. Basically, the SGA stands in the shoes of the insurer.

The funding comes from compulsory funds paid by insurance companies. There is a statutory limit on the amount the SGA will pay toward settlement or adjudication of a claim, thus leaving the physician personally liable for an amount above the statutory-defined maximum.

AN ORGANIZATION'S VIEW ON MEDICAL LIABILITY INSURANCE

A medical organization must protect its assets to maintain viability in the marketplace; managing physician liability is a crucial component of the organization's overall risk management program. Physician behavior can be identified as an asset or a liability in the organization's balance sheet. Surveillance and management of physician activity are critical to minimizing potential liability for the organization.

The organizational structure that is most advantageous to legally protect the medical organization's assets is the corporation, in particular the limited liability corporation (LLC). In fact, the best reason for incorporating is the limited liability (see Table 1). However, there is no such thing as total insulation from liability resulting from doing business as a corporation.

TABLE 1. Advantages and Disadvantages of the Limited Liability Corporation

Advantages • Limited personal liability for the owners: (like a corporation; and unlike a partnership). • No federal taxes (like a partnership). • No limit on the number of stockholders (unlike an S corporation). • More than one class of stock is permitted (unlike an S corporation). • Business losses may be deducted on personal income tax returns (like an S corporation).
Disadvantages • Legal assistance required to set up due to complex paperwork. • No continuity of life as in a regular corporation, so if an owner dies or otherwise leaves, the LLC dissolves (other formal agreements between the owners can overcome this). • Possible requirement that an LLC have more than one member; (based on state).

Every organization needs to identify internal personnel who have expertise in managing physician liability and who devote adequate time to this responsibility. This duty can be assigned to risk managers, the medical director, or interested physicians. The responsible internal person must constantly survey potential and actual events. The monitoring process must be rigorous, comprehensive, and a top priority of the medical organization if the goal is to limit physician, or organization liability.

The strategy must have processes in place that train physicians and non-physician staff on the potential legal pitfalls inherent in daily medical practice. Regular seminars, written materials, and testing of risk management principles to ensure a knowledge base among the staff should help reduce liability.

A structured process must be in place that facilitates reporting to senior leadership the potential and actual liability issues facing the medical organization. There must be a transparent process that allows intervention and action when the organization encounters potential liability. The organization's leadership must be prepared to take appropriate action, including temporary suspension of physicians, mandatory retraining, or termination for individual physicians, depending on the nature and frequency of liability claims.

The medical organization must have organization-wide policies and procedures specifically detailing its requirements and expectations about issues such as content and format of staff communications with patients and coworkers; record-keeping with appropriate documentation; a uniform and robust consent process; systems for monitoring all laboratory, radiology, pathology, and clinical reports, department call schedules, and coverage; and refusing and/or terminating the care of difficult patients. The final issue can be critical in reducing the risk of liability for the physician/medical organization.

Medical organizations may find it helpful to have one internal legal expert assigned to these duties as well as an external legal expert in areas of risk management and physician liability. Because the liability insurance company usually has a local attorney to defend the medical organizations physicians facing liability, it is beneficial to have an in-house attorney who is aware of the claim to provide objective legal advice to the organization and physician on the potential negligence and the decision regarding settlement or trial.

This may be particularly important when the interests of the liability insurance company and those of the physician/medical organization conflict. The insurance company may see settling as advantageous to minimize financial losses; the physician/medical organization may prefer to proceed to trial to protect the reputations of the physician and the organization. The physician may consider prevailing at trial as being important to reduce damage to his or her reputation and to prevent being reported to the National Practitioner Data Bank with all the ramifications related to physician practice, privileges, and job security.

Medical organizations should have their in-house attorney participate in meetings of departments or committees that periodically review preventable errors, or clinical complications. This process allows rigorous analysis to establish best-practice methods without fear of potential litigation, as it is protected from future discovery by the attorney-client privilege.

A large medical organization that has in-depth procedures managing risk, an excellent malpractice history, and a large asset base may choose to be self-insured. Most medical organizations, however, would be prudent to find coverage through traditional physician liability insurance to protect their organizational assets.

CONCLUSION

Physicians practicing as sole proprietors, in partnerships, or as corporations must understand the importance of risk management principles with regard to potential medical malpractice liability. Solo practitioners and large medical organizations alike should take the appropriate steps to protect assets through the various forms of liability insurance. As part of this process, the physician and the organization must review and understand the provisions of their medical liability policies.

CHAPTER 5

Changing Perspectives in Medical Practice: Disruptive Innovation

Disruptive innovation represents a business model that identifies a market location and increases consumer options. Retail clinics may represent a disruptive healthcare innovation that identifies strategies to reduce the cost of healthcare at the primary care level.

The future of healthcare demands disruptive innovation that will allow for the 50 million uninsured members of our society to receive medical care. Disruptive innovative solutions need to ensure access, quality, and reasonable cost.

Retail clinics represent the tip of the iceberg in disruptive innovative thinking. The obstacles that retail clinics must solve will be lessons learned for those that identify future innovative techniques.

At the beginning of the 21st century, healthcare seemed to vanish from the list of national priorities. The horror of the World Trade Center and Pentagon bombings, the threat of global terrorism, the war in Iraq, and the uncertainties of a post-bubble economy consumed the nation's attention. Despite lack of public attention, a national healthcare crisis was brewing.

Medical costs skyrocketed, requiring an increasing amount of the nation's resources. In 1970, healthcare spending represented just 7% of the gross domestic product (GDP). By 2005, the nation's healthcare bill was approximately 16% of the GDP. Projections suggest that by 2020, healthcare spending would consume 21% of the GDP—projections that are being realized in 2021.

Health insurance premiums are increasing four times faster than wages. The data suggest that employers cannot afford to continue to offer health insurance while remaining competitive in the global marketplace. Employees in this economy will not be able to pay escalating premium costs or rising deductibles. Middle class Americans are already "going naked" in insurance industry parlance. Roughly one in three uninsured families earned more than $50,000 per year.

Healthcare inflation has become a pervasive economic problem affecting labor negotiations, jobs, pensions, and our nation's ability to compete internationally. If medical costs continue to outstrip economic growth, eventually there will be no money for education, defense, housing, and the arts.

Healthcare cost reform has been extremely difficult to implement. Perhaps a good first step would be to implement new healthcare innovation strategies that might lead to lower costs at the front door of healthcare access. An example to consider is the potential for meaningful cost savings resulting from retail medical clinics.

THE STATUS OF HEALTHCARE INNOVATION TODAY

There have been numerous innovations in healthcare over the years. Almost all of these innovations, such as fiberoptic endoscopy, minimally invasive surgery, organ transplantation, ultrasound-guided diagnostics, magnetic resonance imaging and positron emission tomography scanning, robotic surgery, and genetic testing and treatment, have resulted in higher quality patient care. All depend on higher levels of specialization and all result in even higher total medical cost. Consequently, almost none of the dramatic innovations in medical care, to date, have lowered the total cost of healthcare.

Disruptive innovations within an industry, on the other hand, result in a more affordable service or product and a new population of consumers using the service or product. Retail medical clinics may represent an example of disruptive innovation in the healthcare industry.

RETAIL CLINICS AS AN EXAMPLE OF DISRUPTIVE INNOVATION IN HEALTHCARE

The number of "in-store" healthcare clinics has increased across the country. These clinics are associated with brand-name mass retailers;

most are independently owned commercial venture chains. The retail clinics see patients without appointments, are demographically well located, have transparent pricing, and have night and weekend hours. They offer preventive care, diagnosis, and treatment. Services are offered through nurse practitioners and physician assistants who operate within electronically driven clinical protocols.

The midlevel provider is given clinical decision-making support with physician consultation available when needed. A specific association with the name Convenient Care Association identifies the niche in which the major retail clinic operators see themselves operating

Retail medical clinics are designed to diagnose and treat "simple" medical problems. These include, but are not limited to, strep throat, upper respiratory tract infections, urinary tract infections, sprains, and strains. Retail clinics offer midlevel provider consultations, laboratory testing, vaccines, and prescriptions, and emphasize preventive care, reassurance, and simple home remedies.

The niche is designed to offer care for the "straightforward" patient visit. These skill-based encounters are meant to consist of low decision density and limited cognitive effort. The practitioners in retail clinics offer solutions that have evolved from collective intuitions and protocols developed over years of practicing the art of medicine. These protocols serve as valuable cognitive tools for midlevel providers and facilitate rapid recognition and treatment of common conditions. Therefore, these intuitions result in the desired outcome when applied to straightforward clinical problems.

These clinics, located in Wal-Mart centers, drugstores, and other large retail chains, empower consumers to make purchasing decisions at the point of care for a limited group of services. The primary goal in establishing retail medical clinics is to provide lower, transparent prices at the point of service through a trusted, reputable retailer. The lower, transparent price makes this a consumer-directed-care model. Retail clinics represent a disruptive innovation that appears to offer lower-cost care relative to other options available to patients seeking primary care medicine.

PRICING, QUALITY, AND ACCESS

Transparent pricing is important to people who are concerned about costs. For some people, uncertainty regarding price may be a significant deterrent to accessing primary care. The retail model lowers cost by reducing fees for medical care; it also reduces childcare costs and minimizes lost wages by providing convenient hours.

In addition to transparency standardization in pricing, retail clinics feature administrative simplification. Retail clinics start with electronic records and work to minimize administrative burden on providers and consumers, decreasing bureaucracy and therefore facilitating a lower price per patient.

The quality issue needs to be monitored, evaluated, and continuously improved to ensure standard-of-care medical practice in the retail clinic. The retail clinic model relies on caring for straightforward problems with low density and uncomplicated reasoning, assisted by clinical protocols that outline evidence-based solutions.

Relatively little medical practice is driven by hard science; substantial variation exists from physician to physician and community to community. In the 1990s, this realization drove large employers to embrace aggressive forms of managed care. Today, individual consumers are seeking value for their money. They may be receptive to "standardized" practice based on clinical protocols and computer-supported decision-making. It may not be difficult to convince consumers to deviate from the current traditional healthcare system to utilize the retail clinic when so many errors occur under our current system.

The retail clinic model is designed to address basic health problems, not serious or acute care needs. When patient care needs exceed the retail clinics' capabilities, quality will depend on the referral practices of the retail clinics. Crucial questions include:

1. How will clinics screen patients who show up for care?
2. Will patients with urgent needs on arrival or after examination receive timely referral to traditional providers?
3. Will patients' continuing medical needs be addressed following retail clinic visits?

If there is a quality concern in the retail clinic movement, it may be about referral rather than about services provided. The success of the referral system will depend on a facilitator model in which both additional primary care and subspecialty care referrals are promptly and appropriately made.

Access to medical care has been a major issue when considering healthcare in the United States, where, according to the Centers for Disease Control and Prevention, in a given 12-month period, almost 50 million people between the ages of 18 and 64 are uninsured. Reducing prices in the marketplace increases demand; therefore, lowering the price for healthcare should expand access at the margin.

The retail model is priced to encourage access even if the patient has no insurance. It offers preventive and primary care services, and the patients decide if the services are necessary and if they are willing to pay for them. Because the expense is relatively low, it will probably appeal to the consuming healthcare public.

In addition to low cost, the retail clinic demographics favor better access. Research indicates 90% of Americans live within 10 miles of a Wal-Mart store, making ease of access a reality. Proximity, convenience, and transparent pricing all encourage retail clinic participation. The model itself facilitates the marketing of these benefits. Retail clinics use point-of-purchase marketing to remind shoppers to buy their preventive and primary care.

THE POSSIBLE ROLE OF RETAIL CLINICS

Retail clinics represent a healthcare innovation that needs further investigation, as they may represent disruptive innovation that can enhance access and decrease skyrocketing costs. They bring customer service innovation to medicine.

A central feature of large retailers is that they constantly reinvent their business model to meet the desires of the consumer/patient, enhancing existing strategies to better serve the customer. The commitment to continuous improvement in services and convenience is more robust than in the healthcare industry. Large retailers adapt to economies of scale with local accommodations. Adaptive skills are likely to prove valuable when reengineering healthcare delivery in communities.

Retail clinics will never dominate healthcare because comprehensive medical care must include inpatient services and specialized services that are not available in a retail setting. Retail clinics, however, have the potential to define preventative/primary care that is available to a large segment of our population. They provide healthcare according to what the community wants in terms of access, quality, and cost.

Today, there are more than 1,500 in-store medical clinic locations, and there will be many more if they prove to be financially, politically, and legally viable. Accomplishing this task at a grassroots level may help attain what has eluded state and federal policy makers.

Developing retail clinics is more than an economic proposition—it leads to questions regarding health insurance, healthcare financing, and healthcare delivery. The debate surrounding these issues will require regulations and statutes that simultaneously facilitate and constrain the development of retail clinics.

Retail clinics will not stabilize health insurance risk pools. Insurance risk will continue to be driven by patients with acute healthcare needs and chronic illness that require high-density decision-making. The preventive/primary care opportunity exists when the axes of healthcare access, quality, and delivery meet at an optimum point on the healthcare supply and demand curve.

Retail clinics offer an affordable alternative to conventional medical care at the preventive/primary care niche and are an attractive option to insurers and cash-paying patients. This model contributes to, but does not solve, the redistribution challenge of financing healthcare for the lower economic strata of the U.S. population. People with no insurance and minimal funds cannot even afford cost-effective, basic care, accentuating the need for additional healthcare innovation.

CHAPTER 6

Risk Management Principles for Physicians

The swift pace of medical practice today makes it imperative for physicians to carry a toolbox jam-packed with risk management principles. The toolbox must be overflowing with utensils that allow a complete execution of the physician's fiduciary responsibility to the patient: all-inclusive informed consent, comprehensive documentation, fulfilling the standard of care, the significance of second opinions, transparency, crisis-management skills, and how to discuss an unfortunate result/outcome.

The rapid-fire pace of medical practice puts physicians at risk for errors in judgment and performance of procedural skills that could result in allegations of malpractice. This discussion focuses on how to limit the potential for malpractice allegations. The problem, succinctly stated, is that practicing good medicine is not enough to avoid allegation of malpractice.

MALPRACTICE CONSIDERATIONS

First, every human being makes mistakes, including physicians. Medicine has evolved into a complex, multidisciplinary model of practice, with multiple players and levels of care, including nurse practitioners and physician assistants assuming a greater role as medical care providers. Risk-adverse physicians must be concerned not only with their own actions and omissions, but also the activity of those ostensibly under their supervision.

Second, even when no error is committed, the discipline of medicine is bursting at the seams with tough choices that frequently must be made in seconds. The complexity lies in the fact that physicians must quickly make tough choices based on imperfect options, and patients, in an emotional and regressed state, must make difficult decisions when confronted with confusing medical terminology regarding unknown diseases.

The susceptibility to "Monday morning quarterbacking" is common in the medical community, where there is an exponential growth of review committees in a medical environment tying reimbursement to "quality." When the outcome of a medical judgment/procedure is suboptimal and emotions are running high, second-guessing is rampant, often irrational, and, in a highly competitive medical marketplace, occasionally vindictive.

Third, even when there is no physician error and the decisions are seemingly predictable; the practice of standard-of-care medicine can occasionally have less-than-desired outcomes. There is always a potential for physical injury, pain, emotional distress, and even death. These adverse outcomes are difficult to ignore, and they bring to the surface suspicion of negligence and a desire for retribution. The unique combination of an untoward outcome, distrustful patient or family, and persuasive plaintiff attorney creates a recipe for an allegation of malpractice despite the medical practice meeting the standard of care.

RISK MANAGEMENT PRINCIPLES

The astute physician must understand how to develop practice patterns and behaviors that prevent patient frustrations from turning into burdensome litigation. Physicians should understand the principles of risk management and develop a coherent plan to implement these principles to minimize the risk of malpractice allegations. Although some of the advice included herein may seem obvious, many physicians wish they could go back in time and apply these basic but vital principles.

The doctor–patient relationship is crucial in defining the likelihood of a medical malpractice allegation. The importance of a warm, genuinely caring relationship with the patient and the patient's family cannot be overstated. Cultivating such a relationship is an essential skill for all physicians involved in patient care. The greater the emotional bond between the patient and the physician, the more likely a trusting relationship will evolve. This will bring to the surface all the information the physician needs to reach the correct diagnosis and provide optimal medical care.

Empirical evidence shows that the patient's perception of the physician's commitment to communication is a major determinant in patient satisfaction with the doctor–patient relationship. Patients sense whether the physician is totally engaged in their medical care. Increasing the emotional connection with the patient enables physicians to provide quality, responsive medical care, and erects a barrier to an allegation of malpractice in cases of questionable outcomes. Conversely, if a physician is perceived as arrogant, disinterested, impatient, or blunt, it becomes easy for the patient or patient's family to believe that the physician is callous or reckless. Any offers of condolence after the fact will fall on deaf ears and will not deter decisions to pursue legal action.

Physicians must develop a manner of communication that cultivates a caring relationship. Specifically, they must educate patients about the process of care with the facilitation of patient/family opinions, check understanding, and encourage dialogue. Remember, in all human relationships, honey works better than vinegar.

INFORMED CONSENT

Carefully articulated and detailed informed consent forms that educate patients about risks and benefits of treatment options, along with documentation, are essential to limiting physician risk. All informed consent documents should be clearly written and easily understood by the patient and/or the guardian. Physicians must ensure that the consent provides a careful and detailed explanation of the medical treatment or procedure with all attendant risks.

In addition to the informed consent form, it behooves the physician to maintain a medical record that reflects that the physician informed the patient of all risks and benefits of the treatment and the patient's understanding and willingness to proceed. A physician should also prepare an informed consent form that documents a patient's refusal of treatment.

In medical malpractice cases, if the consent form does not identify all the risks and alternative approaches to treatment, the physician will have a challenging evidentiary burden proving that the patient was made aware of the risks and alternate approaches to treatment.

DOCUMENTATION

Although often tedious and time consuming, proper documentation of all aspects of medical care is critical. First, it is good medicine and benefits subsequent assessments. Second, proper documentation facilitates more efficient practice because the physician does not need to reinvent the wheel with each patient visit. What's more, the ability to recall the details of the last visit suggests to the patient an engaged, caring physician.

Documentation is often the "lifeline" when claims materialize. Memory and evidence are likely to conflict in key respects, and credibility of evidence may rest on the accuracy of record documentation. The bottom line in medical malpractice cases is if it is not documented, it did not happen.

THE SECOND OPINION

The judicious, discerning physician who wants to minimize exposure to malpractice claims graciously accepts a patient's desire to seek a second medical opinion. The direr the prognosis or complex the medical/surgical issues, the more fertile the ground for second-guessing physician decisions and actions.

It is in precisely such cases that the physician should demonstrate candid commitment to the patient's well-being. The confident, competent physician has nothing to lose and everything to gain by encouraging and facilitating a second opinion. There is always benefit to additional evaluation of complex problems—the cliché that "two minds are better than one" is never so true.

THE STANDARD OF CARE

Employed physicians are facing increasing pressure to conform their care to insurer or employer guidelines and regimens. It is often a Sisyphean effort to determine whether a particular medical test or procedure is authorized. This can lead to the denial of the most accurate test and put the physician in the uncomfortable position of falling below the threshold for meeting the standard of care.

When such conflicts arise, the physician should pursue all available resources to meet the fiduciary responsibility to the patient and document those efforts, as well as the responses.

TRANSPARENCY

Physicians who adopt a mindset of complete transparency will develop approaches to patient management that minimize the potential for adverse outcomes. Reporting medical errors and near misses is an important step in preventing similar errors in the future, and thus improves patient safety. Individual physicians and healthcare institutions should report all medical errors and safety lapses in order to study the adverse effects and learn preventive measures. They also should share their findings with other healthcare professionals. This broad-based sharing can help reveal the root causes of medical errors and help develop methods and guidelines to prevent other physicians from making similar mistakes.

Physicians who join the "transparency team" are engaged in developing protocols, checklists, and strategies to ensure informed consent, comprehensive documentation, crisis-management skills, and effective communications about adverse outcomes.

CRISIS MANAGEMENT

If the course of events in a medical or surgical treatment goes awry, it is imperative that a physician be prepared and equipped to manage the crisis to avoid exacerbating the circumstances and to minimize the potential for harm to the patient. Akin to the captain of a team, the physician must demonstrate leadership by taking charge, assigning priorities, and delegating responsibility. Members of the healthcare team must communicate clearly and concisely and ensure the messages are received and understood. The use of checklists in crisis management is essential because cognitive skills are less precise in life-and-death circumstances.

Teamwork is critical when managing a medical crisis, and all team members must understand their roles and their limitations. The development of good crisis management skills should include in-service training and crisis simulation drills to prepare the staff for unexpected events and outcomes. The time spent drilling these scenarios will result in improved quality of care, minimized risk for the patient, and reduced likelihood of liability for the physician.

DISCUSSING THE BAD OUTCOME

Mr. Brown had his mitral valve replaced, and the surgery and initial post-operative course were uneventful. A tiny bacterial infection found a home on his prosthetic valve—which might or might not have occurred as a result of negligence. The operating physician was unaware of this infection as Mr. Brown had no complaints and was convalescing uneventfully.

Unfortunately, a few weeks after the hospitalization, the bacterial infection embolized to the brain, resulting in a fatal cerebral infarction. The death was completely unexpected, and Mr. Brown's wife and family were in shock. They peppered the physician with questions: "Why did the bacteria develop in the first place?" "Why did the embolism cause his death?" "Was this a preventable situation?" The physician was genuinely shocked at the result and emotionally drained.

Many competing interests must be balanced in these delicate situations. The physician must double his or her efforts to communicate compassionately with the patient and/or the patient's family when an unfortunate outcome occurs. The words chosen should ideally flow from the relationship that had previously been cultivated.

The importance of being caring, sympathetic, and transparent cannot be overstated. Patients and families want to understand what occurred and why. The better their education during the informed consent process, the less likely conflict will surface and bring the potential for allegations of malpractice.

CONCLUSION

These suggestions to physicians living in this digital time—who are wired up and melting down physically and emotionally—may seem simplistic and burdensome. Unfortunately, review of available medical malpractice case law is filled with the real-life stories of physicians who failed to heed them.

CHAPTER 7

Physician Professionalism: Ethical and Moral Duties Physicians Encounter in the New Business Model of Medicine

Physician professionalism is the essence of being a doctor in our society. Physicians have a social agreement with society to act as a fiduciary in the patient–physician relationship. The introduction of managed medicine and the altered medical environment have disrupted that contract. The medical profession is being challenged by an eruption of technology, fluctuating market forces, and problems in the ever-changing landscape of healthcare delivery. These changes make it a real undertaking for physicians to meet their obligations to patients, forcing them to contend with political, legal, and market forces in order to meet their ethical responsibilities to their patients.

Professionalism is the basis of medicine's social agreement with society. The contractual relationship between physicians and society demands that the interests of patients be placed above those of treating physicians. It also obliges physicians to set and maintain standards of competence and integrity and to provide knowledgeable and professional advice to society on matters of health and well-being. Physicians must act as a fiduciary to the patient, which means they must place the interests of their patients above all competing interests.

The medical profession is being challenged to meet its fiduciary responsibilities by erupting technology, fluctuating market forces, and evolving duties in the ever-changing healthcare delivery system. The exponential transformations across an array of technology and market changes make it a real challenge for physicians to meet their obligations to patients. Indeed, the medical profession is confronted with political, legal, and market forces that challenge physicians to meet their fiduciary responsibility to their patients.

The fundamental principles inherent to physician professionalism include patient welfare, patient autonomy, and elimination of discrimination in healthcare, whether based on race, gender, socioeconomic status, ethnicity, or religion. Market forces, societal pressures, and administrative exigencies must not compromise the principles inherent in a true physician–patient relationship.

Physicians must be sincere and trustworthy with patients and empower them to make informed decisions about their treatment options. Patients' decisions about their medical care must be paramount, as long as it is ethical for the physician to comply with those decisions and they do not lead to demands for care that is not appropriate given the clinical presentation.

This chapter describes physicians' obligatory professional responsibilities, their medical and legal fiduciary obligations, and how employed physicians tangled in a web of ascendant market fundamentalism may be caught between the responsibility to maintain patient primacy and their own professional responsibilities.

PROFESSIONAL RESPONSIBILITIES

The physician's professional responsibilities encompass all of the following:

A Commitment to Professional Competence Through Lifelong Learning

Education is crucial in the world of constantly advancing medical knowledge. Physicians must be devoted to lifelong learning and maintaining the knowledge and skills they need to provide standard-of-care medicine. Appropriate mechanisms must be in place for all physicians to achieve this goal. All physicians should pursue the opportunity for continuing medical education services to maintain the highest level of competence in their area of practice.

Integrity in Dealing with Patients

Medical ethics, common law, and, in many states, codified statutory law mandate the informed consent process. Beyond the ethical and legal reasons for informed consent practices, medical informed consent is essential to a true patient–physician partnership. Physicians must participate in the informed consent process so patients and their families can share in the decision-making process. Whenever patients are injured as a result of medical care, they should be informed immediately because failure to inform patients and families compromises patient and societal trust and confidence in the medical profession. Reporting and analyzing medical errors provides a foundation for developing prevention and improvement strategies and equitable compensation to injured parties. Reporting medical errors and injuries is an integral component of informed consent.

Respect for Patient Confidentiality

Safeguarding patient confidentiality is imperative in today's world, where electronic information systems are used to compile and store patient information and data, and where the use of genomic information may affect a patient's ability to obtain insurance and career opportunities. The sanctity of the patient's medical information must be safeguarded. This issue of patient confidentiality is especially likely to arise when providing information to persons acting on a patient's behalf because the patient is not mentally competent to consent. All physician conversations must be measured and well thought through; the commitment to confidentiality occasionally may be trumped by overarching considerations of public interest.

Preservation of the Physician–Patient Relationship

Illness can cause patients to emotionally regress and become dependent on an authority figure. Given the patient's intrinsic vulnerability and the dependency that may arise, physicians must never exploit a patient sexually or for personal financial gain.

Continuous Improvement of Healthcare Delivery

Physicians must be dedicated to continuous improvement in the quality of healthcare they provide. This commitment must involve not only maintaining personal clinical competence, but also working collaboratively with colleagues to increase clinical knowledge, reduce medical errors, increase patient safety, minimize overuse and misuse of healthcare resources, and optimize patient outcomes.

Physicians, individually and through professional organizations, must take the responsibility for ensuring the availability of uniform and excellent standard-of-care medicine across all demographics and socioeconomic classes.

Just Distribution of Finite Medical Resources

Physicians must provide healthcare that is based on judicious and cost-effective management of limited clinical resources and healthcare dollars. The physician's professional responsibility for equitable allocation of resources requires conscientious avoidance of tests and procedures that are unnecessary and financially driven. Providing unwarranted medical services exposes patients to risk and expense and limits the available resources for others in true need of those resources. Physicians and organizations—both "for profit" and nonprofit—should never compromise their professional responsibilities by pursuing personal advantage.

Physicians have a duty to disclose conflicts of interest that arise in their professional work. They also have a moral and ethical duty to disclose unethical behavior of physicians, organizations, and physicians and organizations acting in concert. Physicians as a profession must participate in self-regulation, including remediation and punishment of physicians, administrators, and organizations that fail to meet professional standards.

FIDUCIARY RESPONSIBILITY OF PHYSICIANS

The word *fiduciary* derives from the Latin word for "trust." The covenant of trust between the patient and the physician is vital to the diagnostic and therapeutic process. It is the foundation of the physician–patient partnership. To help physicians make accurate diagnoses and provide optimal therapeutic recommendations, patients must trust that they can communicate all relevant information about an illness or injury without the physician divulging confidential information. The fiduciary relationship is based on accepted codes of professional ethics.

Historically, the physician–patient relationship was understood to be based on the principle of benevolence, played out through the doctrine of medical authoritarianism. Closely aligned to authoritarianism is *medical paternalism, which* has been defined as an action taken by one person in the best interest of another without that person's consent.

The rationale was that the physician alone had the knowledge and experience needed to make a medical decision; it was therapeutically counterproductive for patients to understand their compromised state of health and the risks they faced because such knowledge would jeopardize, limit, and inhibit their recovery. Paternalism pervaded the physician–patient relationship until the middle of the 20th century.

Medical paternalism eventually succumbed to notions of patient autonomy when it was determined that patients had the right to make their own decisions. This has evolved to the concept of shared responsibility, in which the physician and the patient jointly exercise decision-making authority.

In 1914, in *Schloendorff v. Society of New York Hospital*, Justice Benjamin Cardozo wrote, "Every human being of adult years and sound mind has a right to determine what shall be done with his own body; and a surgeon who performs an operation without his patient's consent commits an assault for which he is liable in damages." This landmark decision marked a radical shift toward recognizing patients' rights in the physician–patient relationship. The increased recognition of civil rights in the 1960s permeated and enhanced a range of individual rights, including those of medical patients. The courts ultimately endorsed the position that a physician would be liable if there was failure to obtain informed consent before medical or surgical treatment.

In the seminal case of *Canterbury v Spence* in 1972, the court ruled that a physician has a duty to disclose to a patient any material risk associated with a proposed therapy that a reasonable patient would need to hear to make an informed decision. The informed consent requirement marked the turning point in changing the definition of the physician–patient relationship from medical paternalism to patient autonomy.

Today the pendulum has swung to a position of shared decision-making. Proper healthcare decision - making and management involve detailed communication and exchange of information between patients and physicians; the patient shares his or her symptoms, concerns, personal goals, personal and family history, and lifestyle desires, and the physician shares the risks, side effects, alternative approaches to care, and potential outcomes. This two-way exchange represents a true physician–patient partnership.

INFORMED CONSENT IN AN ERA OF SHARED DECISION-MAKING

The concept of *informed consent* was explained in *Salgo v. Leland Stanford Jr. University Board of Trustees*, where a California Court of Appeals declared in 1957 that "a physician violates his duty to his patient and subjects himself to liability if he withholds any facts which are necessary to form the basis of an intelligent consent by the patient to the proposed treatment." Subsequent to this ruling, informed consent became an ethical and legal duty imposed upon physicians throughout the United States.

This ethical and legal responsibility to inform patients of the potential material risks and benefits of any proposed treatment before obtaining that patient's consent to perform a medical procedure is now considered a fundamental component of healthcare that is incumbent upon—and a universal obligation accepted by—physicians as part of the doctor–patient covenant. It gives patients the right to make the ultimate decision on the course of treatment. This ethical, moral, and legal duty of physician to patient is a critical piece of the professional responsibilities of physicians.

WHEN THERE IS TOO MUCH INFORMATION

In a world exploding with medical information through television advertising and the vast array of telecommunications, physicians must know how to respond to informed patients. Physicians often receive requests for treatments that are not medically necessary from patients who have misinterpreted information they found on the Internet or derived from advertising. Physicians should not lose sight of their prime fiduciary responsibility to promote and protect the best interests of the patient, even at the risk of losing revenue. The law empowers physicians to refuse to provide services that are not medically indicated, an empowerment that serves society well.

THE THREAT TO PHYSICIAN PROFESSIONALISM

As patients have experienced a transition from paternalism to autonomous decision-making, physicians have experienced the opposite: a transition from autonomy to conflict regarding to whom they are a fiduciary.

Physicians today commonly practice as employees of large corporate medical organizations. Ascendant market fundamentalism pressures them to practice as a fiduciary to the organization, not to the patient. Employed physicians report to business-trained managers and may be subject to contractual obligations that threaten quality of care, patient safety, and the professional and fiduciary responsibilities they owe patients. The MBA-degreed administrators insist that physicians let the demands of the marketplace trump other goals because they believe the practices they learned in business school apply equally to the practice of medicine.

In the new era of employed physicians, numerous problematic clauses in their contracts may affect their abilities to meet their professional duties and fiduciary responsibilities.

Confidentiality Clauses

Confidentiality clauses in physician contracts often have the result of hiding quality and safety issues, medical errors, unethical conduct, and malfeasance. These confidentiality clauses are in direct opposition to the physician's professional responsibility to improve the quality of patient care. The commitment to quality must entail reducing all medical errors, increasing patient safety, minimizing overuse and misuse of healthcare resources, and optimizing patient outcomes.

Physicians have an inherent duty to participate in the development of quality-of-care measures and application of quality measures to assess individuals, institutions, and systems responsible for healthcare delivery. The objective of medical care must be the availability of uniform and excellent standards of care across all demographics and socioeconomic classes.

Confidentiality clauses may interfere with the mandates of professional responsibility necessary to maintain the fiduciary responsibilities inherent in a physician–patient relationship.

Incentive Clauses

Most physician contracts include productivity incentives—inducements for activities that primarily increase employer income and tend to inspire overtreatment. These incentive clauses are in direct opposition to the professional responsibility of physicians to maintain the just distribution of finite medical resources. Physicians must provide healthcare based on judicious and cost-effective management of limited clinical resources and huge financial healthcare dollar deficits. The physician's professional responsibility for equitable allocation of resources requires conscientious avoidance of tests and procedures that are unnecessary and financially driven.

The provision of unwarranted medical services exposes patients to risk and expense and limits the available resources for others in true need. Incentive clauses put the just distribution of medical resources at risk. Physicians have been terminated for low productivity or for not meeting these incentives.

Referral Restrictions

Referral restrictions may be referred to as "leakage control." Many physician contracts prohibit referring to providers outside the system, which may prevent appropriate referrals for particular patients, thus decreasing quality of care. Physician offices often have physician navigators who direct the care of patients to specialists within the health system and take control of the referral away from the primary physician. Contractual clauses that prevent referral to the most skilled and elite physicians directly interfere with the professional responsibility of physicians.

Physicians must collectively attempt to eliminate barriers to excellent and equitable medical care. The objective of medical care must be availability of uniform and excellent standard of care across all demographics and socioeconomic classes.

"Gag" Clauses and Termination Without Cause

Clauses that prohibit physicians from revealing quality and safety problems, medical errors, unethical conduct, and problems with electronic medical records directly interfere with a physician's professional responsibility. Termination without cause puts physicians at extreme risk if they stand up for professional responsibilities. Gag clauses and termination without cause are in direct opposition to a physician's professional responsibility.

THE CONUNDRUM PHYSICIANS FACE

Physicians are trapped between professional responsibilities and contractual obligations that limit their ability to meet those professional responsibilities and their fiduciary responsibility to their patients. This conflict is a manifestation of corporate medicine letting the demands of the marketplace undermines the goals of professional and fiduciary responsibility of physicians.

The ascendant market fundamentalism has pressured physicians to become entrepreneurial businesspersons rather than medical professionals. This shift in the physician's fiduciary responsibility to the employer rather than the patient threatens quality of care, patient safety, and physician professional values.

It is a daunting time for physicians, patients, and society. Managers of large healthcare corporations may not be willing to meaningfully negotiate the most egregious provisions in the contractual relationship with individual physicians, leaving those physicians feeling powerless. The intransigence of these organizations reflects their sheer market dominance.

Physician medical/surgical organizations must demand a return of professional values and fiduciary responsibility to the patient. This may require physicians to organize to collectively bargain with uncompromising and unyielding employers.

SECTION 2

The Medical Malpractice Environment Affecting Physicians

CHAPTER 8

Why Patients Sue Physicians: Risk Management Strategies

Physicians may head off allegations of negligence by developing a comprehensive understanding of why patients sue physicians and by appreciating what activities commonly lead to patient injury. With this knowledge, physicians can develop risk management strategies to reduce the likelihood of being named in a negligence lawsuit.

I outline the common reasons why patients sue physicians, and what activities frequently lead to patient harm. The case examples emphasize the factors that can lead to allegations of negligence and patient harm.

Physicians are on the front lines of patient care, providing healthcare and coordinating recommendations of specialty physicians. Communication and coordination of patient care by physicians is vital. Allegations of negligence against physicians often include failure to diagnose, delayed diagnosis, or wrong diagnosis; inadequate or incorrect treatment; medication-related error; inadequate performance of, or delay in performing, a procedure; delay in initiating a treatment; failure to treat; and failure to monitor a response to treatment.

Common factors contributing to patient injury include the timeliness of a diagnosis and the selection of therapies. The clinical decisions made by physicians often depend on the promptness of diagnostic studies being ordered, performed, and interpreted. Another important factor is the timeliness of specialty involvement in a patient's diagnosis and treatment strategy.

Patient symptoms and the findings from physical examination are the first source of information to help physicians establish a correct diagnosis. A detailed medical history and comprehensive physical examination are essential. The integration of the medical history and physical examination findings allows the physician to synthesize a broad differential diagnosis. The ability to integrate and synthesize this historical and examination data epitomizes the skill of a physician. The skilled physician must effectively communicate the differential diagnosis to the healthcare team and implement and coordinate the evaluation, treatment, and monitoring of the patient's care.

Effective communication and coordination of care is the cornerstone of timely and accurate diagnoses. It requires clinical, social, and emotional intelligence. The complexity of the clinical diagnosis process is reinforced by the fact that symptoms overlap between various disease processes.

The common symptom of chest pain, for example, can represent a variety of disease processes, including angina, myocardial infarction, pulmonary embolism (PE), pericarditis, gastroesophageal reflux, and chest wall pain. Symptoms of respiratory distress secondary to pneumonia can mimic PE. Both pneumonia and PE can cause decreased oxygen saturation with altered mental status that can be similar to the findings in a stroke syndrome or hypoglycemia. The possibility of overlapping symptoms across a broad range of clinical presentations highlights the complexity of making an accurate diagnosis and treatment plan.

This chapter provides an overview of the common patient allegations of negligence, common contributing factors to patient injuries, case examples highlighting these allegations and contributing elements to injury, and risk management strategies.

ALLEGATIONS OF NEGLIGENCE

The most common patient allegations of negligence include:

- Failure to diagnose, delayed diagnosis, or wrong diagnosis.
- Improper/wrong treatment strategy.
- Medication-related error.
- Improper performance or delay of a procedure.
- Failure to initiate treatment.
- Failure to monitor the response to treatment.

Failure to Diagnose, Delayed Diagnosis, or Wrong Diagnosis

Case example: A 50-year-old woman presented with a three-day history of atypical chest pain, neck pain, and back pain. The patient was admitted to rule out acute coronary syndrome. The initial electrocardiogram (ECG) and biomarkers for myocardial ischemia were normal. Subsequent blood work demonstrated an elevated troponin level that went unrecognized.

In the early morning on the second day of admission, the patient had substernal chest pain, elevated ST segments in leads V4–6, and elevated biomarkers, suggesting acute infarction. She was immediately taken to the cardiac catheterization laboratory and found to have an occluded left anterior descending coronary artery. The patient experienced a myocardial infarction.

The treating cardiologist was found liable for delay in the diagnosis of a coronary syndrome because ordered blood tests were not followed up in a timely fashion.

Discussion: Conditions that are most commonly involved in delayed diagnosis, or failure to make a diagnosis, include myocardial infarction, cerebrovascular events, vascular insufficiency, sepsis, intestinal obstruction, PE, spinal epidural abscess, viral and bacterial pneumonia, sub-acute and acute endocarditis, and aortic dissection.

The failure to diagnose or a delay in diagnosis often results in a catastrophic event. It behooves all physicians to use a broad differential thought process when confronted with complex medical presentations. Comprehensive thinking allows a physician to consider all possibilities that could account for the presenting symptoms. It prevents silo thinking and anchoring.

Improper or Wrong Treatment Strategy

Case example: A 53-year-old man was admitted with dyspnea and pneumonia. There was a history of intravenous drug abuse. The physician evaluating the case diagnosed acute bronchitis and ordered antibiotics and breathing treatments. Later in the day, the patient's condition deteriorated, his neck became swollen, and he was unable to swallow. He was transferred to the intensive care unit (ICU).

Soon after entering the ICU he experienced respiratory arrest, and intubation was unsuccessful due to his swollen neck. He died after an attempt at resuscitation. An autopsy revealed a mediastinal abscess, and laboratory tests revealed positive blood cultures. The legal judgment found inadequate clinical assessment and lack of recognition of sepsis, particularly in light of intravenous drug use.

Discussion: Examples of improper or incorrect management that commonly occur in clinical practice include inadequate assessment of foot and decubitus ulcers that subsequently result in sepsis and possible loss of limb. Another example is inadequate management of patients with diabetes, resulting in ketoacidosis, pyelonephritis, disseminated intravascular coagulopathy, and, ultimately, loss of lower extremities.

Many of these cases, when reviewed by experts, suggest that the time interval between assessments and management decisions were excessive.

Medication-Related Error

Case example: A 56-year-old woman was admitted with complaints of abdominal pain, nausea and vomiting, dizziness, confusion, and double vision for five days.

She had been discharged from the hospital just 10 days prior to this admission, following placement of a right coronary artery stent that had occurred 12 days before discharge. Prior to the catheterization, her creatinine was normal. She had atrial fibrillation with poorly controlled rate and was treated with atenolol 50 mg per day. She denied any other medication except aspirin and Plavix.

At the time of the second admission, her heart rate was junctional, at 37 beats per minute. She was unresponsive to atropine therapy. Her creatinine was found to be 6 mg/dL (.5-1.2 mg/dl). The patient coded and died.

The legal judgment was failure to recognize digoxin toxicity in a setting of classic presenting symptoms: junctional rhythm unresponsive to intravenous atropine and ECG changes of junctional bradycardia in the setting of acute renal failure. In addition, the physician did not communicate with the primary care physician, who had started digoxin therapy five days earlier to control the ventricular response.

Discussion: Medication error is a common allegation of negligence in a number of situations, including renal failure from medications such as gentamicin and vancomycin; respiratory failure from excessive doses of narcotics; retroperitoneal hematoma and bleeding from failure to discontinue anticoagulants; and failure to adjust insulin doses in the setting of changing a patient's diet.

Frequent review of medications and medication interactions is necessary, as is consultation and communication with the pharmacy team when using multiple medications.

Improper Performance or Delay of a Procedure

Case example: A 49-year-old obese man with known sleep apnea was admitted to the hospital for leg swelling and increasing shortness of breath. Nursing assessment documented in the notes suggested the patient was at high risk for deep venous thrombosis (DVT). Heparin was started, but no testing for DVT was performed.

On the second day, heparin therapy was discontinued, without any note documenting the rationale for the change. That evening, the patient complained of shortness of breath. He was placed on supplemental oxygen, but oxygen saturations continued to decline. A pulmonary physician was consulted and ordered a chest CT, but the patient experienced a respiratory arrest and died. An autopsy revealed a PE as the cause of death.

Legal judgment was critical of stopping heparin and not pursuing an evaluation for DVT and possible PE in a clinical setting where the patient was at risk for PE. Additionally, the delayed specialty consultation was thought to have contributed to the patient's demise.

Discussion: Examples of improper performance allegations include (1) central intravenous line placement resulting in damage to vessels and (2) attempts to intubate patients resulting in esophageal lacerations, or causing tracheal tears or perforations.

Alleged delays in treatment or procedures include (1) delayed transfusions for gastrointestinal bleeding, resulting in hemodynamic compromise, and (2) chest tube placement for pneumothorax that was not done until after the patient experienced respiratory arrest.

Failure to Recognize the Condition or Treat the Condition

Case example: A 77-year-old man with a history of recent right hip arthroplasty presented to the emergency department after sustaining a pulseless electrical activity (PEA) arrest. He was intubated and successfully resuscitated. The physical examination was significant for a heart rate of 121 bpm, and his blood pressure was 76/47 mmHg. The ECG was significant for sinus tachycardia and ST elevation inferiorly with reciprocal posterior changes.

A STEMI (ST elevation myocardial infarction) alert was called. Emergency cardiac catheterization was performed, and a 60% left anterior descending coronary was stented. The patient continued to decline clinically upon return to the floor.

An urgent transthoracic two-dimensional echocardiogram showed severe right ventricular (RV) strain with a flat, D-shaped septum, severe RV dilatation and RV free wall akinesis, and preserved apical contractions. The echocardiographic features were suggestive of McConnell sign, which is a strong indicator of PE.

The patient had contraindications to intravenous thrombolytic therapy and subsequently underwent a pulmonary angiogram with transvenous catheter embolectomy of a massive left pulmonary artery embolism. The patient died on the table in the catheterization lab.

Legal judgment was critical of failure to recognize the clinical features of the PE, which was clear-cut in the eyes of experts.

Discussion: Examples of failure to recognize a diagnosis include patients with cardiac symptoms who are not evaluated and monitored prior to suffering cardiac arrest. Other classic examples include brain damage resulting from failure to monitor blood sugars following changes in insulin doses and respiratory arrest in patients with obstructive sleep apnea following prescribed narcotic pain medications without appropriate monitoring.

Failure to Monitor the Response to Treatment

Case example: A 74-year-old man with known severe coronary artery disease, congestive heart failure, and ectopic atrial tachycardia was admitted to the coronary care unit for evaluation and treatment. The patient had reduced kidney and liver function but no preexisting lung disease.

The patient received a loading dose of amiodarone and then was continued on amiodarone at 400 mg per day. After six months, the patient was experiencing shortness of breath to the point of being able to walk no further than 10 feet. No blood levels were monitored and no chest radiography was done until 18 months after he started therapy.

Finally, a chest radiograph was obtained that revealed new bilateral alveolar/interstitial infiltrates compared with his baseline radiographs; however, there was no change in the cardiac size or vascular pedicle width, and there were no new effusions. The patient underwent chest CT, which confirmed multiple bilateral infiltrates. Despite early corticosteroid treatment after exclusion of all other differential diagnoses, the patient died one month later in the ICU from respiratory failure due to severe pneumonitis.

Legal judgment was critical of failure to recognize new symptoms and failure to follow the patient's lung status while taking a medication that has known pulmonary toxicity.

Discussion: All medications must be monitored and reviewed on a regular basis. A physician should verify at all follow-up visits that all medications are necessary for management of the patient's medical conditions. Medication errors are common and often are the etiology of many adverse medical events, including sentinel events.

FACTORS THAT CONTRIBUTE TO PATIENT INJURY

The most common factors that contribute to patient injury include:

- Patient assessment issues.
- Communication (or lack thereof) among providers.
- Selection and management of therapy.
- Communication between patient/family and provider.
- Failures to obtain a specialty consult.

Patient Assessment Issues

Case example: A 30-year-old woman who was taking a birth control medication presented to the emergency department with fever, chills, and pain radiating into her interscapular region. D-dimer levels were elevated. Her chest radiograph revealed a right lower lobe infiltrate. The presumptive diagnosis was pneumonia, and she was started on antibiotics.

In the early evening she complained of shortness of breath. Subsequently she was confused and her oxygen saturation dropped to 86%. Later in the evening she died suddenly. The autopsy revealed a massive PE.

Legal and expert review identified failure to consider available clinical factors to develop a broad differential diagnosis, failure to consider available information (elevated D dimer), and failure to order appropriate tests as contributing to the patient's death.

Discussion: The failure to develop a broad differential diagnosis, act on available information, and obtain appropriate tests all can contribute to patient injury and, as in this case, death.

Communication Among Providers

Case example: A 49-year-old man was admitted with chest pain, headache, back pain, and numbness and tingling in his lower extremities. Blood pressure was 160/50 mm Hg in the right arm and 105/56 mm Hg in the left arm. The nurse failed to document these abnormal blood pressure findings, and she did not call the findings to the attention of the physician. The physician did not take the patient's blood pressure.

The patient was discharged home and later that evening was found dead. An autopsy revealed an aortic dissection. Lack of communication between the nurse and the physician and the physician's lack of assessment were found to be critical factors in determining liability.

Discussion: Nurses failing to notify physicians of their findings is a common theme in liability determination for serious patient harm. Other cases involve physicians failing to read important clinical information documented in the medical record and therefore being unaware of the changing clinical condition resulting in patient injury. Physician approachability and demeanor can play a critical role in nursing staff communication.

Selection and Management of Therapy

Case example: An 80-year-old woman with chronic obstructive pulmonary disease fell and fractured her femur. The patient successfully underwent rod placement for the fractured femur and recovered without adverse consequences. The family desired placement in a skilled nursing facility (SNF). The patient was discharged to a SNF on a Duragesic patch for pain management.

After two days at the SNF, the patient developed respiratory distress and became unresponsive. The staff did not respond because they believed the patient had a do not resuscitate (DNR) order in place. It was subsequently identified that the patient did *not* have a DNR order.

The patient's family alleged that the patient's death was secondary to failure to monitor the impact of the Duragesic patch on the patient's respiratory status and failure to communicate the orders regarding resuscitation among the nursing staff. The case was settled before legal judgment.

Discussion: Cases of selection and management of therapy arise under various circumstances, including mismanaged pneumonia, sepsis, cardiac rhythm disturbances, and traumatic injuries, to name a few. Also, improper selection of medication, failure to order the most appropriate medication, or ordering the wrong medication are common allegations of contributing factors to a patient's injury or death. Failure to carry out DNR orders fall within this category.

Communication Between the Patient and Family and the Provider

Case example: A 75-year-old woman with dilated cardiomyopathy, atrial fibrillation, and heart failure was hospitalized for increasing shortness of breath. The patient was anticoagulated and had a transesophageal echocardiogram before a cardioversion. The cardioversion procedure resulted in sinus rhythm. The patient was started on amiodarone in addition to maintenance medications of digoxin and warfarin. The patient was discharged with a follow-up appointment in two weeks.

In 10 days, the patient returned after experiencing syncope resulting in a subdural hematoma. Her heart rate was 30 beats per minute. She was found to have digoxin toxicity, and her bleeding time was elevated. The subdural hematoma expanded and she died in the hospital.

The family sued because they were never instructed to decrease the digoxin level, and no digoxin level was ever drawn. They also argued they were never instructed regarding the interactions between digoxin, warfarin, and amiodarone. The case was settled prior to legal judgment.

Discussion: Communication skills challenge our society. It is important for physicians to communicate well, including educating patients and families about their medical conditions and treatment plans. Patient failure to understand medication effects and side effects and treatment plans is a common contributing factor to patient injury. Communication should occur and then be carefully documented in the medical record.

Failure to Obtain a Specialty Consult

Case example: A 62-year-old obese woman was admitted to the hospital with complaints of chest pain radiating into the left arm and shortness of breath. She had had similar complaints two weeks earlier and was admitted to the hospital.

During the prior admission, myocardial injury had been ruled out. On the second admission, her initial ECG revealed nonspecific changes, but the troponin was mildly elevated in the setting of mildly impaired kidney function. The second set of enzymes was significantly elevated, and a STAT echocardiogram revealed a large anterior wall myocardial infarction.

After the echocardiogram was obtained, a cardiology consult was ordered. The critical expert review identified that there was a failure to obtain a timely cardiology consult, which would have resulted in preventing injury to the patient.

Discussion: This category includes two situations: (1) the physician caring for the patient does not recognize the patient's medical condition; and (2) the physician caring for the patient believes he or she can manage the case without assistance.

RISK MANAGEMENT PRINCIPLES

Risk management principles arise directly from an understanding of the common themes seen in allegations of physician negligence and patient injuries. The case examples discussed here allow the reader to develop a collective understanding of the issues that require due diligence to prevent allegations of negligence. The following are the golden rules of risk management when practicing medicine in a fast-paced medical environment:

- Perform a detailed medical history and comprehensive physical examination allowing for a broad-based differential diagnoses.
- Perform a thorough evaluation and order and interpret diagnostic tests in a timely manner in order to arrive at a timely diagnosis.
- Involve other specialists immediately if the generated differential diagnosis has the potential for serious sequelae or death.
- Be accessible and responsive to nursing and paraprofessional staff to ensure proper communication and coordination of medical care.
- Communicate the differential thought process, pertinent performed evaluations, and pending test results to physicians when handing off patients to fellow physicians.
- Emphasize diagnostic dilemmas and patients with deteriorating medical conditions.
- Stay engaged with the specialist as the case evolves.
- Document noncompliance or refusal to follow treatment regimens using exact quotes from the patient and family.
- Take time with every patient. Build a rapport and make the patient understand you have a partnership and that you are his or her fiduciary.
- Review all documentation to ensure awareness of all orders, consults, and changing conditions as reported in the nursing notes.
- Document all medical actions, all activities involved in coordination of care, and all discussions with patients, families, nurses, and physicians
- Document all reviewed test results and action to be taken in response to diagnostic testing.

CHAPTER 9

Malpractice Considerations: New Concerns on the Horizon

Physicians practicing medicine in today's ever shifting and advancing medical world are at risk for malpractice liability. The introduction of a vast array of telecommunication media into the physician world is creating a growing area of malpractice risk for physicians.

This chapter explores the new malpractice considerations facing physicians in our constantly evolving digital world. Although they are novel and just on the horizon, these risks are real, and it is prudent for every practicing physician to consider them carefully.

Allegations of negligence are a major concern to practicing physicians. Generally, malpractice is the breach of a standard of care or a standard of conduct by a member of a profession, such as a physician. The failure to meet a standard of care (negligence) or standard of conduct (misconduct) that is recognized by a profession reaches the level of malpractice when a patient is injured or damaged because of physician error.

The litigious nature of American society is influencing the field of medicine. Overwhelming majorities of practicing physicians believe that their concerns regarding medical malpractice liability impair their ability to provide quality care and cause them to order unnecessary tests and make unnecessary referrals. Many nurses and hospital administrators share this belief. Furthermore, a large majority of physicians, nurses, and hospital administrators believe that these extra tests, referrals, and procedures significantly contribute to escalating healthcare costs.

Physicians practicing medicine face many risks on a daily basis, but many of those can be avoided. Knowing and understanding the potential malpractice risks is a physician's best risk-management strategy. I present here some current malpractice concerns and discuss how to avoid them in today's medical practice environment.

The malpractice concerns include the following:

- Why clinical practice guidelines are a double-edged sword.
- How Accountable Care Organizations (ACOs) may heighten a physician's malpractice exposure.
- Why teams of healthcare professionals may raise liability dangers.
- The perils of social media and smartphones.
- The new dangers inherent in electronic medical records.
- Why telemedicine lawsuits are expected.
- Why complaints to state boards are as damaging as lawsuits.

Understanding these new threats will reduce a physician's risk for liability exposure in today's constantly changing digital medical care landscape.

CLINICAL PRACTICE GUIDELINES: SHIELD OR SWORD

Physicians in today's medical practice arena are expected to follow evidenced-based medical guidelines produced by specialty societies, payers, hospitals, and clinical decision support systems in electronic health records (EHRs). Specialty societies issue medical guidelines that protect physicians against unpredictable standards of care promulgated by expert witnesses engaged by plaintiff attorneys. Unfortunately, this attempt at shielding physicians can become a double-edged sword. Studies have been published supporting the thesis that medical guidelines are used more frequently against doctors than in service of them.

Courts still seem wary of medical guidelines, interpreting them as hearsay unless introduced by an expert witness whom they rely on to vouch for the standard of care, defined as: reasonable and ordinary care exercised by physicians in the same specialty and under like circumstances.

The problem with medical practice guidelines is they are ambitiously trying to capture best practices. They are trying to define the optimal level of medical care, which has the potential of requiring the physician to meet an even higher standard of care in a malpractice case. Beyond that, the basic problem is that medical practice guidelines are variable and frequently fail objective tests of reliability.

In 2013, the *Journal of the American Medical Association* assessed several guidelines on the basis of eight standards for creating medical guidelines set by the Institute of Medicine (IOM) and found that none met all eight standards. Even medical guidelines fashioned by organized medicine do not escape criticism. In a study in 2012 only about one-third of medical guidelines produced by subspecialty societies satisfied more than 50% of the IOM standards.

The American Board of Internal Medicine Foundation's Choosing Wisely initiative has persuaded many specialty societies to identify tests and procedures they consider unnecessary or overused. Unfortunately many of the medical guidelines subject practitioners to a low, but significant risk for missing serious disease" if the guidelines were followed to the letter. Choosing Wisely provides a disclaimer at the end of each guideline: "Use this report at your own risk."

What can the practicing physician do about this risk? Just be aware that medical practice guidelines are not an ironclad safeguard against malpractice allegations. The take-home point is that clinical practice guidelines must be considered judiciously within the context of the entire clinical situation. A single clinical approach does not fit all patients. Think of the practice guidelines as guardrails.

ACCOUNTABLE CARE ORGANIZATIONS

New medical organizational structures may create liability risk. ACOs represent a new frontier in malpractice law. Defined and incentivized under the federal Patient Protection and Affordable Care Act, ACOs allow hospital groups and other medical facilities to partner with smaller healthcare provider groups and individual medical professionals. This is the government's attempt to move healthcare delivery away from fee-for-service reimbursement models toward payment structures governed by the quality and cost-effectiveness of treatments that patients receive. ACOs are in an "embryonic state" and have not existed long enough to generate legal decisions; therefore, we have a paucity of legal precedent to formulate risk management strategies.

ACOs may provide higher risks for threats of malpractice for a number of reasons:

- The new organizational structure yields higher expectations of practitioners.

- More clinical information is available for plaintiff attorneys to use.
- The defined mission of ACOs is to produce savings.
- Legal protection available to health maintenance organizations is lacking.

It will take years for cases to arise and wind their way through the courts, so we have precedents available to formulate risk management strategies.

Risk for allegations of negligence is inherent in the expectation of higher levels of care within ACOs. In ACOs, physicians must develop individualized medical care plans for patients that are more comprehensive than what is typically committed to the patient record. Federal regulations mandate a defined process to meet the higher standard for patient communications and state that clinical knowledge must be presented in a way that takes into account a patient's unique needs, priorities, and preferences. This federal regulation–mandated language has intrinsic risks for the practicing physician because patients' unique needs, preferences, and priorities are open to variable interpretation.

The individualized patient care plans, patient assessments, ACO application materials, procedures, and protocols create a gold mine of material for the plaintiff attorney to inspect for inconsistencies. Additionally, federal regulations direct that an ACO must report internally on quality and cost metrics.

The idea of increasing quality while containing costs is fraught with potential inconsistencies. Whenever quality and cost intersect, there is potential for allegations of negligence. Plaintiffs' attorneys could cite the ACOs' mandates to produce shared savings to demonstrate that corners were cut on patient care for cost savings. The cost-cutting argument is persuasive to many juries. HMOs enjoy legal protection against arguments that they skimped on care to save money, but ACOs do not have that protection because they are involved in the actual provision of medical care.

What can physicians do about these possible risks? Be aware and remember they have not materialized yet. The best protection for a physician working in an ACO is to adhere strictly to all the mandates and recognize that attention to detail can be a lifesaver for the patient and the physician.

HEALTHCARE PROFESSIONAL TEAMS' LIABILITY CONCERNS

ACOs, Patient-Centered Medical Homes, and hospital systems are increasingly using teams of healthcare professionals to provide patient care. Involving multiple caregivers in patient care may create the potential for liability risk. The obvious danger is that no single person is in charge of the patient's care. The doctor–patient relationship gets diluted because no one doctor is accountable to the patient's overall medical care. Even when a physician is not directly involved in a patient error, there is the potential for liability under the concept of vicarious liability. Emanating from vicarious liability is the notion that you are only as good as your weakest link.

Additionally, a problem arises when there are conflicting views of what medical care the patient needs. Physicians caring for critically ill patients often do not feel the responsibility to act because they have a different view of treatment than the physician in charge.

A major risk for liability and an opportunity for "finger pointing" occur when a patient is "handed off" from one team member to the next. When a malpractice issue surfaces, there can be a wide discrepancy among team members as to what was said regarding patient management issues. To limit the potential for conflict between care providers, a team member must be "in charge" of overall patient care, and everyone involved in that patient's care must adhere to the defined management strategy.

In addition, patients must be contacted post-appointment or post-hospitalization to ensure that communication has been effective and to avert errors if there was a breakdown in the communication between the healthcare team and the patient. Medical care teams should develop clear lines of accountability for patient care. Team members must have clear roles, mutual trust, effective communication, and shared goals. If the team does not develop such clear lines of accountability for patient care, there is a high risk for poor outcomes and associated liability risk.

THE RISKS OF ELECTRONIC COMMUNICATION

Everywhere you look, people are peering down at their smartphones reviewing a text, email, or the latest Facebook post. In the hospital, it is common to see physicians lost in their smartphone world as well.

The rise of smartphone technology and use has created a new malpractice risk called the "distracted doctor." When physicians and other medical personnel are engaged with their smartphones, they are no longer fully present in the patient's room. In one example that illustrates the severity of the problem, an anesthesiologist was named in a malpractice case involving a patient's death during heart surgery. The defendant was alleged to have been looking at his iPad and failed to notice plummeting oxygen saturations.

Despite the dangers of using smartphones in the clinic or hospital, there are few regulations on their use in the medical work world. Cell phone distractions are a risk to patient safety.

The best approach to lowering this risk for healthcare professionals is to establish policies that prohibit the use of phones for personal matters at work. A possible solution might be dedicated telecommunication devices that can be used for work issues only. These types of policies would eliminate distractions that lead to mistakes that potentially can harm patients. Human beings function best when engaged in the task at hand; multitasking is just asking for allegations of negligence.

SOCIAL MEDIA AND MALPRACTICE RISK

Facebook, Twitter, and Snapchat have become the dominant media for social interaction. Social scientists have a name for this sort of incessant online contact: ambient awareness. It is, they say, very much like being near someone physically and picking up on their mood through the little things they post or tweet.

Facebook is no longer alone in offering this sort of interaction online. In the past year, there has been a boom in tools for posting frequent tiny updates on what you are doing. The phenomenon is quite different from what we normally think of as blogging, because a blog post usually is a written piece, sometimes quite long—a statement of opinion, a story, or an analysis. But these new updates are something different. They are far shorter, far more frequent, and less carefully considered.

One of the most popular tools is Twitter, a website and messaging service that allows its more than 200 million users to broadcast updates limited to 280 characters, on what they are doing. Other services permit users to report where they are traveling or quickly toss online a stream of the pictures, videos, or websites they are looking at. There are even tools that give the user's location.

Physicians, who are as entrenched as anyone else in social media, must remember that anything they post on Facebook or other social media can be used against them in a malpractice proceeding. Plaintiff attorneys want to portray a defendant physician in a bad light and constant Facebook postings give them ample opportunity. The plaintiff attorney can use any acrimonious postings to establish character deficits. The best advice is to keep personal and professional lives separate and limit access to social media postings to family and trusted friends.

ELECTRONIC MEDICAL RECORDS: A MALPRACTICE PARADOX

Electronic medical records (EMRs) are a medical practice paradox. Since EMRs did not become common until 2011, when the Meaningful Use program was initiated, the malpractice law in this area is in its infancy. The cases that have arisen since 2011 have included computer systems that were not interoperable, tests results not properly routed, faulty data entry, and misuse of copy-and-paste functions.

Clearly when there are so many boxes to check, there is a risk of mistakes and errors than can lead to allegations of negligence. EMRs provide plaintiff attorneys with a treasure trove of new evidence for their malpractice case. Unlike a paper trail, everything is recorded in the metadata, showing time stamps and individual keystrokes.

The best advice to physicians is slow down, despite the rapid-fire pace of today's medical practice. It is imperative to edit and proofread any data they copy and paste. Check the system for errors and do not sign any gag orders from vendors. The malpractice risk associated with EMRs is real for physicians. As the systems become more overloaded with data (as often is associated with regulatory mandates), the risks for the physician increase.

TELEMEDICINE AND POTENTIAL MALPRACTICE RISKS

Telemedicine is possible thanks to telecommunications capabilities that allow patients to consult remotely with their doctors via two-way video, text, or e-mail. Patients can receive some of the care they need from the convenience of their own office desks. More than 36 million Americans have used telemedicine in some way, and as many as 70% of doctor visits can be handled over the phone. The use of telemedicine is common and is here to stay. The COVID pandemic has made telemedicine a front and center approach to patient care. What malpractice risks does it present to physicians?

Telemedicine is another new realm of healthcare for which there are few legal precedents. One area of concern is the reduction in the personal connection between the physician and the patient, which may increase the likelihood of a malpractice action. When the doctor has not talked to and examined the patient in person, it is harder to defend against alleged allegations of negligence. Additionally, because telemedicine involves physicians remotely supervising technicians on site, when concerns develop, the doctor can be implicated on the basis of vicarious liability.

What can the physician do to avoid the medical malpractice risk associated with the new world of telemedicine? First, physicians must understand the malpractice risks associated with a digital relationship. If they assume that risk, it may be beneficial to take a course in conducting a telemedicine session so they identify how to make it a personal experience. Second, they must carefully supervise nurse practitioners, physicians' assistants, and technicians at remote sites. Finally, they must have a malpractice policy that covers digital physician–patient relationships.

STATE BOARD REPORTING AS A LIABILITY RISK

Patient complaints to the state medical board are on the rise and represent another liability concern that may be eclipsing malpractice litigation. These complaints can precipitate disciplinary actions against physicians that are just as hazardous as malpractice suits.

A disciplinary action does not have to involve a patient injury, and there is no payout if the physician is censured. However, as with a malpractice suit, it can involve negligence and may be just as harmful to a physician's reputation. Licensure actions and malpractice actions must be reported to the National Practitioner Data Bank.

The increase in the number of complaints filed against physicians is due to unhappy patients who find it easier to file a complaint than to convince an attorney that they have a meritorious case. The confounding factor for physicians is that board actions are based on allegations of impropriety that might not meet the threshold of malpractice.

The best way to prevent complaints to the state board is by maintaining a quality physician–patient relationship based on adequate time spent with the patient, effective communication, and comprehensive follow-up. The best approach when responding to the medical board is to supply comprehensive, detailed records outlining the patient's history, physical examination, and plan of care.

CONCLUSION

Physicians who are developing risk management strategies to prevent allegations of negligence in the digital medical world must understand the new horizon of potential malpractice allegations outlined in this chapter:

- Why clinical practice guidelines are a double-edged sword.
- Why and how ACOs may heighten malpractice exposure.
- Why and how teams of healthcare professionals may raise a few liability dangers.
- Why social media and smartphones pose new malpractice perils.
- Why there are new malpractice dangers inherent in EMRs;
- Why telemedicine lawsuits are expected.
- Why complaints to state boards are as perilous as malpractice lawsuits.

This understanding will reduce the likelihood of being named in a malpractice action that harms one's reputation as a physician.

CHAPTER 10

Medical Malpractice Stress Syndrome: A "Forme Fruste" of Posttraumatic Stress Disorder

Physicians practicing medicine face many challenges in today's health-care arena. The stress of practicing medicine is increasing exponentially as new medical information explodes on a daily basis and new stresses to practicing occur in a burgeoning telecommunication world.

The impact of rapidly increasing medical information and electronic medical records, which allow physicians to communicate with patients and physicians without the benefit of observing body language or clarifying misunderstandings, has had a huge impact on physician–patient risk for misinterpretation of the electronically transmitted medical information.

The risk of malpractice allegations is real even under the best circumstances. The potential risk to physicians alleged to be negligent has resulted in a clinical entity called medical malpractice stress syndrome—a "forme-fruste" of posttraumatic stress disorder.

Posttraumatic stress disorder (PTSD) is a well-defined feature of acute and chronic illness. PTSD may develop in some people who have experienced a shocking or dangerous event. Fear triggers many split-second changes in the body to help defend against danger or to avoid it; this "fight-or-flight" response originating in the thalamus is meant to protect a person from harm. Everyone experiences a range of reactions after trauma, yet most people recover from initial symptoms naturally. Those who continue to experience problems may be diagnosed with PTSD. People who have PTSD may feel stressed or frightened even when they are not in danger.

Traumatized people may not develop chronic or even short-term PTSD, and PTSD can occur even though a person has not experienced dangerous event. Some experiences that can precipitate PTSD include the sudden, unexpected death of a loved one, a wartime experience, or an observation of a traumatic event. Symptoms usually begin within three months after the incident, but may begin years after the initial emotional trauma. To be classified as PTSD, symptoms must last more than a month and be severe enough to interfere with human relationships or work. Some people recover within six months; others have symptoms that last much longer. In a subset of people, the condition becomes chronic.

Cognition and mood symptoms can begin, or become exacerbated, after an event. These symptoms can make the person feel alienated or isolated from friends or family members. Although it is natural to have some of these symptoms after a dangerous event, people may have very serious symptoms that go away after a few weeks. This is called *acute stress disorder*. When the symptoms last more than a month, seriously affect one's ability to function, and are not due to substance use, medical or mental illness, or anything except the event itself, they might indicate PTSD. Some people with PTSD do not show any symptoms for weeks or months. Depression, substance abuse, and anxiety disorders often accompany PTSD.

PTSD can develop at any age, and may occur in war veterans, children, and people who have been through a physical or sexual assault, abuse, accident, disaster, or other serious events. Women are more likely to develop PTSD than men, and genetic predisposition may make some people more likely to develop PTSD.

Not everyone who lives through a dangerous event develops PTSD. In fact, most people will not develop the disorder. Risk factors can make a person more likely to develop PTSD, whereas other factors, called resilience factors, can help reduce the risk of the disorder.

RISK FACTORS AND RESILIENCE FACTORS FOR POSTTRAUMATIC STRESS DISORDER

Factors that increase risk for PTSD include:

- Living through dangerous events and traumas.
- Being injured emotionally or physically.
- Seeing another person hurt or seeing a dead body.
- Experiencing childhood trauma.
- Feeling horror, helplessness, or extreme fear.
- Receiving little or no social support after the event.
- Dealing with extra stress after the event, such as loss of a loved one, pain and injury, or loss of a job or home.
- Having a history of mental illness or substance abuse.

Some resilience factors that may reduce the risk of PTSD include:

- Seeking out support from other people, such as friends and family.
- Finding a support group after a traumatic event.
- Learning to feel good about one's own actions in the face of danger.
- Developing a positive coping strategy or a way of getting through the bad event and learning from it.
- Being able to act and respond effectively despite feeling fear.

CASE PRESENTATION

A 51-year-old male physician presented to the emergency department with chest pain, dyspnea, and an electrocardiogram suggestive of a myocardial infarction–ST elevation across the precordial leads of the electrocardiogram. Biomarkers for myocardial injury were elevated.

A short history revealed that the patient had recently been served notice of a pending malpractice allegation for the death of one of his young patients. The notice stated he was being sued for $10 million. He had been experiencing severe anxiety and suicidal ideation for the last five days and had been using antianxiety agents and alcohol to suppress symptoms.

The echocardiogram revealed apical hypokinesis of the left ventricle with depressed left ventricular function. Coronary angiography revealed normal coronary arteries. The diagnosis was Takotsubo cardiomyopathy or "stress induced cardiomyopathy" or "broken heart syndrome." The exact cause of broken heart syndrome is unclear. It is thought that a surge of stress hormones, such as adrenaline, might temporarily or, in some cases, permanently damage the hearts of some people.

This patient had experienced severe stress and emotional chaos after receiving notice of a pending malpractice action. The patient's cardiac function returned to normal, but he had persistent restlessness, anxiety, depression, fatigue, difficulty concentrating, irritability, insomnia, and temptation to commit suicide.

His psychiatrist diagnosed the patient with medical malpractice stress syndrome (MMSS) manifesting as a myocardial infarction with persistent emotional and psychological stress.

MEDICAL MALPRACTICE STRESS SYNDROME

MMSS is a "forme fruste" of PTSD. It is a common disorder with a spectrum of presentations, manifestation, and long-term health effects. It is rarely discussed and often is concealed by the physician experiencing the traumatic syndrome.

Medical malpractice suits are emotionally traumatic. Although they are a hazard of medical practice, physicians rarely consider their potential impact because that is something that happens to other physicians. Unfortunately, no physician is immune from an allegation of medical negligence, and most physicians will at some point be affected, directly or indirectly, by an allegation of medical negligence.

Consequently, it is important to discuss the syndrome so every physician is aware of its presentation, works proactively to prevent allegations of malpractice, and, if faced with such an allegation, is prepared to cope with the psychological and physical effects. It is important to remember that most malpractice suits are decided in favor of the defendant physician.

Even though medical malpractice lawsuits are common, most physicians are ill equipped to deal with the devastating and demoralizing psychological trauma they experience. They also fail to anticipate the impact such a suit will have on their family and friends, and their medical practice. This stress-type syndrome can escalate to severe depression, which may even lead to suicide.

The primary manifestations of MMSS are emotional symptoms; a secondary manifestation may be physical findings such as the "broken heart syndrome," as seen in the case example. The emotional and physical manifestations of MMSS may represent a new disorder, or the aggravation of a preceding disorder.

Physicians may develop feeling of shame, guilt, irritability, distrust, loneliness, and diminished self-esteem. They often react by emotionally detaching themselves from family, friends, and medical colleagues. Often an emotionally damaged physician becomes insecure, concerned about his or her knowledge and skills, and finds it difficult to make medical decisions. Sadly, the accused may remedy the situation by resorting to alcohol and self-medication. He or she also may experience deterioration in any preexisting medical conditions, such as coronary artery disease, diabetes, or gastrointestinal disease.

The physician experiencing MMSS must first acknowledge this fact and then seek medical and psychiatric medical care. This can be difficult because the physician often is severely depressed and ashamed. The affected physician must act to ameliorate the psychological and physical manifestations in an attempt to reverse the agonizing mental turbulence. Reducing the stress symptoms and physical manifestations allows the physician to think and act with greater objectivity, permitting focus and a healthy perspective on the approaching litigation process. Additionally, the physician must reestablish normal relations with family, close friends, and medical colleagues.

PREVENTION OF MEDICAL MALPRACTICE STRESS SYNDROME

Physicians can help prevent MMSS by practicing due diligence. Understanding and dealing with the pervasive presence of standards and guidelines is a requirement for 21st-century healthcare delivery. Evidence that applicable standards of practice were followed is the key to preventing a successful legal challenge after a suboptimal patient outcome. If the physician deviated at all from the practice standards or guidelines, there should be a carefully documented discussion of the rationale and reasoning for this variation.

Because this is a medical-legal analysis, it must start with the legal definition of what constitutes a proper medical standard of care. *Negligence* in regard to the conduct of a physician means the failure to use ordinary and customary medical care, which is defined as failing to do that which a physician of ordinary prudence would have done under the same or similar circumstances. *Ordinary care,* when used with respect to the conduct of a physician, means that degree of care that a physician of ordinary prudence would use under the same or similar circumstances.

Juries decide whether the healthcare provider followed the standard of care as defined by expert witnesses. Sound judgment, reasonable caution, and evidence of caring are the key factors woven into evaluating the standards of care. The "strictest medical scrutiny" is for avoiding common human failings: being careless, forgetful, inattentive, or indolent.

Prudent Physicians Understand Clinical Guidelines

What could be more compelling to establish the proper standards of medical care than the criteria used to license every healthcare facility or to determine what level of medical care should be reimbursed for millions of American citizens? Enter the Joint Commission (JCAHO) and the Centers for Medicare & Medicaid Services (CMS). By adopting the standards purportedly developed using evidence-based medicine, the private accreditation arm of healthcare facilities and the reimbursement services of the federal government may have taken over the definition of proper medical care.

Prudent Physicians Know the Levels of Evidence and Class of Recommendations

It is left to the trial judge to evaluate the admissibility of evidence-based clinical guidelines based on their proven integrity, as scored using level-of-evidence and class-of-recommendation parameters. The court hears "evidence of the evidence" to determine whether conflicts in clinical guidelines actually identify the proper standard of care.

Evidence is categorized into three levels:

- Level A: Recommendation based on evidence from multiple randomized trials or meta-analyses.
- Level B: Recommendation based on evidence from a single randomized trial or nonrandomized studies.

- Level C: Recommendation based on expert opinion, case studies, or standards of care.

After the level of evidence is valued, the relative strength of the recommendation must be quantified using a risk/benefit analysis and an evaluation of the conflicting findings that may be present in different studies. A class of recommendations is thus established:

- Class I: Conditions exhibiting evidence or general agreement that a given procedure or treatment is useful and effective.
- Class II: Conditions exhibiting conflicting evidence or a divergence of opinion about the usefulness/efficacy of a procedure or treatment.
- Class IIa: Weight of evidence is in favor of usefulness/efficacy.
- Class IIb: Usefulness/efficacy is less well established by evidence or opinion.
- Class III: Exhibiting evidence or general agreement that the procedure is not useful or effective, and in some cases, may be harmful.

Of the Class I recommendations, only approximately 20% are based on Level A evidence. Most of the recommendations are Class II, and they are most commonly supported by Level C evidence. Clearly, practitioners are not limiting their medical decisions to criteria derived from Class I recommendations and Level A evidence. For example, 30% of percutaneous coronary interventions and 39% of cardiac catheterizations were recently performed under Class II indications.

One fact persists about evidence-based medical care: there must be some *evidence* that it was utilized. Thus the emphasis shifts onto what some say is the foremost medical advancement of the 21st century: electronic medical records (EMRs). Physicians must recognize that if there is no documentation in the EMR, it is assumed to not have occurred.

Rarely has there been such excitement about the virtues of a technology for information transfer. By initial accounts, EMRs should speed medical care, stop pharmacy errors, provide real-time access to medical advancements, improve quality of care, enforce clinical guidelines, encourage best practices, ensure proper billing and reimbursement, eliminate fraud and coding abuse, and provide administrators and credentialing bodies with immediate access to the data required to ensure regulatory compliance and to effect certification for an operation.

In fact, there is anecdotal evidence that all of these goals, and more, may be realized by the creation of a universal medical database that is interoperable among practitioners, facilities, and allied healthcare providers. EMRs will be very important in avoiding medical negligence claims once the constraints, both fiscal and physical, have been worked out.

Prudent Physicians Avoid "Never Events"

A "never event" is a serious medical error or adverse event that should *never* happen to a patient, such as wrong-site surgery or hospital-acquired pressure ulcers. CMS defines never events as "serious, preventable, and costly medical errors." They are certain surgical mistakes, medical errors, and preventable complications—also labeled "reportable adverse events" by CMS. Refusal to pay for such occurrences will inevitably lead to medical–legal questions as to whether proper standards of care were employed in the treatment that led up to the events.

Being on the provider end of any of the following CMS-identified categories will almost certainly be followed by the dreaded certified letter with notice of intent to file suit for medical negligence:

- Surgery performed on the wrong patient.
- Surgery performed on the wrong body part.
- Invasive surgery scheduled but wrong procedure performed.
- Objects left in the patient's body after surgery.
- Air embolisms.
- Blood incompatibility.
- Pressure ulcers.
- Falls in the hospital.
- Catheter-associated urinary tract infections.
- Catheter-associated vascular infections.
- Mediastinitis after coronary artery bypass graft.
- Inadequate glycemic control.
- Surgical site infections.
- Deep vein thrombophlebitis and pulmonary embolism.
- Drug-induced delirium.

Defense against liability for any of these events may be possible only if written guidelines for preventive measures are documented in the patient's medical records. Compliance with relevant clinical guidelines seems to be the only meaningful defense when charged with the occurrence of a never event with one of your patients.

FINAL THOUGHTS

What can physicians who are the target of a medical negligence challenge do to increase their chances of prevailing? More importantly, what could they *have done* before the litigation process began to lessen the chances of being sued?

- The primary criterion for determining whether a jury of peers might find a defendant negligent often is whether he or she is *likeable*. If the practitioner is amiable, remorseful, sincere, and articulate in offering his or her feelings, a jury is less likely to find that his or her care was negligent. This is the case even if the medical error was relatively unmistakable.
- A practitioner or facility administrator cannot hope to "turn on the charm" after a bad outcome has occurred. In other words, genuine compassion and caring go a long way in communicating that even failed efforts to achieve optimum results are, nonetheless, our profession's best efforts.
- The best place to begin evaluating your personal malpractice risk is with close personal scrutiny. Do you *care*, without qualifications? Are you positive, upbeat, and encouraging about your patients' health? Are you honest, both in demanding your own best efforts and in holding your patients accountable for a substantial portion of their own well-being?

This is a time of patients' rights and of shared healthcare information, but also of shared responsibility between providers and patients. The threat of medical negligence claims will persist for years to come. Being informed about the source of complaints and remaining vigilant in following the proven standards of our specialties and subspecialties offer the surest form of insurance against liability claims. Awareness of MMSS allows physicians to adapt their practice patterns such that the risk of an allegation of negligence is reduced.

In addition, physicians must empower themselves though awareness of the emotional symptoms and physical manifestations of stress and prepare themselves to handle stress by participating in wellness training programs.

Wellness is defined as a dynamic process involving self-awareness and healthy choices resulting in a successful, balanced lifestyle. Wellness incorporates balance among the physical, emotional, and intellectual realms of daily living. Wellness results in a sense of accomplishment, satisfaction, and belonging. The importance of connectedness cannot be overemphasized. This wellness community offers protection from the unique demands of medical training and defines a lifestyle that offers life-long protection against the many stressors of daily living. Maintaining wellness requires feelings of empowerment and engagement.

The ultimate answer to the question of how to avoid medical negligence claims lies in *prevention*. Ideally each physician should carefully document his or her rationale in all decision-making and clinical care. Any deviations from medical standards or guidelines should be carefully documented, explaining the rationale for the deviation. This strategy will reduce the likelihood of allegations of negligence and the potential for MMSS.

CHAPTER 11

Liability of Physicians Supervising Non-physician Clinicians

Physicians confront a variety of liability issues when supervising non-physician clinicians (NPC) including: (1) direct liability resulting from a failure to meet the state-defined standards of supervision/collaboration with NPCs; (2) vicarious liability, arising from agency law, where physicians are held accountable for NPC clinical care that does not meet the national standard of care; and (3) responsibility for medical errors when the NPC and physician are co-employees of the corporate enterprise.

Physician–NPC co-employee relationships are highlighted because they are new and becoming predominant in existing healthcare models. Because of their novelty, there is a paucity of judicial decisions determining liability for NPC errors in this setting. Knowledge of the existence of these risks will allow physicians to make informed decisions on what relationships they will enter with NPCs and how these relationships will be structured and monitored.

The demand for healthcare services continues to increase with the aging population and the influx of newly insured individuals after implementation of the Patient Protection and Affordable Care Act. The additional demand is presumed to exceed the capacity limits of the traditional physician-centric model of primary and subspecialty care.

One response to meeting this increased demand has been the introduction of non-physician clinicians (NPCs) into the healthcare system. Healthcare strategists believe this new practice model will help meet patient demand, decrease overall healthcare costs, and increase practice productivity. This new paradigm may also add a complex level of responsibility and risk/liability for NPCs, often not recognized by the supervising physician. This is particularly true given the absence of a definite legal framework identifying how the co-employee relationship will affect the assignment of liability when negligence occurs.

This chapter examines the education, training, and role of NPCs; explores the type and extent of risk/liability that physicians may assume in these relationships; and, in light of the paucity of judicial decisions and the variable interpretations of the agency relationship between NPCs and physicians, identifies possible approaches to limit physician liability for NPC error.

The chapter also examines the uncertainty in how courts will analyze the relationship of physicians and NPCs as co-employees of the corporate enterprise. And where physicians and NPCs interact as part of the organization, but not in an employer–employee relationship, I describe a case similar to those that populate physicians' offices daily.

In this discussion, an NPC will be limited to nurse practitioners (NPs) and physician assistants (PAs), as these two providers are the most prevalent physician extenders in clinical care in today's healthcare models. There are distinctions between these providers in terms of education, training, licensure, and certification.

SCOPE OF THE PROBLEM

Litigation against physicians and NPCs is increasing; claim settlements are in the millions of dollars in the aggregate for PAs and NPs. Physician payment of all claims involving physicians and NPCs is approximately 98%. The lack of judicial decisions, due to settlement of claims before trial and appeal, represents an obstacle to establishing a medical-legal framework for physicians and NPCs. Measured inferences from available cases create insights for practicing physicians and NPCs to avoid potential liability.

NEGLIGENCE

The most common form of malpractice action against a healthcare provider, physician, or NPC is the tort of negligence. A "tort" is defined as a civil wrong for which there is a remedy in the form of damages. The plaintiff's attorney must prove four elements to be successful in a medical negligence lawsuit:

1. The physician has a duty of care to the individual;
2. The duty was breached by treatment that fell below the threshold to meet the standard of care;
3. The physician omission or commission was the proximate cause of the alleged harm; and
4. The plaintiff suffers compensable damages.

Expert testimony is needed to establish the standard of care and that the negligence is the cause of the injury.

CLAIMS AGAINST PHYSICIANS FOR NPC MEDICAL ERRORS

The claims against physicians for NPC negligence in the traditional employer–employee relationship are well described in the literature. These claims are a foundation to understanding the responsibility of physicians working in concert with NPCs.

Malpractice claims of negligence typically are based on the acts of commission or omission by NPCs. Alleged malpractice claims against physicians for errors of NPCs include:

- Lack of adequate supervision by the physician.
- Tardy or absent referral to a subspecialty care.
- Incorrect diagnosis or failure to identify the correct diagnosis.
- Physical examination/evaluation that is cursory or not performed.
- Misrepresentation of the credentials of the clinician.
- Lack of due diligence in hiring the NPC.

These claims all fall within the "rubric of negligent-supervision" used to hold "masters" liable for the wrongful acts of "servants."

Cursory or Absent Supervision

When an NPC has limited or absent supervision (or limited or absent documentation of supervision) by a physician, the risk for allegations of negligent practice surfaces. Absent specific statutory or regulatory requirements, the question of appropriate supervision is a question of fact that is decided by the jury. Thus practice context may be vital to a determination of the appropriateness of the supervision.

One physician supervising multiple NPCs increases the potential for a determination of inadequate supervision. One court found insufficient supervision by a physician who did not investigate a report by a patient that the care received from a PA was inappropriate. [*Andrews v. US* 598 F Suppl. 603,612 (1982).] The facts determined that the PA–patient interaction was inappropriate, and the physician was held liable for the actions of the PA under the theory of substandard supervision.

Tardy in Time or Absent Referral to a More Sophisticated Level of Care

An allegation of failure to properly diagnose/manage may be made when the NPC misinterprets the clinical history provided by the patient, resulting in a flawed or absent diagnosis, and/or when attempts to treat a complicated medical/surgical illness are beyond the NPC's level of training and skill.

A pertinent example of an alleged malpractice claim based on failure to diagnose and tardy referral involved a patient treated at a U.S. Air Force base medical facility for months for a hiatal hernia with reflux. [*MacDonald v United States* 853 F Suppl. 1430 (M.D. Ga. 1994).]

The plaintiff, a woman in her early 30s, had undergone medical care between 1980 and 1989 for diverse medical reasons, including complaints of sore right leg; dry skin patches on right arm, right leg, and stomach; rash over right calf; warts; hiatal hernia; elevated blood pressure; obesity; smoking; reflux; hip bursitis; and dyspepsia.

Because the medical care history resembles many of the complex patient scenarios medical providers confront, it is instructional to examine the facts. Below is a summary of the court's accounting of the plaintiff's medical care for the relevant period at the U.S. Air Force medical facility:

On June 4, 1988, a patient presented with vomiting. The defendant physician evaluated diarrhea and hip pain. The physician diagnosed the plaintiff with chronic nausea. On June 17, 1988, the plaintiff visited the

PA complaining of pain in her hip and side, and continued pain in the area of her hiatal hernia. The PA diagnosed dyspepsia and prescribed Mylanta, Tagamet, and Motrin.

On September 8, 1988, the plaintiff complained of stomach bloating and heartburn to the PA. The PA diagnosed hiatal hernia with reflux. The PA prescribed Tagamet, Reglan, and Mylanta. The plaintiff's hip complaint was reviewed with the supervising physician. A CT scan and x-rays were ordered.

On October 7, 1988, the plaintiff saw the same PA for follow-up of her stomach and hip complaints. An upper GI revealed reflux and probable duodenitis. The PA continued the prescription for medication and prescribed a follow-up with the physician for hip pain. On October 12, 1988, the plaintiff saw the physician for evaluation of her hip pain.

On January 29, 1989, at 8 a.m., the plaintiff awoke with severe upper abdominal pain. The plaintiff visited the emergency department with "crunching" pain in her upper abdomen and radiating up into her neck and down both arms. A GI cocktail did not alleviate her symptoms.

A physician ordered an abdominal x-ray series. The physician reviewed the x-rays and diagnosed constipation and gave the patient a laxative. The physician recommended discharge but the plaintiff refused because she was in too much pain to go home. After further examination, an electrocardiogram was ordered that revealed an evolving myocardial infarction.

The treatment for the plaintiff's condition was not available and the attempt at transfer to a hospital was delayed in time. Upon arrival at the hospital, despite the referring physician's diagnosis of evolving myocardial infarction, the hospital physician initially treated the plaintiff for a hiatal hernia.

The plaintiff alleged medical negligence against the PA and physician and sought recovery from the defendants' employer, the United States. Based upon the plaintiff's expert testimony, the court concluded, among other things, that the PA had substituted his judgment for that of a physician and that the physician was negligent for lack of supervision of the PA's performance throughout the series of earlier appointments for multiple complaints.

Misrepresentation

Misrepresentation occurs when the patient is not informed that the NPC is not a physician. In one case, the jury found liability on this theory when a NPC prescribed medication that resulted in an anaphylactic reaction leading to multi-organ system failure.

The plaintiff alleged she was unaware she had been treated by a PA. She was not told when scheduling her appointment a PA would see her, and she was not corrected when she introduced the PA to her husband as "doctor." She claimed not to have noticed his name badge, business card, and signs inside and outside of the office identifying him as a PA. [*Oliver v. Sadler* Jury Verdicts (Oct 1994).]

Negligent Hiring

Physicians and/or employers have a duty to use "due diligence" when hiring NPCs. Due diligence requires verification of educational background, licensure, and clinical experience.

One court revoked a physician's license for "aiding and abetting" the unauthorized practice of medicine when it found he had not met the due diligence required when hiring an NPC. The physician had hired the PA based upon the individual's attestation and did not independently verify the credentials.

[*Khan v. Medical Board of California* 16 Cal Rptr 2d 385,392 (Cal App. 1993).]

LEGAL THEORIES

The legal underpinnings for the above-described malpractice allegations arise from three legal theories: (1) vicarious liability; (2) negligent supervision; and (3) negligent hiring. The legal theories are the conceptual framework used by the judicial review process to determine negligence/liability.

Vicarious Liability

Vicarious liability imposes liability for a medical error by the wrongdoer (here, the NPC) to the principal (physician), the person on whose behalf the wrongdoer acted. The law of agency assigns vicarious liability under the respondeat superior and borrowed servant notions. The principal–agent relationship intrinsic to a vicarious liability claim under the theory of respondeat superior requires that the master have the right to control the servant and that both parties voluntarily consent to the agent acting on behalf of the master. The Restatement (Second) Agency states that the master must have the right to voluntarily choose—to select and dismiss—the alleged servant.

Throughout the nation, the courts' interpretation of agency law as applied to physician–NPC relationships is mixed. An Alabama court in 2006, reviewing an alleged, imputed claim of negligence, found that when there was no voluntary consent for a co-employee—a nurse anesthetist—to work on behalf of the co-employee—an anesthesiologist—the anesthesiologist would not be held liable. [*Ware v. Timmons*, 954So. 2d545 (2006).]

A Wisconsin court reached the contrary conclusion in 2009 when it found a surgeon could be vicariously liable for a nonemployee PA under the theory of respondeat superior. The court stated that respondeat superior, while typically arising in an employer–employee relationship, is not limited to only those situations. [*Petzel v. Valley Orthopedics*, 770N.W. 2d 787 (2009).]

In the Wisconsin case, an orthopedic surgeon performed hip surgery on the plaintiff's severely arthritic hip. A PA assisted the surgeon during surgery. After the surgery, the plaintiff had a new paralysis of the foot. The allegation was that negligent surgery resulted in the paralysis.

The standard of care issue revolved around whether the paralysis resulted from the sciatic nerve or the peroneal nerve, which is a branch of the sciatic nerve. Sciatic nerve injury was a known potential complication and would not constitute a deviation from the standard of care.

The Appeals Court held that the surgeon's supervising role, required by the Wisconsin Administrative Code, might have been enough to conclude that the PA was acting under the physician's control and supervision even though there was no employer–employee relationship. The appellate court remanded the case back to the trial court to determine if the facts supported a finding of the required control by the surgeon over the PA for an imposition of vicarious liability.

In this case, the fact that there was no employer–employee relationship did not dispose of the potential for a finding of vicarious liability on the physician for the actions of the PA.

The new corporate business medicine model alters the relationship between the NPC and physician. Under the corporate model, both are employees of the corporate organization. This Wisconsin appellate court decision suggests that in some states, the assignment of liability will be with the physician, who is presumed to control the actions of the NPC, despite the absence of an employer–employee relationship. The Alabama court reached a polar-opposite conclusion.

Negligent Supervision

The second legal underpinning for assignment of liability when physicians are working with NPCs is negligent supervision. This applies when the NPC performs clinical duties under the direction/supervision of the physician. Statutory law in certain states requires direct supervision and may determine whether the physician must be in the same location as the NPC. Physicians must strictly adhere to the statutory provisions to limit risk.

Negligent Hiring

The third legal underpinning for assignment of liability is negligent hiring. This occurs when an employer/physician hires an NPC but fails to use reasonable care to discover the NPC's lack of competence to perform the duties included in the clinical work. [Harris 385 N.C. at 387, 438 S.E. at 735.]

NURSE PRACTITIONERS WORKING WITH PHYSICIANS

Although the potential liability for actions of an NP in a retail clinic setting has been reviewed, there is no review of NP liability when physicians are working with NPs in clinic and hospital settings, and there is limited available judicial review on this topic.

Although physician supervision and collaboration requirements are the dominant provision in most states, in some states, NPs have the ability to diagnose, treat, and manage patients independently of physicians. Collaboration and supervising statutory schemes vary from state to state. The traditional requirement is that the NP work in connection with a physician to develop defined, written protocols under which the NP practices.

Typically the NP and the physician must spend onsite time together and have chart review requirements. These regulations appear to create a master–servant relationship which, as articulated in the Restatement (Second) of Agency, could be subject to vicarious liability under respondeat superior.

POLICY ISSUES

The dominant paradigm is that the NPC and physician are co-employees of the corporate enterprise. It is the corporate entity, not the physician, that likely is imposing certain controls over what and how NPCs can perform and which patients they see. It is the employing entity that has control over which individuals are hired, retained, and assigned to work together. The present-day policy of focusing on improving efficiency and finances through the use of NPC in the delivery of care is an admirable goal, but possibly at a cost of providing less sophisticated care.

In deciding to accept this sacrifice in exchange for efficiency and cost-savings, policymakers will have to entertain the question as to who bears the liability when medical errors are made by the NPC. In addition to the negligent NPC, should the co-employee, supervising physician be vicariously liable?

A major goal of the tort law system is to limit the likelihood that similar errors of omission or commission will recur in the future. Shifting risk away from the NP and toward the supervising physician may hamper that goal. Eliminating the vicarious liability of the physician in this circumstance makes sense when the employing entity will likely provide the "deep pocket" for any uncompensated recovery from the negligent NPC.

TABLE 1. NP and PA Education, Training, Licensure, and Certification

	Education	Training	Licensure	Certification
NP[3]	4-year bachelor's degree Master's degree	Under NPA Dx, Rx, and M	Licensed	Nationally
PA[4]	4-year bachelor's degree	2 years	Certification	U.S./District of Colombia

Dx, diagnosis; Rx, treatment; M, management; NP, nurse practitioner; NPA, Nurse Practice Act; PA, physician assistant.

PA graduates are required to take a national certifying examination. PAs must complete 100 hours of continuing medical education every two years and take a recertification examination every six years. The PA education is two years and is validated by the Accreditation Review Committee on Education for Physician Assistants.

CONCLUSION AND GOLDEN RULES

Physicians and NPCs working as co-employees of the corporate enterprise are navigating uncharted waters. Physicians would be prudent to understand the risks associated with a supervisory role over NPCs.

Initially, physicians must realize they may be unwittingly assuming this liability risk. They should assume that a judicial review would identify the physician as having control over an NPC's actions, even though the physician does not employ the NPC. Accordingly, the following are some golden rules for physicians:

- Become familiar with and knowledgeable of the state rules, regulations, and requirements for the NPC in the state in which they practice.
- Affirm that the NPCs they work with meet all educational requirements and have the experience and training needed to fulfill the position—including checking all credentials and references to ensure accuracy and veracity (see Table 1).
- Make efforts to properly teach, train, and monitor NPCs in areas of responsibility to ensure safe, high-quality patient care.
- Ensure that the ratio of physicians to NPCs is commensurate with the number prescribed by law.
- Through the development of a system of high standards for NPCs, including regular review of patient management, focus on proper

diagnosis, treatment, surveillance, and comprehensive mechanisms and documentation to ensure these standards are met.
- Insert language in their contract indemnifying them and holding them harmless for liability that may impose for the negligence of the NPCs.

The physician performing these due diligence actions will minimize the risk for liability when working in conjunction with NPCs.

CHAPTER 12

Professional Liability Pertinent to Graduate Medical Education: The Intersection of Medical Education, Patient Care, and Law

Physicians in training, nurse practitioners, physician assistants, attending physicians, and institutions that sponsor medical education, are all at risk for potential professional liability issues. The unique relationship between healthcare providers and their sponsoring institution generates complex and evolving legal issues for all participants in medical education training.

The law has played an instrumental role integrating quality care and patient safety with excellent medical education for training physicians, while providing an avenue for relief when a medical error occurs. The intersection of law and medicine, while allowing for optimal medical education and patient care, exposes participating medical providers and the sponsoring institutions to specific professional liability issues. This chapter addresses these medical education settings and their potential professional liability issues.

Physicians in training (i.e., interns/residents, fellows), advanced practitioners (i.e., nurse practitioners [NPs] and physician assistants [PAs], are employed by the medical institutions that sponsor their medical training program. The institution may be a community hospital or, more commonly, a hospital affiliated with an academic center. Due to varying levels of medical qualifications, physicians in training and advanced practitioners work under the supervision of attending physicians in a hierarchical fashion. The attending physicians either are employees of the institution or have a contractual relationship to teach the physicians in training.

Under common law, the employer has the right to dictate to the employee what to do as well as where, when, and how. This type of strict employee–employer relationship typically exists between the training program and the healthcare trainee. In exchange, the institution or training program must provide to its employee continuing medical education, an environment where responsible patient care can be practiced, and protection against the medical-legal system during this critical learning period. It is because of this interwoven relationship that the physician in training, advanced practitioner, attending physician, and sponsoring institution of the graduate medical education are all at risk for allegations of negligence and are potential defendants in a lawsuit.

INTERSECTION OF MEDICINE AND LAW

Physicians in training and advanced practitioners must be licensed to practice medicine and are subject to personal medical malpractice risk for providing care that does not meet the identified standard of care in the medical community.

The greatest concern for physicians in training and physician extenders is the potential for personal encounters with the law. Examples that demonstrate the sometimes tortuous relationship between medical education and the law include: the antitrust lawsuit against the Association of American Medical Colleges, the federal regulation of resident work hours, Medicare and Medicaid's ever-changing compliance regulations, the complexities of the Health Insurance Portability and Accountability Act of 1996, and the growing concern with the legal ramifications of the electronic medical record and the exponential growth in rules and regulations associated with guideline and metric medicine.

The attending physicians and sponsoring institutions are aware of and concerned about the potential for professional liability. The complex relationships between physician trainees, NPs, attending physicians, and sponsoring institutions make the legal issues an important topic for discussion. The Accreditation Council for Graduate Medical Education

(ACGME) requires accredited institutions that sponsor residency and fellowship programs to provide professional liability insurance. In the future, graduate medical education will continue to be constrained by current and evolving rules of law.

THE STANDARD OF CARE

Healthcare providers and graduate medical education institutions share a responsibility to provide high-quality and safe patient care in accordance with standards of care established in medicine. The law has not, and will not, proffer a lower threshold for meeting the standard of care for physicians in training or advanced practitioners. Physicians in training are held to the same standard of care as attending physicians. This principle encourages physicians in training to seek supervision and inspires attending physicians to provide close, vigilant oversight.

Attending physicians are exposed to malpractice allegations for the care they provide directly and indirectly through their supervision of physicians in training. Attending physicians may be held vicariously liable for the negligence of a physician in training under their supervision and directly liable for insufficient supervision. The adequacy of supervision is continually being elevated to higher standards as the public's attention to patient safety continues to escalate. The graduate medical education institutions and program sponsors bear legal responsibility for the care they deliver and for the negligence of their employees. They also face liability for failure to administer safe systems of care. Physicians in training, advanced practitioners, attending physicians, and graduate medical education organizations all must understand and meet these substantial legal standards.

PHYSICIANS IN TRAINING STANDARD OF CARE

What standard of care should apply to a physician in training? Courts have ruled that trainees should be held to the same standard of care as attending physicians. Courts walk a slippery slope when determining where to hold trainees accountable using an objective, equitable standard of care that facilitates the essential educational mission of training, yet ensures patient safety and an opportunity for patients to seek redress for their injuries [*Parmlee v Kline*, 579 So2d 1008 (La Ct App 1991)].

Modern jurisprudence favors holding the trainee/advanced practitioner/attending triad to the standard of care of an attending in that particular specialty. This is a reasonable and sensible standard given that the education and training process depends on the attending physician's teaching and supervisory role.

The rationale for insisting on this standard for training physicians is grounded in a public policy that protects the safety of patients. Courts have noted a benevolent dual purpose: (1) creating an incentive for physicians in training to seek supervision and (2) incentivizing attending physicians to provide the highest quality supervision. Physicians in training should expect to be held to the same standard of medical care as a reasonable attending physician in their specialty based on the precedent of the available case law.

Graduate medical education institutions must ensure risk management considerations, bolstering patient safety by mandating that training physicians seek attending physician advice whether certain or uncertain about the patient's medical conditions. Attending physicians must be available to give the supervision necessary to provide the highest quality of care. The discussion between the trainee and the attending physicians has great value in evaluating the appropriateness of the trainee's thinking and plan of medical care.

PROFESSIONAL LIABILITY INSURANCE FOR PHYSICIANS IN TRAINING

In general, the ACGME requires accredited institutions that sponsor residency and fellowship programs to provide professional liability insurance to cover all claims arising within the scope and duration of the training. This *occurrence-based* coverage provides for a defense and financial protection against claims connected to medical care implemented during a training physician's activities while participating in a graduate medical education program.

The ACGME standards do not mandate that the policies apply to medical practice outside the graduate medical education program. Sponsoring institutions must provide appropriate clinical support for trainee physicians in compliance with collaborative, supervisory agreements with attending physicians.

ADVANCED PRACTITIONERS' STANDARD OF CARE

PAs and NPs, or physician extenders, are considered legally liable for actions or omissions concerning patients they treat and, therefore, are required in all states to carry adequate medical liability insurance.

Physicians providing medical direction or supervision also may be held liable for the actions or omissions of PAs and NPs, even if no patient–physician interaction occurred. Such liability exists in three separate manners: *negligent selection, negligent supervision,* and *respondeat superior.*

The medical director or other party responsible for hiring a PA or NP may be accused of *negligent selection*, meaning that the party responsible for hiring the physician assistant or nurse practitioner knew, or should have known, issues in the PA's or NP's past that might have predicted future performance insufficiencies. Diligent research and reference review, with adequate documentation of the same, should help prevent and protect from such claims.

Negligent supervision may be alleged against the supervising physician of record, claiming that the supervising physician did not follow state, hospital, or departmental supervision regulation/policies/guidelines, or if the plaintiff's expert believes the physician's supervision was otherwise below the standard of care.

To decrease ambiguity, emergency departments using advanced practitioners should establish guidelines specifying supervising physician responsibility, including factors that trigger when a PA or NP should seek supervising physician consultation, and when a supervising physician should physically attend to a patient evaluated by a physician extender.

If not named for any of the aforementioned reasons, a supervising physician may be included in a medical liability action against a physician extender under the *respondeat superior* claim.

Respondeat superior, Latin for "let the master answer," is the primary vehicle used to assert vicarious liability of the supervising physician for the alleged negligent acts of physician extenders. Under this principle, the supervising physician may not have been present or even aware of the patient encounter, but as the "master of the ship" may be considered liable. Should no claim of negligent selection or supervision be raised, supervising physicians named under the concept of *respondeat superior* often will eventually be dismissed from the case.

Historically, there have been few medical liability cases brought against physician extenders. In 2009 a review of 17 years of records from the United States National Practitioner Data Bank (1991–2007). During the study period, the probability of making a malpractice payment was 12 times less for PAs and 24 times less for NPs as compared with physicians.

ATTENDING PHYSICIANS STANDARD OF CARE

Attending physicians who are supervising training physicians in a graduate medical education setting are subject to the same liability exposure they face when they personally direct and deliver care outside the graduate medical education arena. The attending physician's liability risk is unaffected by the nature of the relationship with the sponsor of the training program.

Attending physicians are exposed to two additional types of liability when assuming a supervisory role: (1) vicarious liability for the physician in training's negligence under the *respondeat superior* notion and (2) direct liability for failure to supervise.

Vicarious liability is the law's imposition of liability on a person or institution for the negligence of another (e.g., trainee/nurse practitioner) based on the relationship between the parties. An employer may be held liable for the negligent acts of employees acting within the scope of their employment, even if the employer acted appropriately. An attending physician acting in a supervisory role can be held liable for the acts of the trainee. [*Brown v Flowe*, 496 SE2d 830 (NC Ct App 1998).]

Courts focus on the nature and extent of the attending physician's control over the practice setting, and the control of the institution under which the training physician is working. [*McCullough v Hutzel Hospital*, 276 NW2d 569 (Michigan Ct of App 1979).]

Frequently, both the attending physician and the sponsoring institution may be vicariously liable. Additionally, attending physicians may be held liable for negligent oversight and supervision of the care provided by training physicians and advanced practitioners.

PRESENT-DAY MEDICAL PRACTICE

These growing and evolving legal standards are juxtaposed with the fact that physicians working in hospitals are being asked to do more in less time—the impact of corporate medicine and the RVU as the metric of productivity. The arsenal of tests, technologies, and therapies is expanding at an exponential rate. Concerns over neglectful medical decisions made under extreme fatigue have resulted in reduction of resident work hours, leading to an increasing number of "handoffs" of patients between changing shifts and potentially compromising continuity of care.

This change in the healthcare landscape has mandated that attending physicians and their extenders be more aware of the details of each patient's health status to better coordinate the care of patients being cared for by physicians in training.

Inpatient care at hospitals has become a relay race among training physicians, advanced practitioners, and attending physicians—the patient is the baton, and coordination of the patient's care is a challenge. These changes have led to a more turbulent work environment. Medical care is susceptible to the level of emotional, biological, and physical resilience of attending physicians, NPs, and physicians in training.

Physicians need an internal compass to cope with the changing landscape of medical care to preserve the sanctity of patient care. The large number of variables involved in patient care leaves them susceptible to medical errors and to potential allegation of negligence.

Allegations of Malpractice

Like any physician practicing medicine, physicians in training, PAs, and NPs can find themselves named in an allegation of medical malpractice. In a medical malpractice case, the plaintiff-patient must prove to the trier of fact that the defendant physician breached the professional standard of care. Expert testimony generally is required to establish the prevailing standard of care for a particular specialty.

Although the physician in training's liability ultimately depends on many competing factors, a complicating fact is that there is a paucity of case law discussing the standard of care for training physicians. [*McCullough v Hutzel Hospital*, 276 NW2d 569 (Michigan Ct of App 1979).]

Courts have tended to treat physicians in training as attending physicians when it comes to the professional standard of care in medical malpractice cases. [*Rush v Akron General Hospital*, 71 NE2d 378 (Ohio Ct App 1957); *Jenkins v Clark*, 454 NE 2d 541 (Ohio Ct All 1982); *Centman v Cobb*, 581 NE2d 1286 (Indiana Ct App 1991).] NPs and PAs need to understand that they also will be held to the same standard, as this incentivizes these advanced practitioners to seek supervision from the attending physician. Attending physicians must understand the scope of practice of physician assistants and nurse practitioners and support them to practice within that scope.

Courts have tried to hold physicians in training to an equitable standard of care in medical malpractice cases, being mindful of the educational purposes of graduate medical education, the need for adequate supervision, and the overriding policy to provide a proper channel of relief for patients who have been harmed. [*Pratt v Stein*, 444 A2d 674 (Pa Super Ct 1982); *Jistarri v Nappi*, 549 A2d 210 (Pa Super Ct 1988); *Bahr v Harper Grace Hospitals*, 479 NW2d 526 (Michigan Ct App 1993); and *Gonzalez v St. John Hospital & Medical Center*, 739 NW 2d 392 (Michigan Ct of App 2007).]

Negligence

Negligence is well defined in tort law. To demonstrate negligence, a plaintiff must prove four elements under a "greater probability than not" standard:

1. The defendant owed the plaintiff a duty.
2. The defendant breached that duty.
3. The plaintiff sustained an injury or harm.
4. The injury/harm was a direct consequence of the defendant's breach.

Physicians breach their duty when their actions or omissions of behavior fail to meet the standard generally expected for a physician in similar circumstances.

IMPACT OF A LAWSUIT

Physicians in training, PAs, and NPs must realize that being named in a lawsuit can result in onerous and time-consuming processes that affect work and home life. The impact of lawsuits on the relationship among healthcare professionals can be extremely disruptive and contentious. Litigation has the potential to bring severe unrest and tension to the graduate medical education setting.

Being aware how the law impacts medical practice is a first step in attempting to prevent the possibility of a lawsuit. The sponsoring institutions must also recognize the importance of developing a risk management program that will help all members of the healthcare team understand the potential pitfalls that could result in allegations of negligence.

CONCLUSION

Professional liability considerations are important for physicians in training, PAs, NPs, teaching attending physicians, and graduate medical education institutions. All members of the healthcare team are at risk for allegations of negligence. All physicians working in graduate medical education must be aware of the issues related to professional liability. Based on collaborative efforts involved in the medical care provided to patients, *all healthcare providers*, no matter their level of qualification or certification, are held to the same standard of medical care. This is grounded in a public policy incentivizing trainees and advanced practitioners to seek supervision, and for attending physicians to provide appropriate supervision.

The student and teacher must see and examine the patient and discuss the potential etiologies of the patient's symptoms and physical findings. The physician trainee and PA or NP must be able to articulate underlying pathophysiologic principles resulting in symptoms, physical findings, and potential treatment options.

The attending physician must ensure that the decision-making processes made by students under his or her supervision are accurate and safe. These laws help provide the legal foundation for the medical education of trainees and physician extenders while providing assurance to the general public that the medical education system produces medical providers who practice clinically appropriate, high-quality, and safe medical care.

CHAPTER 13

The Anatomy of a Lawsuit

Litigation is a physician's nightmare, disrupting his or her personal and professional life. Physicians feel personally and professionally attacked. Even if a physician prevails at trial, the victory is lost in the devastating emotional cost of alleged liability; ultimate victory can feel like defeat. No amount of advance knowledge or preparation can alleviate the anxiety and emotional toll of litigation; however, knowing the nuisances of the process can help a physician navigate and endure the process.

The journey through the lawsuit process outlined here will affect how physicians practice medicine and give them a new respect for the importance of meeting the standard of care on every patient they encounter in medical practice.

THE CASE STUDY

You are a family medicine doctor covering the emergency department. A 49-year-old male arrives with chest pain. He has no risk factors for coronary artery disease. The nurse relays to you that the vital signs are normal. Blood pressure is 140/85 mm Hg, and the heart rate is regular at a rate of 80 bpm.

You interview the patient, who reports 3/10 mid-sternal chest pain waxing and waning for the past 24 hours. You identify no precipitating or alleviating factors to explain the chest pain. The patient appears tense. He denies any significant emotional stress.

The cardiopulmonary physical examination is normal. The electrocardiogram (ECG) is normal, as is the chest x-ray. The blood tests, including a troponin level, are normal. The patient states the pain has resolved and he believes it is anxiety related. He wants to be discharged.

You decide the patient is low risk based on symptoms, physical examination, ECG, and blood tests. You discharge the patient from the emergency department and recommend follow-up with his family physician. The next day you learn the patient died of an apparent heart attack.

THE LAWSUIT: THE BEGINNING

The insurance carrier frequently resolves claims of negligence without a lawsuit ever being filed. These claims are typically clear-cut examples where the standard of care was breached. When it is unclear whether there was a violation of the standard of care, the litigation process often moves forward. The query surfaced by the allegation of negligence often involves determining who bears responsibility for the alleged negligence. Alternatively, the claimant and insurance companies, and/or physicians cannot agree on the valuation of the claim.

When a patient, or the family of a deceased patient, has determined that the physician's malpractice carrier will not resolve a claim for medical malpractice, the patient or the administrator/executer of the estate initiates formal legal action by filing a complaint. The patient or executor, known as the plaintiff, will hire an attorney to file in state court a complaint describing the factual and legal basis for the lawsuit.

There are specific time limitations by which a lawsuit must be filed. A physician should never consider a potential claim "dead" until advised by the insurer, or his or her attorney, that the applicable time to file a lawsuit has expired.

An action against a physician does not begin until the complaint is filed with the court and officially served upon the physician. The proper means of serving a complaint is governed by each state's law and includes being served personally or by registered or certified mail. The timing and manner of service is important, as errors in the process of serving the complaint can result in the lawsuit being dismissed.

When a physician receives a letter or other notice of an asserted claim alleging malpractice, the insurance carrier and physician's attorney should be notified immediately, and copies of the lawsuit papers should be forwarded to each. It is imperative for the physician's attorney to know the exact circumstances under which the complaint was received, to whom it was delivered, who signed for receipt of the complaint, and the exact date and time of such receipt.

The named defendant physician must maintain emotional composure when reviewing the allegations of the complaint point by point and preparing to discuss them with counsel. A medical malpractice complaint is difficult reading for the defendant physician because the allegations frequently include punitive language that is often insulting, such as *willfully*, *wantonly*, and *recklessly*. The complaint purposely presents only one side of the story—it's biased. The defendant will have an opportunity to respond in a factual matter and attempt to accurately depict the circumstances surrounding the allegations.

Upon notice of the malpractice claim, it is prudent for the defendant physician to transfer the plaintiff's care to another physician with similar training and expertise. After transfer to another physician, the defendant physician should have no contact or communication with the plaintiff or legal representative for the plaintiff, except to provide copies of medical records to the patient or patient's designated representative as formally requested. All copies of records should be sent by certified mail. The physician should prevent any loss of or tampering with medical records.

INSURANCE COVERAGE ISSUES

When the malpractice insurer decides not to resolve the claim, control of the case shifts from the insurance company to the attorney retained to serve as independent counsel for the defendant physician. Defense counsel will be the physician's primary source for information about pertinent law and the progress of the case.

The issues regarding the claim of negligence are directed to the defense counsel, and the attorney has a duty to keep the physician and insurance carrier informed about the progress of the case. The physician must be certain his or her counsel has no conflict of interest.

A professional liability insurance policy requires the company to provide a defense for the insured physician on all claims for which there may be potential coverage. If there is uncertainty surrounding a potential coverage issue, the carrier will issue a "reservation of rights" letter informing the physician that the company is providing defense counsel for the insured, but is reserving its rights to deny any coverage for any adverse settlements should the facts identified in the litigation support a denial.

Among other reasons, the insurance company may deny coverage because some or all of the treatment occurred outside the coverage period, or the physician was treating outside his or her specialty, did not give proper notice when the claim arose, or had defaulted on payment and premiums.

A physician should retain separate counsel to review any reservation of rights by the insurer, to provide advice about rights and obligations under the policy, and, if necessary, to litigate against the insurance company in the event of wrongful dismissal of coverage.

MEETING WITH DEFENSE COUNSEL

Physician's Overview of the Case

Defense counsel will meet with the physician in person to find out about the particular facts underlying the claim, provide an overview of legal standards and issues that will be controlling, and discuss upcoming actions in the case. The physician should arrange for the attorney to have all medical records, bills, devices, and instruments that are pertinent to the claim, and a list of all medical personnel involved in the patient's evaluation and treatment.

The physician must be prepared to describe in detail the diagnosis and treatment of the plaintiff, identify what personnel handled which aspects of treatment, and explain all notes and abbreviations in the medical records. The physician must familiarize the attorney with the normal causes, symptoms, and progression of the disease or condition at issue, and how the diagnosed disease or condition is typically treated. The attorney must be well educated about the condition and treatments in question.

The physician must be completely candid with the attorney. If defense counsel is assuming false information to be true, he or she is primed for exposure that will cost credibility with the judge or jury, and will certainly decrease the likelihood of winning the case or settling it favorably. True facts are critical for the defense counsel to evaluate the case and construct a defense. The attorney-client privilege, whereby the attorney and attorney's staff are ethically bound not to reveal any confidential communications, exists to specifically promote such full disclosure and will be violated only in situations such as to prevent the commission of fraud or a future crime.

Identification of Other Parties

The physician's initial interview with counsel will allow identification of parties named in the lawsuit and their roles in diagnosis and treatment. Plaintiff attorneys look for as many potential sources of recovery as possible, thereby naming all involved medical personnel and the clinic or hospital where medical care was rendered. The defense attorney needs to identify healthcare professionals or institutions involved in the patient's care that already settled claims against them.

The individual institutions need to be nominally named in the lawsuit for purposes of allocations of fault. The physician named in the lawsuit may want to file a cross claim against other parties or add new unnamed parties. In this scenario, the physician would allege that the other defendant(s) are solely responsible for the plaintiff's injury, or if the physician is found liable to the plaintiff, that the other defendants or cross claimants should be obligated to reimburse him or her for the damages he or she has to pay.

Evaluation of Procedural Pretrial Defenses

One of the procedural defenses to be considered is invalid or improper service of process. That is why it is imperative that the physician's attorney know the precise circumstances under which the complaint was received, to whom it was delivered, who signed for receipt of the complaint, and the exact date and time of such receipt. If the method or timing of service were improper, the defense attorney may file a motion to dismiss the suit. This decision depends on the gravity of the improper services and the demeanor of the judge who decides the motion.

The remedy for an improperly served complaint may be granting of additional time to allow proper service. Generally, unless the improper service is grossly abnormal, the defense counsel will move to the merits of the case as a possible reason for dismissal.

A motion to dismiss may be filed if the claim was filed beyond the statute of limitations, or if the plaintiff failed to comply with procedural or other statutory requirements. The statute of limitations on a medical malpractice action varies from state to state, ranging from two to four years. It sets the time limit for filing suit; the clock does not begin until the alleged harm/injury has manifested itself.

The statute of limitations may be longer temporarily for claims involving minors, foreign objects left in a patient's body, or claims where the harm was not reasonably discoverable for some period of time based upon the facts. Some states operate by a statue of repose. This sets out the maximum amount of time within which a lawsuit can be filed; the time when harm or injury manifests is not relevant.

Some states have statutes that require a plaintiff to certify that a competent medical professional in the same area of medical/surgical expertise has reviewed the claim and would be willing to testify as to the breach of the standard of care before a lawsuit can be filed.

Procedural defenses may be litigated as pretrial motions to dismiss. A motion to dismiss asks the court to find that even if everything in the complaint is true, the defendant is not liable and should not be required to defend the lawsuit as a matter of law. The defendant physician may have to sign an affidavit, or sworn declaration, describing the circumstances supporting a motion to dismiss.

Each side has an opportunity to present its legal argument on such a motion as legal briefs or oral arguments at a hearing, and the judge will issue an order with a ruling.

Evaluation of the Merits of the Case and Substantive Legal Defenses

Substantive legal issues in the malpractice arena will allege issues such as negligence, improper informed consent, or an intentional tort, such as battery (operating on wrong appendage/organ). The elements of medical negligence are simple. The plaintiff must establish that the physician breached the standard of care in his or her evaluation and/or treatment, and that such breach was the proximate cause of the patient's alleged injury.

The plaintiff tries to establish that the physician did not act as a reasonable physician with similar training would have under similar circumstances, and that the physician's error or omission made the patient's condition worse, slowed recovery, or caused injury or death.

The plaintiff will have to present testimony by expert witnesses that the standard of care was breached. The expert practicing in the relevant field of expertise will testify about the optimal evaluation and/or treatment of the particular condition and identify any deviation from the standard of care. Expert testimony must also establish that the alleged negligence proximately caused the injury or illness, pain, and suffering allegedly endured by the plaintiff.

Assuming the case does not settle, the defendant physician will have the opportunity to present both factual and expert testimony, including experts retained to testify that the defendant physician followed the pertinent standard of care under the circumstances. The issues of breach of the standard of care and proximate cause will often boil down to the dueling of the experts, and the outcomes will depend on which experts present the most knowledgeable, objective, and credible testimony.

The two most straightforward and frequently asserted defenses are that the defendant physician did not breach the standard of care and/or that any error that the defendant physician may have made was not the proximate cause of patient's injury or condition progressing, or failing to improve. The burden lies with the plaintiff to establish these elements. The defense must present evidence disproving either or both of these elements.

Other defenses can shield the defendant physician even when all elements of negligence are proven, such as independent intervening negligence and contributing negligence, which requires proving that despite the defendant physician's negligence, a co-incident or subsequent negligent act or omission was the real cause of the plaintiff's continued illness, injury, or death.

Contributory and comparative negligence are defenses to liability when it can be shown that the plaintiff failed to act with the care of a reasonable person and in so doing, caused or contributed to his or her death or injury. The patient's negligence may be a partial or complete defense to liability.

Additionally, every state has enacted some form of a Good Samaritan law, which shields a medical professional from liability for negligence. In Florida, a statue codifies a form of charitable immunity that state healthcare providers who offer free medical care to indigents are immune from a lawsuit for negligence.

Evaluation of the Plaintiff's Claim and of the Defendant Exposure

Medical malpractice plaintiffs are permitted to seek reimbursement for economic damages, non-economic damages, and punitive damages. Economic damages include lost earnings and expenses for medical treatment incident to and necessitated by the alleged act of negligence. Non-economic damages refer to pain and suffering. Punitive damages are additional sums of money awarded to deter intentional, malicious, or reckless behavior. Past economic damages typically include the dollar amount spent for alleged negligent care, any remedial care, and lost wages from work.

In cases where the degree and cost of future medical care or future lost earnings potential are involved, each side will rely on expert testimony to establish what type and level of future care the plaintiff will need, and the potential for future gainful employment. This may require expert testimony from an economist to assist the jury in determining the award. Non-economic and punitive damages are much more of a wild card than economic damages.

Pretrial Discovery Procedures

Once the complaint has been filed and answered, any procedural pretrial motions resolved, and a litigation strategy mapped out, the pretrial discovery process begins. The interval from the time of alleged negligence to commencement of a malpractice claim may be several years. The discovery process usually consumes the largest portion of time once the lawsuit is filed.

It is in the discovery process that the lawsuit is frequently won or lost. The attorneys typically control the discovery process. The court is involved to the extent necessary to set timetables for completion of discovery or to resolve any disputes among the parties about the propriety of requests or the timeliness and completeness of responses. The trial judge makes the ultimate determination of what evidence may be considered by the jury at the trial.

The rules of civil procedure govern the discovery process and provide two methods to identify what evidence or expert opinions the adversaries plan to offer at trial: written requests for information and live testimony of witness at deposition.

Written Discovery

Written discovery requests include requests for admission, requests for documents, and interrogatories. Requests for admission are statements of facts that the recipient is asked to admit or deny under oath. If the recipient of the request fails to respond, the statement is automatically admitted as true. The recipient is typically instructed to provide a full explanation of the factual basis for his or her denial of any particular request.

Requests for documents are the means by which the plaintiff obtains copies of the physician's notes, records, bills, test results, and imaging results. Conversely, the defense attorney may serve similar requests upon the plaintiff, asking for all of the records of treatment by other physicians before, during, and after the defendant physician's treatment. Additional requests can include opinion letters, reports prepared by the plaintiff's expert witnesses, and evidence of payment of the plaintiff's damages from other sources.

Interrogatories are written questions submitted to the parties - asking for general information regarding the case, including explanations of the defendant's view of the facts, lists of people believed to have knowledge of the facts of the case, and information regarding previous claims filed against the defendant and the previous claims filed by the plaintiff. The responding party must obtain interrogatories under oath and they may be used at trial as if live testimony.

The defense attorney reviews all incoming written discovery requests and identifies response deadlines. The defense attorney and defendant physician should draft the responses together. The attorney identifies any requests that will not lead to admissible evidence and objects in writing to such requests. If opposing counsel disagrees, he or she may file a motion asking the presiding judge to rule on whether information sought is discoverable.

The defendant physician reviews the responses of the plaintiff to interrogatories to evaluate accuracy and credibility and to identify any medical or factual mistakes and information omitted or unaccounted for. The defendant physician must review the reports of plaintiff experts to facilitate the defendant attorney's understanding as he or she prepares to depose the plaintiff's expert witnesses.

Depositions

A deposition is a witness's recorded testimony, given under oath, when questioned by the attorneys for the parties in the case. The deposition allows the attorneys to find out what facts and opinions the witness will testify to at trial.

The plaintiff attorney takes the deposition of the defendant physician, the physician's expert witnesses, and any fact witnesses the physician has identified. The defense attorney takes the depositions of the plaintiff and the plaintiff's witnesses. If the witness is one of the parties to the lawsuit, his or her attorney will be present to object to any allegedly improper questions, learn how his or her own witness presents, and ask follow-up questions to clarify the witness's answers or any misimpressions created on the record.

The attorneys use the deposition to lock down the witness's testimony to keep it from changing, to identify and explore any weaknesses, and to assess the witness's overall credibility and jury appeal. The strength or weakness of a witness or expert's deposition testimony is a crucial factor in a party's decision to settle the case or press forward to trial.

A witness physician must thoroughly prepare for deposition by having an in-depth knowledge of the patient's medical history and treatment. The plaintiff's attorney will use lack of in-depth knowledge to imply carelessness, callousness, indifference, and ignorance of the defendant physician. The defendant physician counsel will help the witness prepare for the deposition by telling him or her what to expect and by identifying possible questions the opposing counsel will ask.

Dispositive Motions

Upon completion of discovery, either or both parties may file a motion for summary judgment, asking the court to rule in favor as a matter of law, even if the opposition's vision of the facts is considered to be true for purposes of the motion. The party moving for summary judgment must prove no genuine issues of material fact and therefore no need to proceed to trial. The moving party will file discovery depositions, transcripts, and legal briefs outlining his or her argument. Once the moving party has met its burden, the nonmoving party must file its own brief demonstrating a genuine issue for trial.

When the court considers summary judgment, it must view the undisputed facts and the inferences drawn from those facts in a light most favorable to the party opposing the motion for summary judgment. It is rarely granted in medical negligence cases because of the many factual issues and conflicting expert opinions.

Alternative Dispute Resolution/Mediation

Increasingly, courts encourage resolving disputes by agreement rather than trial. The judge may conduct a settlement conference or appoint a neutral third party to be a mediator or arbitrator of the dispute.

The most common form of dispute resolution in medical malpractice cases is mediation. At the mediation, all parties to the lawsuit, attorneys, and representatives from insurance companies meet in person with a neutral third-party mediator appointed by the court or agreed upon by the disputing parties. The mediator does not decide the case, but attempts to get the parties to agree to settle on mutually agreeable terms. An excellent mediator will bring the parties together for an open, honest discussion about the merits of the case.

The physician's demeanor will communicate to the plaintiff whether he or she is genuinely concerned for the plaintiff's well-being. What the physician says and how it is communicated will greatly affect whether a favorable agreement can be reached.

The mediation session offers each party an opportunity to speak with impunity. The statements made in the course of the mediation are privileged and may not be used by either party if the case proceeds to trial. It is an opportunity for the defendant's physician to express that he or she is sincerely sorry about the outcome.

The mediation will conclude when an agreement is reached or the communications come to an impasse. In a typical settlement agreement, the parties agree that the physician's settlement of the claim does not constitute an admission of liability, and the terms of the agreement are kept confidential.

A physician should go into mediation with an open mind and willingness to explore all avenues of a peaceful resolution.

THE TRIAL

The trial begins with selection of a jury. A large pool of potential jurors will be questioned together and individually by the attorneys for each side about the potential juror's background, work experience, jury experience, and prejudices that may impair their ability to render a fair decision. Once the final composition of the jury is determined, the jurors will be sworn in and presentation of the case will begin.

In a medical liability case, the plaintiff carries the burden of proof, which in a civil trial requires establishing the elements of the case by a preponderance of the evidence. Thus, the burden is on the plaintiff to present evidence and persuade the jury. The defendant bears the burden of proof in affirmative defenses, such as whether the plaintiff acted to cause or contribute to the injury.

Plaintiff counsel will call the plaintiff's witnesses and direct questions to elicit their direct testimony. Defense counsel will cross-examine each witness, attempting to undermine credibility, demonstrate bias, or point out facts the witness did not acknowledge in testimony.

When the plaintiff has finished presenting witnesses and evidence, the judge will entertain any motions by the defense for a direct verdict. This motion asks the judge to rule that the plaintiff has not provided sufficient evidence to allow the case to go to jury. Again, it is a rare circumstance that this motion is granted.

The defense attorney will then begin to present his or her evidence, including testimony of the defendant physician and supporting experts. The plaintiff's attorney will have an opportunity to cross-examine the defendant physician and supportive experts. The defendant physician must remain composed when the plaintiff attorney attempts to discredit the physician during cross-examination. The attorneys will object to the admission of certain testimony or pieces of evidence as appropriate, and the judge will sustain or overrule this objection on the spot.

At the conclusion of the defendant's presentation of evidence, the defendant may again request that the judge decide the case based upon the law and not submit to the jury. If the case moves forward, the attorneys conduct a conference during which they discuss and argue the elements of the instructions to the jurors. Then each attorney presents a closing argument to the jury.

The judge will instruct the jury as to applicable law to the case and how they are to deliberate and arrive at a verdict. The jury then retires to deliberate. The foreman announces the verdict or impasse (hung jury). If a hung jury, the case may need to be retried.

POST-TRIAL MOTIONS AND APPEALS

After the jury trial, the losing side may move that the judge enter judgment notwithstanding the verdict. The threshold for this motion to succeed is extremely high, as the party so moving must establish no reasonable juror could have found in favor of the moving party based upon the evidence in the record. The losing side has a statutorily defined time period in which to file notice of its intention to appeal the verdict. The parties may settle before appeal.

SECTION 3

The Importance of "Basics" in Limiting Allegations of Physician Negligence

CHAPTER 14

The Physician Fiduciary: Understanding Trusteeship

Physicians must, as fiduciaries and trustees to patients, have a physician–patient relationship that will achieve high-quality care, excellent health outcomes, and contained cost. Responsible caring physicians understand the importance of being a fiduciary and trustee to their patients in a complex healthcare arena that has changed from palpable public responsibilities to a profit maximization business model.

As physicians, we live in a complex, ever-changing medical landscape. The goal of maximizing profits percolated into the healthcare sector that was once based upon the "common good" of our patients and society. What is the common good? It consists of our communal values, about what we owe one another as citizens, bound together in the same society seeking the rules and principles we seek to achieve together. A concern for the moral good is an ethical attitude recognizing we are all in it together. If there is no common good there is no society.

A century ago, hospitals and health insurers had palpable public responsibilities. The original purpose of health insurance plans, devised at Baylor University in the 1920s, was not to maximize profits. The original intent of the health insurance plan was to share the risk of illness across all demographics and to cover as many people as possible (maximize the common good).

The nonprofit Blue Cross and Blue Shield accepted everyone who wanted to be a member. Unique to this plan was the idea that every member paid the same rate, irrespective of age or health. In the 1960s, Blue Cross was providing hospital coverage to more than 50 million Americans.

Then, in the 1970s, "entrepreneurs" seized an opportunity to make vast sums of money by exploiting the common good. This change in the health insurance landscape adulterated the charitable mission of Blue Cross and Blue Shield. These entrepreneurs founded for-profit insurance companies like Aetna and Cigna that accepted only younger and healthier patients. This profit-driven mission allowed them to lower their premiums below the Blues' while running to their depository with hefty profits. The Blues were unable to compete, so in 1994 they surrendered and became for-profit. This ended the era of nonprofit health insurance.

This tragic transition led to a new paradigm where the American health insurance system zealously insured the healthful and avoided the sick population like the plague. When the only motive is to make as much money as possible in a short time frame, the common good is easily displaced.

As physicians, we have been thrust into this dismal situation of trying to identify how we reinstate the common good back into the healthcare of America. A daunting challenge, but one physicians must accept individually and as a group.

The present-day healthcare pact has put physicians in a triangle composed of administration, healthcare providers, and patients. We must resist the urge to become tribal. Tribalism is the behavior and attitudes that stem from strong loyalty to one's own tribe or social group. Ignorance of tribalism led American policymakers to underestimate the importance of cultural identity in Vietnam in the 1960s, Venezuela in the 1990s, and Afghanistan in the 2000s. As physicians, we must understand the cultural, political, and financial identities of the stakeholders sitting at the healthcare policymaking table. We must act as leaders through trusteeship.

What is a trustee? Trustee is a legal term that, in its broadest sense, is a synonym for anyone in a position of trust or responsibility for the benefit of another. Physicians are the trustees of patients. Physician leaders must be the stewards of the once-unwritten rules we took for granted—the common good.

One-half century ago, healthcare leaders understood that corporations were not just for shareholders, but also for employees, communities, customers, and the public. Health insures existed to provide coverage to everyone who needed it, not to cherry pick the young and healthy. Over time and through tumultuous change in the healthcare arena, leaders seem to have forgotten that their legitimacy depends on advancing the common good, and that type of leadership is a public trust.

Physician leaders have a duty to teach physicians about the importance of being a fiduciary in the doctor-patient relationship. They have a duty to meet with administrators and patients to discuss how to restore the common good in healthcare and to serve the common good of our nation. Leadership as trusteeship extends beyond ethics. It requires a different way of thinking about the central obligation of leaders. Its essence is restoring trust in the healthcare system.

CHAPTER 15

Physician Professionalism

Professionalism is the basis of medicine's social agreement with society. This contractual relationship demands placing the interests of patients above those of physicians, setting and maintaining extraordinary standards of competence and integrity, and delivering knowledgeable and professional advice to society on matters of healthiness and well-being.

The medical profession is being challenged by an eruption of technology, fluctuating market forces, and problems in the ever-changing healthcare delivery. Indeed, the medical profession must contend with political, legal, and market forces that challenge physicians to meet their fiduciary responsibility to their patients.

The fundamental principles inherent to physician professionalism include patient welfare, patient autonomy, and elimination of discrimination in healthcare, whether based on race, gender, socioeconomic status, ethnicity, or religion. Market forces, societal pressures, and administrative exigencies must not compromise the principles inherent in a true physician–patient relationship.

Physicians must be sincere and trustworthy with patients and empower them to make informed decisions about their treatment options. Patients' decisions about their medical care must be paramount, as long as the care is ethical, and the patients' decisions do not lead to demands for incongruous care given the clinical presentation.

I describe here the necessary physician professional responsibilities, the medical and legal fiduciary obligations of physicians, and how employed physicians tangled in a web of ascendant market focus may be wedged in a conundrum of how to maintain patient primacy and their own professional responsibilities.

PROFESSIONAL RESPONSIBILITIES

Physician professional responsibilities should encompass a commitment to professional competence, integrity when dealing with patients, patient confidentiality, preservation of appropriate personal and financial relations, access to medical care, highest quality medical care, equitable distribution of finite resources, and maintenance of trust by avoiding conflicts of interest for personal or financial gain.

Physicians must be devoted to pursuing lifelong learning and maintaining the knowledge and skills to provide standard of care medicine. Education is crucial in the world of ever-advancing medical knowledge, and all physicians should pursue continuing medical education to maintain the highest level of competence in their area of practice.

Medical ethics, common law, and, in many states, codified statutory law mandate the informed consent process and physicians should be knowledgeable in these areas. Patients should participate in the informed consent process to understand the risk-benefit relationship for the proposed treatment strategy; this understanding is essential because patients are often psychologically regressed secondary to the realization that they are confronting a life-preserving procedure.

Whenever patients are injured as a result of medical care, the physician should immediately inform the patient and family because failure to inform them compromises patient and societal trust and confidence in the medical system. Reporting and analyzing medical errors provides a basis and foundation for developing prevention and improvement strategies and apt compensation to injured parties.

The sanctity of the patient's medical information must be safeguarded. Safeguarding patient confidentiality is imperative in today's world, where electronic information systems are used to compile and store patient information and data, and where the use of genomic information may affect a patient's ability to obtain insurance and career opportunities.

Patient confidentiality can be an especially slippery slope when the patient is unable to make his or her own decisions and conversations must be had with person(s) acting on the patient's behalf. All conversations must be measured and thought through. The commitment to confidentiality may occasionally be trumped by overarching considerations of public interest.

The physician–patient relationship is inherently vulnerable because illness allows patients to emotionally retreat and become dependent upon an authority figure. Given this intrinsic vulnerability and dependency, physicians must be careful to not exploit a patient sexually or for personal financial gain.

Improving the quality of patient care is a core value for every physician. Physicians must be dedicated to continuous improvement in the quality of medical healthcare. This commitment includes maintaining personal clinical competence and requires collaboration with all colleagues to increase clinical knowledge, reduce medical errors, increase patient safety, minimize overuse and misuse of healthcare resources, and optimize patient outcomes.

Physicians have an inherent duty to participate in the development of quality-of-care measures and application of quality measures to assess individuals, institutions, and systems responsible for healthcare delivery. Physicians, individually and through professional organizations, must assist and maintain mechanisms to encourage continuous improvement in knowledge and quality of care, including breaking down barriers to excellent and equitable medical care. The objective of medical care must be the availability of uniform, excellent standards of care across all demographics and socioeconomic classes.

Physicians must promote the just distribution of finite medical resources by providing healthcare that is based on judicious and cost-effective management of limited clinical resources and huge financial healthcare dollar deficits.

The physician's professional responsibility for equitable allocation of resources requires conscientious avoidance of tests and procedures that are unnecessary and financially driven. Unwarranted medical services expose patients to risk and expense and limit the available resources for others in true need.

Across profit and nonprofit organizations, physicians and organizations have many opportunities to compromise their professional responsibilities by pursuing personal advantage. They have a duty to disclose conflicts of interest that arise in their professional work as well as a moral and ethical duty to disclose observed, unethical behavior of physicians and medical organizations, whether acting in isolation or in concert, and pursue their remediation when they fail to meet professional standards.

FIDUCIARY RESPONSIBILITIES

The word "fiduciary" derives from the Latin word for "trust." The covenant of trust between the patient and the physician is vital to the diagnostic and therapeutic process; it is the foundation of the physician–patient relationship.

To facilitate physicians making accurate diagnoses and providing optimal therapeutic recommendations, the patient must trust he or she can communicate all relevant information about an illness or injury without the physician divulging confidential information. The fiduciary relationship is based on accepted codes of professional ethics.

Historically, the physician–patient relationship was created upon the principle of benevolence, played out through the doctrine of medical authoritarianism. Medical paternalism eventually succumbed to notions of patient autonomy when it was determined that patients had the right to make their own decisions. This has evolved to the concept of shared responsibility where the physician and the patient jointly exercise decision-making authority.

Medical paternalism has been defined as an action taken by one person in the best interest of another without their consent. The rationale was that the physician alone possessed the knowledge and experience needed to make a medical decision and that it was therapeutically counterproductive for a patient to understand their compromised state of health and the risks they faced because it would jeopardize, limit, and retard recovery. Paternalism pervaded the physician–patient relationship until the middle of the 20th century.

In 1914, in *Schloendorff v. Society of New York Hospital*, Justice Benjamin Cardozo wrote, "Every human being of adult years and sound mind has a right to determine what shall be done with his own body; and a surgeon who performs an operation without his patient's consent commits an assault for which is liable for damages."

This landmark decision marked a radical shift toward recognizing patients' rights in the physician–patient relationship. The increased recognition of civil rights in the 1960s permeated and enhanced a range of individual rights, including those of medical patients. The courts ultimately endorsed the position that a physician would be liable if there was failure to obtain informed consent before medical or surgical treatment. In the seminal case of *Canterbury v. Spence*, the court ruled that a physician has a duty to disclose to a patient the material risk associated with a proposed therapy that a reasonable patient would need to know to make an informed decision. The informed consent requirement marked the zenith of the shift in the nature of the physician–patient relationship from paternalistic to autonomous patient.

Today the pendulum has swung to a position of shared decision-making. Proper healthcare decision-making and management involves a detailed communication and exchange between patients and physicians where the patients share their symptoms, concerns, goals, personal and family history, and lifestyle desires; and the physicians share the risks, side effects, alternative approaches to care, and potential outcomes. This is a two-way exchange that represents a true physician–patient partnership.

Informed consent is a physician's obligation to the patient ethically, morally, and legally. The term "informed consent" was coined and explained in *Salgo v. Leland Stanford Jr. University Board of Trustees*, where a California Court of Appeals declared that "a physician violates his duty to his patient and subjects himself to liability if he withholds any facts which are necessary to form the basis of an intelligent consent by the patient to the proposed treatment." Subsequent to this ruling, informed consent became an ethical and legal duty imposed upon physicians throughout the United States.

Physicians now consider informed consent universally accepted fundamental component of healthcare. Physicians have an ethical and legal responsibility to inform patients of the potential material risks and benefits of any proposed treatment before obtaining a patient's consent to perform a medical procedure, with the patient given the right to make the ultimate decision of the course of treatment. This ethical, moral, and legal duty is a critical piece of the professional responsibilities of physicians.

In a world exploding with medical information through television advertising and the Internet, physicians must know how to respond to informed patients. Physicians often encounter requests for unnecessary medical care by patients who have misinterpreted the Internet or advertising. Physicians should not lose sight of their prime fiduciary responsibility to promote and protect the best interests of the patient, even at the risk of losing revenue, the law empowers physicians to say no to services that are not medically indicated—an empowerment that serves society well.

THE THREAT TO PHYSICIAN PROFESSIONALISM

As patients have experienced a transition from paternalism to autonomous decision-making, physicians have experienced a transition from autonomy to conflict regarding who their fiduciary is. Physicians increasingly practice as employees of large corporate medical organizations, and ascendant market fundamentalism has pressured them to practice as fiduciaries to the organization. Employed physicians report to business-trained managers and may be subject to contractual obligations that threaten quality of care, patient safety, and the professional and fiduciary responsibilities they owe patients. These MBAs demand that the physicians succumb to market goals because they believe the theories they learned in business school apply to the practice of medicine.

In the new era of employed physicians, numerous problematic contractual clauses impede physicians' professional duties and fiduciary responsibilities.

Confidentiality Clauses

These clauses in physician contracts often attempt to hide quality and safety issues, medical errors, unethical conduct, and malfeasance. These confidentiality clauses are in direct opposition to the professional responsibility of physicians to improve the quality of patient care.

Physicians' commitment to continuous improvement of quality medical care must entail reducing all medical errors, increasing patient safety, minimizing overuse and misuse of healthcare resources, and optimizing patient outcomes across all demographics and socioeconomic classes. The confidentiality clause can prevent physicians from meeting their professional, ethical, and moral responsibilities.

Incentive Clauses

Most physician contracts include productivity incentives. These clauses provide inducements primarily for activities that increase employer income and tend to promote overtreatment—in direct opposition to physicians' professional responsibility to pursue the just distribution of finite medical resources. Providing unwarranted medical services exposes patients to risk and expense and limits the available resources for others in true need.

Referral Restrictions

Many physician contracts forbid referring outside the system—what's called "leakage control." This prohibits appropriate referrals for some patients, thus decreasing quality of care. Many physician offices have physician navigators that direct the care of patients to specialists in the health system and take the control of referral away from the primary physician.

Contractual clauses interfering with referral to skilled, elite physicians directly oppose the professional responsibility of physicians to encourage continuous improvement in quality of care.

"Gag" Clauses and Termination Without Cause

Clauses that prohibit physicians from revealing quality and safety problems, medical errors, and unethical conduct, and that bar physicians from revealing problems with electronic medical records that result in healthcare quality and safety issues (often emanating from confidentiality clauses in the contracts between hospital employers and electronic record vendors) directly interfere with a physicians' professional responsibilities.

Clauses that allow termination without cause put physicians at risk for standing up for professional responsibilities and to maintaining their fiduciary responsibility to the patient when it conflicts with the employer. The gag clauses and termination without cause clauses are in direct opposition to physicians' commitment to reduce medical errors, increase patient safety, minimize overuse and misuse of healthcare resources, optimize patient outcomes, and stand up to the organization when behaviors surface that interfere with physician professionalism and fiduciary responsibility.

THE CONUNDRUM PHYSICIANS FACE

Physicians are juxtaposed between professional and fiduciary responsibilities to their patients and contractual obligations that limit their ability to meet those responsibilities. This juxtaposition arises from manifestations of corporate medicine that allow the demands of the marketplace to pressure physicians to become entrepreneurial businesspersons. This shift in the physician's fiduciary responsibility to the employer threatens the quality of care, patient safety, and physician professional values.

It is a daunting time for physicians, patients, and society. Given that the managers of large health corporations may not be willing to meaningfully negotiate the most egregious provisions in the contractual relationship with individual physicians leaves physicians feeling impotent. The refusal of these organizations to compromise reflects their sheer market dominance.

What can physicians do to combat this loss of professional values and fiduciary responsibility? They may need to organize to collectively bargain with uncompromising and unyielding employers.

CHAPTER 16

Should Doctors Still Examine Patients?

The physical examination skills of young physicians in training need careful examination, as advancing technology seems to have replaced those skills compared to prior generations of physicians.

A question to ponder is how should medical education address the convincing evidence that physician trainees of today are less astute at the physical examination than those that came before them? This inquiry must address whether the decline in physical examination skills hinders accurate, cost-effective, and timely diagnoses. Additionally, it must consider whether the absence of a comprehensive physical examination impairs the patient–physician relationship.

This type of inquiry leads to the conclusion that the physical examination and technology must be merged as the clinical situation dictates to provide accurate, cost effective, and accurate diagnoses. The carefully performed physical examination in conjunction with a detailed history should dictate the use of our ever-advancing technologic advances in medicine.

> "Learn to see, learn to hear, learn to feel, learn to smell and know by practice alone you can become an expert"
>
> — Sir William Osler

Physicians once relied on seeing, hearing, and touching a patient to make a diagnosis. Technology has enhanced and sometimes replaced those skills, but many doctors lament their decline. A question to ponder is how should medical education address the convincing evidence that physician trainees of today are less astute at the physical examination than those who came before them?

Technology is constantly redefining the practice of medicine. New devices and laboratory tests from sophisticated testing in tertiary care centers to advanced technology available in outpatient settings have changed how we practice medicine. The question we posed is whether the advanced technology of echocardiography replaces the stethoscope in disease diagnosis.

DIAGNOSTIC ACUMEN

Physicians still diagnose as well as generations of physicians did before them. Few physicians, however, would trade a certain echocardiographic diagnosis of a mitral diastolic murmur, complete with color flow, Doppler velocities, and leaflet visualization and ejection fraction, for a probable diagnosis by physical examination.

Clearly, advanced technology aids diagnosis, but determining what must be confirmed or ruled out depends on a comprehensive history and physical examination.

ETHICAL CONSIDERATIONS

Is it ethical for advanced technology to be the sole actor in disease diagnosis? An environment of soaring healthcare costs, unaffordability, and the consideration that most information gleaned from technology can be ascertained from an astute physical examination suggests it is not ethical for advance technology to supplant the history and physical examination.

The time spent listening, examining, and physically touching the patient builds a robust patient–doctor relationship. Physical diagnosis must be fused with technology when necessary to diagnose and treat patients.

LEGAL CONSIDERATIONS

Current billing regulations by Medicare and Medicaid mandate that physicians perform key components of the physical examination. Physicians who want to be paid must confirm that they performed these components. Failure to perform the physical examination is unethical and unlawful.

Furthermore, studies have shown that the best approach to avoiding legal proceedings is to have a strong, trusting, and caring relationship with one's patients

THE ROLE OF ECHOCARDIOGRAPHY

Echocardiography should be an extension of a comprehensive history and physical examination, including auscultation, and should never be a replacement for a comprehensive history and physical examination including auscultation. Echocardiography should be a confirmatory test that increases the understanding of the degree of valvular abnormality detected on physical examination. The cardiac sounds appreciated with the stethoscope can only be adequately evaluated if the clinician knows the patient's symptoms and all aspects of the cardiovascular examination.

A comprehensive assessment of the blood pressure, arterial pulses, venous system, heart sounds, and lung sounds permits the clinician to determine the patient's cardiovascular status.

CARDIOVASCULAR PERFORMANCE

Cardiovascular performance is dependent upon the patient's autonomic tone, preload, afterload, and left and right ventricular contractility. Knowledge of these variables allows the clinician to understand where the patient lies on the Frank Starling curve and the Force Tension curve.

A careful, critically performed physical examination allows a detailed understanding of the individual patient's autonomic tone, pre-load, afterload, and cardiac contractility.

- The patient's jugular venous pressure is a surrogate measure of preload and is dependent upon total blood volume, venous tone, supine/standing position, atrial function, skeletal muscle contraction, and pericardial pressure.
- The patient's systolic blood pressure is a surrogate measure of afterload. Afterload represents the work load the contracting myocardium faces on each cardiac cycle. The afterload is dependent upon the left ventricular geometry, left ventricular (LV) pressure, and systemic vascular resistance.
- The carotid upstroke is a surrogate measure of the LV performance (contractility). It is a rough measure of the LV ejection fraction. The LV contractility is dependent upon the preload and afterload.

Contractility is influenced by many parameters including circulating catecholamines, the autonomic nervous system function, extrinsic abnormalities, metabolic factors, and degree of functioning myocardium

A synthesis of the information ascertained from the clinical history and physical examination allows the clinician to determine the patient's cardiovascular status and performance. That understanding in conjunction with the auscultator's finding with the stethoscope allows for a determination of whether the echocardiogram is needed as an extension of the stethoscope.

THE STETHOSCOPE AND AUSCULTATION

The invention of the stethoscope in 1816 by French physician René Théophile Hyacinthe Laennec was the most revolutionary step in the clinical auscultation of humans. With this invention, many new heart sounds could be heard.

Physicians and healthcare providers often feel obligated to evaluate these extra sounds for organic heart disease. In most cases, the distinction between an innocent/benign and pathological/malignant murmur can be made at bedside. Murmurs are characterized as systolic, diastolic, or continuous, based on the portion of the cardiac cycle the murmur occupies in relationship to the first (S1) and second (S2) heart sounds. Differentiating S1 and S2 is accomplished by palpating the carotid artery during auscultation. Palpation of the carotid upstroke occurs simultaneously with S1.

Systolic murmurs occur between the S1 and S2 heart sounds, while diastolic sounds occur after S2 and before S1. Diastolic murmurs often require further assessment with an echocardiogram.

The same is true for continuous murmurs, which are heard throughout the cardiac cycle, unless the auscultator is confident the continuous murmur is due to venous hum or mammary soufflé of pregnancy, which are benign conditions.

One should be able to determine the etiology of the murmur based upon comprehensive physical examination. Clues are the area on the chest wall where a murmur is best heard, the timing of the murmur in the cardiac cycle, the location to which it radiates, and changes in the characteristics of the murmur in response to maneuvers that alter cardiac hemodynamics by alteration in preload and afterload (dynamic auscultation).

Benign murmurs are typically related to turbulent blood flow during systole. These turbulent sounds may relate to high flow states secondary to medical conditions such as anemia and hyperthyroidism. These flow murmurs are typically related to aortic and pulmonary flow.

The velocity of blood flow in healthy individuals is highest during early systole so these benign murmurs are best heard at this stage, but not beyond mid-systole. Bedside maneuver such as Valsalva decreases preload with reduced velocity of blood flow, resulting in decreased murmur intensity.

These are short, crescendo–decrescendo, grade 1–2 sounds with no associated diastolic component. These flow murmurs are generally common in young individuals, but can be heard in all age groups. Accordingly, medical education must not de-emphasize the importance of the physical examination in disease diagnosis.

ECHOCARDIOGRAPHY

Pathologic systolic murmurs include aortic (AS) and pulmonic stenosis (PS), mitral (MR) and tricuspid (TR) regurgitation, and the murmurs of hypertrophic obstructive cardiomyopathy (HOCM), mitral valve prolapse (MVP), and ventricular septal defect (VSD). Their verification and quantitation often requires the use of echocardiography. Dynamic auscultation, with alteration in loading conditions, is used to differentiate these various murmurs. Inspiration, which increases venous return, increases the intensity of right-sided murmurs. Standing and Valsalva decrease preload and decrease the intensity of these murmurs; the exceptions being HOCM and MVP which will have increased intensity.

The intensity and timing of a murmur may determine whether it requires further evaluation. Murmur intensity is gauged with a system originally proposed by Samuel Levine in 1934, grading the murmur on a 1–6 scale based on its noise intensity.

A grade 1 murmur is very faint, and can only be heard with special effort. Grade 4–6 murmurs are loud, are associated with a palpable thrill, and can be distinguished based upon whether the stethoscope needs to be on the chest to hear the murmur. Grade 4 murmurs are loud, but require the stethoscope to be on the chest for auscultation. A grade 5 murmur can be heard with the stethoscope partially off the chest wall, and a grade 6 with the stethoscope completely removed from contact with the chest wall. Most murmurs grades 3–6 require further evaluation with an echocardiogram.

Clinical evaluation of murmurs includes obtaining a comprehensive clinical history to determine whether patients have symptoms. Any cardiac symptoms associated with grade 3–6 systolic murmurs and diastolic murmurs warrant an echocardiogram. A history of cardiovascular issues, such as prior myocardial infarction or symptoms of exercise induced rhythm abnormalities, may indicate a need for an echocardiogram. Examples of significant exercised-induced findings include shortness of breath, syncope, and angina. Additionally, on rare occasions the echocardiogram may be necessary because the patient's body habitus precludes an accurate physical examination.

CONCLUSION

An echocardiogram is an extension of a comprehensive history and physical examination. It is not needed for benign flow murmurs, but is indicated for cardiac murmur associated with cardiac symptoms, diastolic murmurs, and systolic murmurs with grade ≥3 intensity, and systolic murmurs associated with other abnormal physical exam findings.

Ultimately, the echocardiogram should confirm the physical examination findings and determine the hemodynamic significance of the abnormal turbulent blood flow. The echocardiogram should only serve as an extension of a comprehensive history and physical examination and not to eliminate the stethoscope. Physical examination and technology must be merged as the clinical situation dictates.

CHAPTER 17

The Importance of the Medical Record: A Critical Professional Responsibility

Comprehensive, detailed documentation in the medical record is critical to patient care and to a physician when allegations of negligence arise. Physicians, therefore, would be prudent to have a clear understanding of this documentation. It is important to understand who is responsible for documentation, what is important to document, when to document, and how to document. Additionally, it should be understood who owns the medical record, the significance of the transition to the electronic medical record, problems and pitfalls when using the electronic medical record, and how the Health Information Technology for Economic and Clinical Health Act affects healthcare providers and health information technology.

> "Medicine is the only world-wide profession, following everywhere the same methods, actuated by the same ambitions, and pursuing the same ends."
>
> —Sir William Osler

Recent attempts to improve patient healthcare include scientific breakthroughs, medical innovations, and technological advances. Medical records occupy the last category; they are a portal through which all medical staff can investigate the history of the patient to learn about prior medical care, understand the established diagnoses and response to outlined treatments, and synthesize this information in preparation for further evaluation and treatment approaches.

A well-documented medical record serves two worthwhile purposes: (1) it reflects the patient's history and corresponding medical care, thereby allowing for continuity of care; and (2) it can provide a defense for a physician facing allegations of malpractice by detailing adherence to the standard of care.

Current technologies are bringing medical records into the 21st century through innovative software and hardware computer programs. As healthcare professionals, we must understand that despite the changing platform by which we interact with the medical record, the basics of the medical record remain the same, as does its purpose: to provide information that allows for optimal patient care.

This chapter reviews who is responsible for documentation, what is important to document, when to document, how to document, who owns the medical record, the transition to electronic medical records, problems and pitfalls when using the medical record (EMRs), and how the Health Information Technology for Economic and Clinical Health (HITECH) Act affects healthcare providers and health information technology.

WHO IS RESPONSIBLE FOR DOCUMENTATION?

Succinctly stated, everyone who provides care to a patient is responsible for documenting the care and recommendations that have been provided and articulated to the patient. Medical records are legal documents that are used to demonstrate the thought process leading to the diagnosis and treatment options. All patient encounters should be documented, whether the encounter is in person, over the telephone, or by electronic communication. The documentation should be created contemporaneous with the discussion.

Documentation can be delegated to an assigned recorder during an emergency situation such as cardiac resuscitation. The delegated documentation should be carefully reviewed for accuracy immediately after the event, while the details of the resuscitation are fresh. This is important because even if good care was provided, incomplete documentation can give the opposite impression. The paper medical record recommendations also apply to the EMR, which has been adopted by healthcare entities across the country.

WHAT TO DOCUMENT AND WHY

Clinical notes should be well thought out, be clearly written, and give a detailed picture of the clinical situation. They must include important information such as the patient's name, age, and gender; the source of the information; and the date and time of the encounter. Additionally, relevant history and details of the physical examination with pertinent positive and negative findings should be clearly stated in the medical record.

The conclusions should include a working differential diagnosis and working plan of action, such as investigations, consultations, treatment, follow-up, and rationale for the workup and treatment. It is important to document all information shared with the patient, both written and verbal, and to define the patient's understanding of the plan of action and any refusal or disagreement. The provider should sign the medical note.

Good clinical practice and informed consent are inseparable. Respect for patient autonomy in clinical practice is of great moral significance in our society. The moral and legal responsibility of obtaining medical informed consent depends on transmission of appropriate information to the patient.

I believe patients' choices must be made independently and based on the full spectrum of medical knowledge, and not coerced by members of the healthcare team or by third parties, such as family, friends, or payers. Equally, I believe patients must be competent to consent: they must understand, remember, consider, and believe the clinical information given to them about the specific and alternative treatments.

The moral foundation for the requirement of medical informed consent in general is not disputed. The medical record must stand on its face to document the clinical, moral, and legal responsibility of the physician to provide the patient with the information to make an informed decision. It is the fiduciary responsibility of the physician to meet this standard.

Physicians and all healthcare providers must recognize that informed medical choice is an educational process and has the potential to affect the healthcare provider–patient alliance to their mutual benefit. Healthcare providers must give patients equity in the covenant of informed choice by educating them to make informed choices.

This type of healthcare team–patient relationship becomes a true partnership with shared decision-making responsibility for treatment approaches and outcomes. The medical record must reflect this informed decision-making between the healthcare provider and the patient.

Special Situations

When transferring the care of patients for the evening, the weekend, before a vacation, or for any other reason, remember that the individual assuming the responsibility for the patients' ongoing medical care does not have the same depth of understanding about their medical conditions as the healthcare provider who is handing off the patients.

The handoff should document, verbally and in the medical record, the expectations regarding the patients' condition, the ongoing care required, any pending investigations, any pending consults or reports, any unsolved medical or social issues, and what is anticipated for long-term care. The record should clearly document who is assuming responsibility for medical care, including start and end times with specific dates.

Discharge Summaries

At the time of discharge, it is paramount to document the detailed hospital course, including treatments, complications, and intercurrent illnesses. Clearly document what people were consulted, their recommendations, and all actions taken in response to those recommendations. Identify all investigations and actions taken. Identify pending investigations and who is responsible for following these results. All follow-up actions should document what was done, by whom, and when.

WHEN TO DOCUMENT?

It is best to document contemporaneous with the events, because memory about details fades with time, other events may occur, and there may later be disputes concerning their sequence.

Case Study: Delay in Documentation

A patient is discharged from the hospital, and the discharge summary has not been completed before the patient is readmitted under the same physician. The patient's second admission is complicated, with prolonged hospitalization ending in death.

When the physician completes the discharge summaries for both events, laboratory findings for the second admission are inadvertently included in the first discharge summary.

At a subsequent mortality review, there is an inference of a delay in responding to these lab results, with delayed diagnosis and treatment resulting in the adverse outcome of death. Only after detailed review of both admissions was the true sequence of events established and the inference of malpractice negated.

The lesson learned is that a delay in documentation can result in uncertainty regarding the sequence and timing of actions. This can have negative consequences for healthcare providers in terms of reputation and potential for litigation.

ELECTRONIC MEDICAL RECORDS

The EMR is here to stay. Healthcare providers must take the time to learn how to use the software and give the same attention to documenting patient care in the EMR as when using a paper record.

A significant disadvantage arises because of the length of the EMR, which can make it difficult and time consuming for healthcare providers to find the signals among the noise. A major advantage of the EMR is that it includes tools to help with decision-making and to alert the user to potential problems such as drug interactions.

When using such tools, it is vital to write a clear note in the record that documents the thought process that led to the chosen treatment options. The EMR must identify a true partnership between patient and provider, with shared, informed decision-making responsibility for treatment approaches and outcomes. Informal interactions can become a healthcare provider's nightmare.

Remember that patients have a legal right to see the content of their own medical record at any time and for any reason, although the physical record belongs to the person or organization responsible for its creation, which is the physician's office or the healthcare corporation or hospital. The owner of the physical record is responsible for controlling access by others in accordance with privacy law.

PROBLEMS AND PITFALLS

Informal interactions can become a healthcare provider's nightmare. Information given or received by telephone without documentation often is forgotten, but can be vital to patient care and prevention of allegations of negligence. Informal discussion in the hallway or supermarket may lead to decisions to do or not do something. If there is an adverse outcome, the reasoning and lack of documentation will be missing.

It is important to correct the medical record with precision. In the EMR it is important to indicate the reason for the change and carefully enter the correct information. An EMR should have an audit function that will indicate who made any entries or changes and when these changes occurred—both date and time. If an EMR allows deletion, it should store and permit access to deleted text.

The golden rules of correcting the medical record are as follows:

- Never allow others to use your password.
- Never use someone else's password.
- Never make changes after a patient complaint, or after learning of a legal action.

A common cause for legal action is improper handling of lab results or diagnostic tests: for example, a test wasn't performed, the results weren't reported, the information was sent to the wrong location, the diagnostic test wasn't interpreted, results were filed before they could be reviewed, or information was not acted upon.

Healthcare teams must have a fail-safe system to track, file, and document the results of these tests and how they acted on the results.

Case: A Case of True Syncope

An emergency department physician (EDP) diagnosed a concussion in a 14-year-old female basketball player who struck her head after experiencing true syncope while playing pick-up basketball. The paramedics had documented a rapid dysrhythmia that resolved spontaneously. The EDP noted an epsilon wave on the electrocardiogram (ECG).

The EDP forwarded the ECG to a pediatric cardiologist for a second opinion. The pediatric cardiologist highlighted the abnormality on the ECG and documented the possibility of arrhythmogenic right ventricular dysplasia (ARVD). There was no direct communication between the physicians. The pediatric cardiologist intended to send a report to the EDP, but it was sent to a different physician with the same surname. The patient's family physician never received a report of the ECG.

A year later, the patient suffered sudden death playing high school basketball. The autopsy revealed that she had ARVD. The lessons learned are all directly related to communication errors. There was no direct communication between the EDP and the pediatric cardiologist; as a result, the pediatric cardiologist did not communicate the possibility of a serious medical condition to the EDP, and no one arranged follow-up for a potentially dangerous medical condition. The EDP did not follow up because he or she received no communication on the concerning ECG in this patient with true syncope and documentation of a rhythm disturbance.

HITECH ACT

The HITECH Act was signed into law in February 2009 (HITECH Act, 42 U.S.C. & 300jj-11). Its purpose is to promote the adoption and meaningful use of health information technology in healthcare. The HITECH Act includes incentives for healthcare providers to accelerate adoption of the EMR among providers.

Importantly, the HITECH Act gives the government more bite in its ability to prosecute healthcare providers who violate the Act. The Act is a powerful tool for attorneys to use when requesting an individual's medical records; it directs healthcare providers to provide the requested information within a short period of time and at a reasonable cost.

CONCLUSION

Healthcare providers must understand who is responsible for documentation, what is important to document, when to document, how to document, who owns the medical record, the impact of changing to electronic medical records, problems and pitfalls when using the medical record, and how the HITECH Act impacts healthcare providers and health information technology. Healthcare providers must implement practices and policies that will meet all the documentation policies outlined in this article.

CHAPTER 18

Heightened Malpractice Risk for Hospitalist Physicians in the United States—What to Know and What to Do

Hospitalists, nurse practitioners, physician assistants, and institutions are all at risk for potential professional liability issues. The unique relationship between healthcare providers and their sponsoring institution generates complex and evolving legal issues for all participants.

The law has played a great role integrating quality care and patient safety with physicians, while providing an avenue for relief when a medical error occurs. The intersection of law and medicine, while allowing for optimal patient care, exposes participating medical providers and the sponsoring institutions to specific professional liability issues.

This chapter addresses the heightened medical practice risk that hospitalist physicians' encounter in today's practice of hospital medicine.

Experts have argued that patients receive a higher level of care when physicians specialized in hospital medicine take the primary attending role for all hospitalized patients. The Society of Hospital Medicine defines a hospitalist as a physician whose primary professional focus is the general medical care of hospitalized patients. Their activities include providing medical care of hospitalized patients, teaching, doing research, and providing leadership related to hospital medicine. Hospitalist physicians may be employees of the hospital or independent contractors who have a contractual agreement with the hospital to provide medical care to the patients in the hospital.

Hospitalists function independently in the management of hospitalized patients. Emanating from the established doctor-patient relationship is fiduciary responsibilities to the patient. Hospitalists make autonomous medical decisions including whether to consult specialists.

As the practice of medicine continues to transition to performance-based payment systems, the number of mergers of hospitalists and specialists has surged. Payment models that focus on clinical outcomes and best practices link payment to the ability of physicians to provide efficient, quality healthcare and improve patient outcomes.

These payment systems are changing the way healthcare services are delivered by demanding better patient care at a lower cost. The result is increasing pressure on physicians to meet operational and quality goals or receive less reimbursement for their services.

Studies have shown that the effective use of hospitalists can improve standardized patient care. Hospitalists also provide value to specialists by freeing up time so they can focus on their area of expertise. As a result, co-management arrangements between hospitalists and specialists have become a popular tool to define working relationships and improve the quality of patient care.

In the beginning, hospitalists were perceived as a hazard to primary care physicians and specialists. To overcome these negative connotations and prove their worth, hospitalists began co-managing patients for surgical specialists, who soon realized the significant value hospitalist services provided. Not only do they share in the responsibility of care provided to patients, but they also reduce readmissions and costs associated with providing healthcare.

Hospitalists add value by helping to alleviate the burden on specialists—providing emergency department coverage, assisting in the operating room, and rounding on patients. They evaluate surgical patients for medical issues, reconcile medications across the spectrum of a patient's care, and standardize the patient discharge and communication processes.

Providing these services frees specialists from rounding and allows them to concentrate on their specialty. Hospitalists do not have office-based practices, which allows them to spend their time in the hospital caring for admitted, pre-operative, and post-operative patients.

It is in the pre-operative and post-operative environments where hospitalists have established their extreme value to specialists. Under co-management arrangements, hospitalists are able to ensure that all pre-operative tests are conducted, reports are dictated, and the patient's medical history is available. Pre-operative evaluations allow the hospitalist to develop a post-operative plan of care and proactively address many medical concerns. Also, the hospitalist is available to see patients immediately after surgery, allowing immediate evaluation and treatment for high blood pressure, issues with diabetes, and a plethora of medical issues that arise post procedure and operation.

The hospitalist is responsible for the medical care of the specialist's patients, and the specialist is able to focus on the specialty services he or she provides. Providing these services gives hospitalists the opportunity to anticipate problems and overcome issues, which results in more efficient care, shorter lengths of stay in the hospital, and improved patient satisfaction. Such results make hospitalists critical to success in performance-based payment systems.

THE REALITY OF HOSPITALIST WORK

Hospitalists work demanding schedules, seeing a broad mix of patients who generally are very ill. Superimposed on this schedule is increasing pressure from hospital administration to see more patients each day. In today's medical environment, reimbursements are declining and hospitalists are a high fixed cost. This tension between reimbursements and costs puts a strain on the hospital administration to keep costs down.

Hospitalists are seeing on average 18–20 patients per day. This workload tests the mandate for the highest quality care. As the number of patients seen each day increases, the physician has less time to spend with each patient. This leads to less time for reviewing the patient's history and all aspects of the medical record, less time for performing a comprehensive physical examination, less time for talking to families, and less time for documentation. Each aspect of less time puts the hospitalist at risk for omissions that may lead to alleged negligence.

The magnitude of this problem grows to a greater magnitude in a relative value units (RVU) system where hospitalists are often seeing 30–35 encounters per day. The formula under this structure is to make more RVUs to enhance income. This type of practice is a formula for medical care that falls below the standard of care and subjects the practitioner to potential negligence.

Another important issue when considering hospitalist potential for liability is inadequate supervision of nurse practitioners. Many hospitalists have nurse practitioners that help share the workload; however, the extent of supervision is an issue. Each state has a its own rules governing the required supervision, but ultimately the physician is respondent superior and not having adequate time to supervise is a huge legal concern.

UNDERSTANDING NEGLIGENCE IS CRITICAL

Negligence is well defined in tort law. To demonstrate negligence, a plaintiff must prove four elements under a "greater probability than not" standard:

- The defendant owed the plaintiff a duty.
- The defendant breached that duty.
- The plaintiff sustained an injury or harm.
- The injury or harm was a direct consequence of the defendant's breach.

Physicians breach their duty when their actions or omissions of behavior fail to meet the standard of care generally expected for a physician in similar circumstances.

HOSPITALIST PHYSICIAN *STANDARD OF CARE*

Attending physicians supervising nurse practitioners and physician assistants are subject to the same liability exposure they face when they personally direct and deliver care. The attending physician's liability risk is unaffected by the nature of the relationship with the mid-level providers.

Attending physicians are exposed to two additional types of liability when assuming a supervisory role: (1) vicarious liability for the physician extenders negligence under the respondeat superior notion and (2) direct liability for failure to supervise.

Vicarious liability is the law's imposition of liability on a person or institution for the negligence of another (physician extender) based on the relationship between the parties. An employer may be held liable for the negligent acts of employees acting within the scope of their employment, even if the employer acted appropriately. An attending physician acting in a supervisory role can be held liable for the acts of the physician extender. Courts focus on the nature and extent of the attending physician's control over the practice setting and the control of the institution under which the mid-level provider is working.

Frequently, both the attending physician and the sponsoring institution may be vicariously liable. Additionally, attending physicians may be held liable for negligent oversight and supervision of the care provided by advanced practitioners.

ADVANCED PRACTITIONERS' *STANDARD OF CARE*

PAs and NPs, or physician extenders, are considered legally liable for actions or omissions concerning patients they treat and, therefore, are required in all states to carry adequate medical liability insurance.

Physicians providing medical direction or supervision may also be held liable for the actions or omissions of PAs and NPs, even if no patient–physician interaction occurred. Such liability exists in three separate manners: negligent selection, negligent supervision, and respondeat superior.

The medical director or other party responsible for hiring a physician assistant or nurse practitioner may be accused of negligent selection, claiming that the party responsible for hiring the physician assistant or nurse practitioner knew, or should have known, prior issues in the PA's or NP's past that might have predicted future performance insufficiencies. Diligent research and reference review, with adequate documentation of same, should help prevent and protect from such claims.

Negligent supervision may be alleged against the supervising physician of record, claiming that the supervising physician did not follow state, hospital, or departmental supervision regulation/policies/guidelines, or if the plaintiff's expert believes the physician's supervision was otherwise below the standard of care.

To decrease ambiguity, hospitalists using advanced practitioners should have guidelines specifying supervising physician responsibility, including factors that trigger when a PA or NP should seek supervising physician consultation and when a supervising physician should physically attend to a patient evaluated by a physician extender.

If not named for any of the aforementioned reasons, a supervising physician may be included in a medical liability action against a physician extender under the *respondeat superior* claim.

Respondeat superior, Latin for "let the master answer," is the primary vehicle used to assert vicarious liability of the supervising physician for the alleged negligent acts of physician extenders. Under this principle, the supervising physician may not have been present or even aware of the patient encounter, but as the "master of the ship" may be considered liable. Should no claim of negligent selection or supervision be raised, supervising physicians named under the concept of *respondeat superior* often are dismissed from the case eventually.

Historically, there have been fewer medical liability cases brought against physician extenders. A review of 17 years of records from the United States National Practitioner Data Bank, from 1991 through 2007. During the study period, the probability of making a malpractice payment was 12 times less for PAs and 24 times less for NPs as compared with physicians.

CONCLUSION

Professional liability considerations are important for hospitalists, PAs, NPs, and healthcare institutions. All members of the healthcare team are at risk for allegations of negligence. Based on collaborative efforts involved in the medical care provided to patients, all healthcare providers, no matter their level of qualification or certification, are held to the same standard of medical care. This is grounded in a public policy incentivizing advanced practitioners to seek supervision, and for attending physicians to provide appropriate supervision.

The advanced practitioner and the hospitalist must see and examine the patient and discuss the potential etiologies of the patient's symptoms and physical findings. The PA or NP must be able to articulate underlying pathophysiologic principles resulting in symptoms, physical findings, and potential treatment options. The attending physician must ensure that the decision-making processes made by mid-level providers under his or her supervision are accurate and safe. These laws help to provide the legal foundation for the physician extenders while providing assurance to the general public that the medical system results in medical providers who practice clinically appropriate, high quality, and safe medical care.

It behooves hospitalist physicians to be prudent and communicate to the healthcare team members and the patients the rationale, risks and benefits, and alternative approaches for all medical decisions and treatment strategies. These communications must be clearly documented in granular detail in the medical record.

Additionally, it should be documented that the patient understood the rationale for the decisions made and agreed with the outlined approach to the patient's medical issues. Patients and the healthcare team members deserve nothing less. This comprehensive approach has the potential for high-quality medical care and low likelihood of alleged negligence.

GOLDEN RULES

- Hospitalists and physician extenders must understand negligence.
- Hospitalists and physician extenders must understand the standard of care.
- Hospitalists and physician extenders must take comprehensive histories and physical examinations and then discuss the differential diagnosis and plan of care and timing of follow up.
- Hospitalists and physician extenders must understand communication is critical to high-quality care.
- Hospitalists and physician extenders must choose work environments that allow the time to meet the standard of care.
- Hospitalists and physician extenders must seek subspecialty evaluation if the patient's problem exceeds their expertise.

Reprinted with permission: Paterick ZR, Paterick TE. Heightened Malpractice Risk for Hospitalist Physicians in the USA: What To Know and What To Do. *Postgrad Med J*. 2019 Oct;95(1128):531–533. doi: 10.1136/postgradmedj-2019-136713. Epub 2019 Aug 1. PMID: 31371462.

CHAPTER 19

Physician Alert: The Legal Risks Associated with "On-Call" Duties in the United States

On-call physicians encounter a diverse aggregate of interfaces with sundry persons concerning patient care that may surface potential legal peril. The duties and obligations of an on-call physician, who must act as a fiduciary to all patients, creates myriad circumstances where there is a risk of falling prey to legal ambiguities.

The understanding of the doctor–patient relationship, the obligations of physicians under the Emergency Medical Treatment and Labor Act, the meaning of medical informed consent, and the elements of negligence will help physicians avoid the legal risks associated with the various encounters of being on call.

Being on call is time-consuming and arduous. While on call, physicians have a duty to act morally and ethically in the best interest of the patients. On-call physicians would be prudent to understand how to meet their duties and obligations when they interact with other physicians, nurse practitioners, physician assistants, nurses, the answering service, and patients.

Furthermore, physicians must understand that interpreting medical data, making a diagnosis, advising a course of treatment, and recommending follow-up surveillance and treatment while serving as the on-call physician must be carefully and comprehensively documented. Additionally, physicians must understand the importance of documenting all phone and personal conversations, the rationale for medical decisions, and the rationale for prescribed follow-up.

Fundamental to understanding and meeting their duties and obligations, physicians on call must understand the doctor–patient relationship, the Emergency Medical Treatment and Labor Act (EMTALA), medical informed consent, and the fundamental elements of negligence. These duties and obligations are the ethical and moral duties physicians have to their patients in the United States. Understanding them will limit the potential for liability.

THE DOCTOR–PATIENT RELATIONSHIP

The physician–patient relationship is a fiduciary relationship in which mutual trust and confidence are essential. The physician acting as a fiduciary to the patient must act in the best interest of the patient. Physicians are held to a standard of medical care defined by the accepted national standards of practice. Some of the obligations of a physician's responsibility of due care include the obligation to:

- Fully inform the patient of his or her condition.
- Continue to provide medical care once the physician–patient relationship has been established.
- Refer the patient to a specialist, if necessary.
- Obtain the patient's informed consent to the medical treatment or operation.

Informed consent evolves from a shared decision-making process between the physician and the patient. Confidentiality laws protect the physician–patient relationship and the patient's consent must be obtained before medical records may be released.

Generally, an affirmative act on the part of the physician must exist before a legal duty arises. Once the physician–patient relationship has been established, it continues until it is ended by the consent of the parties or revoked by the dismissal of the physician, or until the physician's services are no longer needed.

Without proper notice of withdrawal, affording the patient ample opportunity to seek alternative care, the physician's termination of services to the patient could be held to be abandonment, subjecting the physician to the charge of negligence and liability to the patient for any damages proximately caused by such negligence.

Succinctly stated: The physician–patient relationship can be defined as "a consensual relationship in which the patient knowingly seeks the physician's assistance and in which the physician knowingly accepts the person as a patient." That fundamental relationship is the buttress of good medical care as it reflects a shared decision-making process between the physician and the patient.

EMERGENCY MEDICAL TREATMENT AND LABOR ACT (EMTALA)

EMTALA was enacted to prevent hospitals from refusing to treat patients or prevent transfer of patients just because they could not pay for their care. EMTALA requires Medicare–participating hospitals with an emergency department (ED) to provide a screening examination to determine whether a patient has an emergency medical condition — an illness that necessitates immediate medical attention to prevent serious jeopardy to the patient's immediate and long-term health.

The clinical condition is such that there is not adequate time to transfer a patient without posing a threat to the health or safety of that patient. Under EMTALA, the on-call physician must appear in person to evaluate and stabilize the patient if summoned by the ED physician requesting consultation. Failing to come, or directing transfer without an evaluation, may be in violation of EMTALA and subject the hospital and physician to a fine.

There are no further EMTALA obligations or duties once a patient is admitted, stabilized, or transferred to another hospital. When a transfer is deemed appropriate, a physician must endorse that the benefits of transfer outweigh the risks. A patient is stabilized when it is unlikely that his or her condition will deteriorate as a result of during transfer.

The physician must use expert medical judgment when making decisions regarding stabilization. This is an area of legal risk. There is not an expectation of ongoing medical care, but the hospital is expected to provide patients with the information they need to obtain appropriate follow-up care to prevent a relapse or deterioration of their medical condition. Failure to provide that information would fall below the standard of care and violate EMTALA.

MEDICAL INFORMED CONSENT

Medical informed consent is essential to the physician's ability to diagnose and treat patients as well as the patient's right to accept or reject clinical evaluation, treatment, or both. Medical informed consent should be an exchange of ideas that buttresses the patient–physician relationship. The consent process should be the foundation of the fiduciary relationship between a patient and a physician.

Physicians must recognize that informed medical choice is an educational process and has the potential to affect the patient–physician alliance to their mutual benefit. Physicians must give patients equality in the covenant by educating them to make informed choices. When physicians and patients take medical informed consent seriously, the patient –physician relationship becomes a true partnership with shared decision-making authority and responsibility for outcomes.

Physicians need to understand informed medical consent from an ethical foundation, as codified by statutory law in many states, and from a generalized common-law perspective requiring medical practice consistent with the standard of care. It is fundamental to the patient–physician relationship that each partner understands and accepts the degree of autonomy the patient desires in the decision-making process.

Ethically and legally, all physicians have a mandatory obligation to understand the medical informed consent process. Understanding this process allows for the exchange of ideas in medical practice that will yield informed decisions and will lead to the best outcomes on the basis of shared information. Further, informed consent limits the potential for negligence cases brought for lack of informed consent.

NEGLIGENCE

Negligence requires that four elements be established for liability of the physician-defendant: (1) a duty of the physician to meet a particular standard of care, (2) the physician's failure to perform that duty, (3) a causal connection (proximate cause) between the physician's failure and the patient's injury, and (4) an injury for which monetary compensation is adequate relief. An allegation of negligence can only be asserted if there is a doctor-patient relationship.

On-call physicians who fail to respond when called may also be subject to adverse action under any on-call services agreement. Such agreements generally require compliance with EMTALA and/or other applicable laws, and may have specific requirements for responding to calls. The on-call physician may be liable to the hospital for resulting damages the hospital may incur, including but not limited to the cost of responding to EMTALA investigations, EMTALA penalties, and suits by individuals. Failure to meet these obligations puts the physician at risk for allegations of negligence.

ON-CALL ACTIVITIES THAT POSITION PHYSICIANS AT RISK FOR LIABILITY

Legal Risks Associated with Your Answering Service

The answering service may be an asset or liability for physicians. The answering service is a necessary component of medical practice. It is the nexus between the patient, physician, nurse practitioner, physician assistant, and nurse to the on-call physician. The potential liability is when a physician does not respond in a timely and appropriate manner to a patient's medical emergency.

An example will highlight this malpractice risk. You are busy rounding on the medical wards with incoming pages from nurses and attending to patients who are ill. A patient's daughter calls your answering service asking to speak to the physician on call because her father is experiencing left-side numbness, blurred vision, and confusion. The daughter had called yesterday with similar concerns and an ER visit occurred with no diagnosis identified.

You contact the daughter three hours later and learn the patient has had a stroke. Tissue plasminogen activator is not administered within the three-hour window, paralysis ensues, and you are sued for malpractice and abandonment. You are now faced with defending yourself on the timeliness and appropriateness of your response and the advice you gave the patient.

You also may be placed in the position of defending the standard of care of your answering service. A patient calls with a headache and says it is not an emergency, but later is diagnosed with a ruptured cerebral aneurysm. You will have to show that the failure of the answering service to call you was reasonable given the clinical scenario.

The answering service is regarded as an agent of the physician. Therefore, under agency law, the physician is responsible for the selection, training, and monitoring of the answering service. Ultimately, the physician is responsible.

A pattern of chaotic message forwarding may include untimely calling, not dating and timing the calls, calling the wrong physician, transposing a number, or misinterpreting a message. A plaintiff's attorney may allege negligence for a physician who does not correct this pattern of chaotic messaging.

The answering service must know who is on call and how to contact that person; therefore, the answering service must have complete information for on-call schedules and for hospital and medical practice arrangements for coverage.

If you are the physician on call, you should provide all your contact information including: your cell phone number, text-messaging information, email address, home phone, beeper number, and alternative person you designate in case you cannot be reached. The message is loud and clear: Be available.

The answering service operators must be human beings who have good communication skills and empathy for a patient in distress. It is imperative operators understand that they never diagnose maladies or prescribe treatments. They should have the autonomy to tell patients to call 911 or go to the emergency room if the physician cannot get back to the patient in a reasonable amount of time.

Malpractice Risks Associated with Your Answering Service

Patient satisfaction is critical to your practice and the answering service creates a significant impression on patients after hours. The operators must respond in a timely manner and have good communication skills, empathy, patience, and follow-through. How can you protect yourself? Scrutinize your answering service — call as a patient and check the efficacy, efficiency, and accuracy of your operators. If you are not satisfied, make changes immediately. You have a legal duty to reach patients in a timely fashion. The standard of care is that physicians in a similar circumstance would have reached the patient in a similar time frame and would have given similar advice.

Answering service cases often are argued from a claim of proximate cause, which is defined as a causal connection between the alleged departure from the standard of care and the patient's damages. The question that will be posed is: "Did the failure to respond to the patient in a timely manner and/or give reasonable advice within the patient's clinical context cause the patient's injuries?" Alternatively, "Would the progress of the disease have been the same regardless of the alleged malfeasance of the physician or his or her answering service?" In the event of a lawsuit, your documentation of your meeting the standard of care in terms of timeliness is critical. All communications between the answering service and patients must be carefully documented in the medical record. Additionally, all communication between a physician and other physicians and patients should be carefully documented with date and time.

LEGAL RISKS ASSOCIATED WITH PHYSICIAN TO PHYSICIAN AND/OR PHYSICIAN TO NON-PHYSICIAN CLINICIANS CALLS

Physician-to-Physician Calls

When a physician receives a call from an ER physician, urgent care physician, or hospitalist physician, he or she must answer promptly, listen carefully, and communicate harmoniously. It is important to succinctly reiterate what you have heard so it is abundantly clear that your understanding of the clinical discussion resonates with the calling physician.

If the calling physician desires a consultation, the on-call physician should respond promptly to evaluate the patient and make recommendations based on an integration and synthesis of a comprehensive history, physical examination, and laboratory and imaging data. If the requesting physician is calling for advice, without an in-person consultation, there must be a clear of understanding of the patient's clinical condition and then comprehensive documentation of recommendations and the rationale for the decision-making and recommendations.

The on-call physician making recommendations without a personal history and physical examination is always at risk for liability if medical advice is rendered. It is always better to see the patient and make recommendations based on an in-depth history and physical examination. There should be comprehensive documentation of all discussions with date and time noted.

Non-Physician Clinicians Calls

When a physician receives a call from a non-physician clinician (nurse practitioner, physicians assistant) he or she must answer promptly, listen carefully, and communicate harmoniously. It is important to succinctly reiterate what you have heard so it is abundantly clear that your understanding of the clinical discussion resonates with the calling non- physician clinician.

It is safest in these situations to always personally evaluate the patient before making recommendations. The rationale is that in the event of an adverse outcome, the physician will be considered the respondent superior. The common-law doctrine of respondent superior was established in the 17th century to define the legal liability of an employer for the actions of an employee. The doctrine was adopted in the United States and has been a fixture of agency law. The non-clinician physician is considered an agent of the physician. The physician is considered the principal and is responsible for the agent's actions.

Physicians should always fully participate in the medical evaluation, medical care, and decision-making of a patient to prevent the potential for alleged negligence and possibly liability. Again, all communication and decision-making must be carefully and comprehensively documented. There are no short cuts to high-quality care.

Physician Response to Nurse Calls

The on-call physician must remember that nurses are the critical piece to great patient care. They spend an enormous amount of time talking to and examining the patient. Therefore, nurses develop an intimate and detailed knowledge of the patient's symptoms, concerns, fears, and hopes. This in-depth relationship between the nurse and the patient demands a physician's recognition and respect. Excellent physicians understand they can gain great insight into the patient's clinical condition if they communicate well with the nursing staff.

When nurses request to speak to the on-call physician there should be a prompt response and a large ear. Physician listening skills are essential. The changing nature of a patient's condition is most apparent to the nurse who is providing minute-by-minute care. Listen carefully to the nurse's assessment and communicate with careful thought and compassion. It is important to succinctly reiterate what you have heard so it is abundantly clear that your understanding of the clinical discussion resonates with the nurse.

If there is concern about a changing medical status, it is prudent to evaluate the patient immediately and comprehensively. If the call does not deem an immediate evaluation, but there is communication of critical medical information, it is prudent to carefully document the conversation and decision-making. Nurses will make or break a physician. If they feel you are not listening and lack compassion, they will stop communicating with you and, again, through agency law, you are responsible.

THE ON-CALL PHYSICIAN AND THE NOVEL LEGAL RISKS OF TELEMEDICINE

The telecommunication era has introduced us to telemedicine. Physicians on call are often forced to respond to patient calls from rural areas. Physicians who practice telemedicine have to consider state laws, payment issues, and licensing regulations. But another important consideration is medical liability. As the practice of telemedicine is growing exponentially, so are the legal risks associated with virtual care.

Telemedicine can fuel a wide spectrum of legal issues, including malpractice, product liability claims, data exposure, and credentialing risks. A central problem to telemedicine is that a uniform standard of care does not exist. Does the standard of care for services provided in person apply to the virtual care model? How do we determine whether informed consent occurred with virtual medicine? How does credentialing occur when the academic medical center doctor provides medical care for the patient in a rural hospital?

These novel legal concerns should be considered before participating in telemedicine. Remember, you're a provider for the health system until there is a lawsuit—then you are the physician.

CONCLUSION

Understanding the meaning and nature of the doctor–patient relationship, EMTALA law, medical informed consent, and negligence will help the on-call physician cope with the myriad situations and circumstances that occur when on call and being summoned by the answering service, the ER, physicians, non-physician clinicians, and nurses. Succinctly stated: To reduce legal risk, be prompt, listen intently, reiterate for clarity, go in promptly when the situation dictates, perform a comprehensive assessment, and document in granular detail your conversations, examinations, and decision - making. Being on call is a rigorous, time-consuming job that requires complete attention to detail.

Reprinted with permission, Paterick ZR, Patel NJ, Paterick TE. Physician Alert: The Legal Risks Associated with 'On-Call' Duties in The USA. *Postgrad Med J*. 2018 Jul;94(1113):411-414. doi: 10.1136/postgradmedj-2018-135847. Epub 2018 Jun 13. PMID: 29898914.

CHAPTER 20

Improving Health Outcomes Through Patient Education and Partnerships with Patients

"Each patient carries his own doctor inside him."

—Norman Cousins, *Anatomy of an Illness*

To improve healthcare outcomes, physicians must spend more time with patients. The teaching physician's interaction with the patient must be enthusiastic, motivated, and responsive to the individual patient's needs. For individual members of our society to realize the benefits of physician health education, there is a need for a robust, hearty engagement between patients and physicians.

Interventions to improve self-care have led to documented improvements in self-efficacy. Self-efficacy is defined as one's belief in one's ability to succeed in specific situations, or accomplish certain tasks. One's sense of self-efficacy plays a major role in how one approaches goals, tasks, and challenges regarding one's health. Clinical benefits have been seen in trials of lifestyle intervention within a wide range of conditions such as diabetes, coronary heart disease, heart failure, and rheumatoid arthritis.

In the context of escalating healthcare costs and shocking future cost projections, the potential for improved health outcomes through patient education and self-management programs is immense. In the early 1990s, it was estimated that 50% of the annual mortality toll in the United States was premature. Tobacco use, poor diet, a lack of physical exercise, alcohol consumption, exposure to microbial agents, use of firearms, risky sexual behavior, motor vehicle accidents, and illicit drug use were the culprits causing premature death. Approximately 80% of premature deaths were due to tobacco use, dietary patterns, and a low physical activity level.

Clearly, these are all behaviors we could modify to reverse the trends. For those individuals who do not smoke, eat healthy food, and participate in regular exercise programs, the hazard ratio for diabetes, myocardial infarction, stroke or cancer was 0.22.

There is a belief in the medical community that physical activity and diet can reduce the risk of developing coronary artery disease, hypertension, diabetes, and the metabolic syndrome. A comprehensive systematic review reinforced this notion by revealing that there is irrefutable, convincing evidence for the benefit of exercise in improving clinical outcomes in metabolic disorders, coronary heart disease, and heart failure.

Physicians must promote patient education and engagement through improvement in patients' health literacy. Health literacy is defined as the capacity to seek, understand, and act on health information. The presumption has been that low health literacy means that physician communication is poorly understood, leading to incomplete self-health management and responsibility and incomplete healthcare utilization. It is the responsibility of physicians to proactively enable patients to have more accessible interactions and situations that promote health and well-being.

Health literacy is the primary responsibility of physicians, given that it is physicians who determine the parameters of the health interaction, including physical setting, available time, communication style, content, modes of information provided, and concepts of sound healthcare decision crafting and acquiescence. There are communication methodologies and behaviors that physicians can implement to ameliorate the potential risks associated with limited patient health literacy, including avoiding medical jargon, engaging in patient questions, explaining unfamiliar forms, and using "teach back" as a method to ensure understanding.

Critical to any educational process is time. The development of patient health literacy is crucial to our proven health prevention measures of exercise and diet. Patients must have a deep understanding of the impact healthy interventions can have on their present and long-term health. Physicians will need to spend time and energy educating patients to see behavioral change that results in improved health outcomes and reduced morbidity and mortality due to preventable chronic diseases such as diabetes, obesity, and coronary and cerebrovascular disease. As physicians, we will know when we have reached the threshold of being an excellent teacher by observing responsible patients.

The partnership between a physician and patient requires dual responsibility. Physicians have a duty to inform patients how to achieve health and wellness, and patients have a responsibility to act on the information provided in their best health interest. Medical informed consent is essential to the physician's ability to diagnose and treat patients, as well as the patient's right to accept or reject clinical evaluation, treatment, or both.

Medical informed consent should be an exchange of ideas that buttresses the patient–physician relationship. The consent process should be the foundation of the fiduciary relationship between a patient and a physician. Physicians must recognize that informed medical choice is an educational process and has the potential to affect the patient–physician alliance to their mutual benefit. Physicians must give patients equality in the covenant by educating them to make informed choices. Patients must use the educational process to make rational health choices.

When physicians and patients take medical informed consent seriously, the patient-physician relationship becomes a true partnership with shared decision-making authority and responsibility for outcomes. Physicians need to understand informed medical consent from an ethical foundation, as codified by statutory law in many states, and from a generalized common-law perspective requiring medical practice consistent with the standard of care. It is fundamental to the patient-physician relationship that each partner understands and accepts the degree of autonomy the patient desires in the decision-making process.

Reprinted with permission, Timothy E. Paterick, Nachiket Patel, A. Jamil Tajik & Krishnaswamy Chandrasekaran (2017) Improving Health Outcomes Through Patient Education and Partnerships with Patients, Baylor University Medical Center Proceedings, 30:1, 112-113, DOI: 10.1080/08998280.2017.11929552

CHAPTER 21

Implications of Good Samaritan Laws for Physicians

Good Samaritan laws are designed to encourage individuals, including physicians, to gratuitously render medical care in emergency situations. Through these laws, immunity from civil liability is provided to physicians who act in good faith to provide emergency care gratis.

Historically, emergency care involved medical assistance given to persons in motor vehicle crashes or other emergency situations in which bystanders were present. Protection of physicians from allegations of negligence was a tactic of the legislative and judicial systems to encourage active clinical participation, rather than cautious nonparticipation, in emergency care. In some states and under defined circumstances, the immunity may apply in the hospital setting, as well as in the physician's office.

Legislatures have continued to amend the statutes to expand the protection provided to physicians who offer emergency care. Judicial construction of the nature and scope of physician immunity has similarly expanded.

Most states have enacted Good Samaritan statutes to encourage persons, including physicians, to provide emergency medical care without fear of civil liability (see Table 1). The definition of emergency care varies by statutory definition or by circumstance. However, it can be broadly defined as the initial evaluation and the immediate assistance, treatment, and intervention rendered to an injured person before care can be transferred to professional medical personnel with access to standard medical equipment and support staff. Many statutes make an exception to immunity if the rendered emergency care is grossly negligent or a medical injury results from a willful or wanton act by the caregiver. This issue is not addressed in this chapter.

TABLE 1. Statutes on Good Samaritan Acts and Doctrines

U.S. Legislative Territory	Statute Reference
Alabama	Ala Code 1975 & 6-5-332
Alaska	Alaska Stat & 09.651090 (Mich)
Arizona	ARS & 32-1471, ARS & 32-1472
Arkansas	Ark Code Ann & 17-95-101
California	Cal Health & Safety Code & 1799.102
Colorado	CRSA & 13-21-108, CRSA & 12-29.3-101
Connecticut	CGSA & 52-557b
Delaware	16 DelC §6801, 24 DelC §1767
District of Columbia	DC Code Ann 7 §-401
Florida	FS 7 §68.13
Georgia	Ga Code Ann §51-1-29
Hawaii	Haw Rev Stat §663-1-5
Idaho	IC §5-330, IC §5-332
Illinois	745 ILCS 49/25 (West 2000)
Indiana	IC 34-30-12-1
Iowa	ICA §613.17
Kentucky	KRS §411.148
Louisiana	LA RS 37:1731
Maine	32 MRSA §2594 (generally) and 14 MRSA §164
Massachusetts	MGLA 112 §12 B
Michigan	MCLA 691.1501
Minnesota	MN ST §604A.01
Mississippi	Miss Code Ann §73-25-37
Missouri	VAMS 537.037
Nevada	NRS 41.500
New Hampshire	NH Rev Stat §329.25
New Jersey	NJSA 2A:62A-1
New Mexico	NMSA 1978, §24-10-3; NMSA 1978, §24-10-4
New York	NY Pub Health Law §3000
North Carolina	NCGSA §20-166
North Dakota	ND Cent Code §32-03
Ohio	RC §2305.23
Oklahoma	59 Okl St Ann §518
Oregon	Or Rev Stat §30.801
Pennsylvania	42 PaCSA §8331

(table continues)

TABLE 1. Statutes on Good Samaritan Acts and Doctrines *(continued)*

U.S. Legislative Territory	Statute Reference
Puerto Rico	P de la C 1375, Law No. 152
Rhode Island	Gen Laws 1956, RI ST & 9-1-27.1, §5-37-14
South Carolina	SC ST §15-1-310
South Dakota	SDCL §20-9-3
Tennessee	TCA 63-6-218
Texas	VTCA Civil Practice & Remedies Code §74.151
Utah	UCA 1953 §58-13-2
Vermont	12 VSA 519
Virginia	Va Code Ann §8.01-225
Washington	West s RCWA 424.300
West Virginia	W Va Code Ann §55-7-15
Wisconsin	WSA 895.48
Wyoming	WS 1977 §1-1-

The purpose of Good Samaritan statutes is to encourage individuals to provide emergency care to an injured person through the granting of immunity from common-law liability if the caregivers fail to exercise reasonable diligence when rendering the emergency care in good faith. Some of the common elements of these statutes require that the care be "emergency care" rendered "in good faith" "at the scene of the emergency." However, the statutes differ from state to state.

Initially, many jurisdictions provided immunity to physicians and laypersons who provided emergency care gratis at the scene of motor vehicle crashes. Over time, some jurisdictions broadened the definition of what constitutes an emergency scene to which Good Samaritan protection is extended. An emergency occurring in a hospital or medical office may, or may not, qualify for protection when a non-attending physician voluntarily and without pay offers emergency care. Outside the medical setting, the emergency scene may encompass a friend's home to which an injured person goes first after an accident.

Some jurisdictions, although providing immunity for physicians and other medical providers, do so for a layperson only when the layperson holds a certificate in first aid or advanced life support. Accordingly, for comprehension of a state's Good Samaritan protection, a review of one's own state statutes and case law would be prudent.

EXTENSION OF GOOD SAMARITAN IMMUNITY

The following cases exemplify how the scope of civil immunity has expanded to reflect the legislative and judicial desire to encourage the provision of medical aid to preserve health and life.

In *Mueller v McMillian Warner Insurance Company*, the Wisconsin Supreme Court held that the state's Good Samaritan statute sets forth three elements: (1) emergency care must be rendered at the scene of an emergency; (2) the care rendered must be emergency care; and (3) any emergency care must be rendered in good faith. The court stated that if all three elements are met, the caregiver shall be immune from civil liability for his or her acts or omissions in providing such emergency care.

The issue in *Mueller* was whether care given to a person injured in an all-terrain vehicle crash by a layperson at the layperson's home was emergency care rendered at the scene of an emergency. In discussing the elements of the state statute, the Wisconsin Supreme Court held that the care given at the home constituted care at the "scene of an emergency" because the phrase is sufficiently broad to cover emergency care at a location where care is needed. However, the court found that the care rendered was not emergency care; it consisted of putting the injured person to bed and checking on her throughout the night. The court held that it exceeded "emergency care" because it went beyond the initial evaluation and immediate assistance, treatment, and intervention during the period before care can be transferred to professional medical personnel. (Undisputed was the fact that professional assistance could have been summoned immediately after the person arrived at the home.) Thus, immunity was not granted to the lay caregiver.

A 1980s Illinois case addresses the nature and scope of Good Samaritan protections afforded to physicians. In *Johnson v Matviuw*, the plaintiff, who was 37 weeks' pregnant, was admitted to the hospital with pain and numbness in the right lower leg. During hospitalization, she suffered cardiopulmonary arrest, and a code was sounded. Defendant Matviuw, a physician, was attending to one of his patients and was summoned by the nurses to attend to the plaintiff. He inserted a breathing tube and initiated cardiopulmonary resuscitation. The code team and the plaintiff's attending physician arrived and informed Matviuw that they would take over and that no additional assistance was needed. Approximately 50 minutes after the plaintiff went into cardiopulmonary arrest, resuscitation efforts ceased, and the plaintiff and her fetus were pronounced dead.

A medical malpractice lawsuit was initiated against Matviuw, alleging that he was careless and negligent in his treatment and failed to recognize the life-threatening condition of the fetus by failing to both initiate fetal monitoring and perform a timely cesarean delivery. The defendant filed a motion for summary judgment, asserting he was immune from civil liability under the Good Samaritan statute. In a supporting affidavit, Matviuw claimed that he provided emergency care to the plaintiff and her fetus, that provision of the care was his sole contact, and that his emergency assistance was gratis. The trial court granted summary judgment for the defendant.

The appellate court affirmed and addressed critical elements of the Good Samaritan statute. The court observed that, in Illinois, the issue of a physician responding to an emergency in a hospital was one of first impression. The court stated, "No one in this case has suggested that the circumstances involving Matviuw with decedent constituted anything other than an emergency. It is beyond this court's power to limit the ordinary meaning of the word emergency by adding except when occurring in a hospital." The court declared "the statute clearly applies to a physician who, in good faith and without prior notice of the illness, renders emergency care without charging a fee. This is precisely the situation in the present case." Thus, the court expanded the traditional notion that Good Samaritan laws were intended to provide civil immunity for emergency care at the scene of roadside crashes, extending it to emergency care rendered by a physician gratuitously to a victim of an emergency that occurred in a hospital.

The case of *Rivera v Arana* extended the Illinois court's expansion of immunity to the medical office. The aunt, who was also the legal guardian, of three-year-old Osvaldo Rivera asked defendant Arana, a physician, to examine Osvaldo for "infected feet," although she did not have funds to pay for medical care and did not have a public aid medical card. The aunt asked whether Arana would see Osvaldo "as an emergency," and he agreed. The examination lasted 15 minutes, and Arana noted that the child was in normal health, except below ideal body weight for his age. The physician found the surfaces of Osvaldo's feet slightly infected, with no open wounds, odor, or pus. Arana gave the aunt a prescription for an antibiotic and a topical ointment. The patient's chart read, "Return in 1 week, and then no charge for the visit because the aunt did not have any money. This woman was poor, and she requested to be seen as an emergency, as an add-on-case," stating "she didn't have a Public Aid card."

The mother of Osvaldo, alleging that Arana failed to take an adequate history or perform an adequate examination, brought a malpractice suit against Arana. Arana moved for summary judgment, asserting that the Illinois Good Samaritan Act barred the plaintiff's claim and that he was immune from civil liability. The trial court granted summary judgment for Arana on the basis that the physician was immune from civil liability under the state act. On review, the appellate court emphasized that a three-part test is used to determine whether the Good Samaritan Act is applicable: "First, the doctor must not have notice of the illness or injury; second, the doctor must provide emergency care; and third, the doctor must not charge a fee."

Observing that no Illinois case addressing the Good Samaritan Act had defined the terms *emergency* or *emergency care*, the appellate court made the following statement: "We believe that whether an emergency situation exists is to be resolved based upon the unforeseen, unexpected combination of circumstances presented which require the need for immediate action, assistance, or relief." On the basis of the facts of the case, the court concluded that the case constituted an emergency. The court stated that "Osvaldo had an inflammation and . . . could have turned into a more serious and severe infection absent treatment." In addition, the physician provided emergency care and performed the service gratis. The court affirmed the summary judgment in favor of the physician on the basis of the Good Samaritan Act.

In Illinois, the courts have clearly extended immunity to the hospital and office settings. The Illinois legislature recodified the Good Samaritan Act in 1997 without altering the holdings of the *Johnson* and *Rivera* cases. Thus, Good Samaritan immunity can apply to emergency care rendered gratis in the hospital or medical office.

Some states have passed statutes with specific language to delineate when immunity extends to an emergency in the hospital or physician office. For example, California and New York do not allow Good Samaritan protection in the medical setting. California excludes "emergency departments and other places where medical care is usually offered" from its definition of a "scene of an emergency."

To the contrary, by statute it provides that in "any action for damages involving a claim of negligence against a physician and surgeon arising out of emergency medical services provided in a general acute care hospital emergency department, the trier of fact shall consider, together with all other relevant matters, the circumstances constituting the emergency, as defined herein, and the degree of care and skill ordinarily exercised by reputable members of the physician and surgeon's profession in the same or similar locality, in like cases, and under similar emergency circumstances." This language appears to codify the regular medical standard of care that is required to be rendered in the emergency department.

New York also by statute denies immunity in the hospital setting. It limits Good Samaritan protection to emergencies "outside a hospital, doctor's office or any other place having proper and necessary medical equipment. . . ."

Wisconsin's Good Samaritan law appears to be less sweeping in its limitation of civil immunity for persons providing emergency care in a hospital or medical setting. Its statute includes the following statement: "Any person who renders emergency care at the scene of any emergency or accident in good faith shall be immune from civil liability for his or her acts or omissions in rendering such emergency care.

This immunity does not extend when employees trained in healthcare or healthcare professionals render emergency care for compensation and within the scope of their usual and customary employment or practice at a hospital or other institution equipped with hospital facilities, at the scene of any emergency or accident, enroute to a hospital or other institution equipped with hospital facilities or at a physician's office."

Thus, in Wisconsin, civil immunity does not appear to apply at a hospital or doctor's office when the care is for compensation and within the scope of the physician or provider's employment. However, if the care is within the scope of employment but is not performed for compensation, does immunity apply?

Florida brings a different approach to civil immunity for medical professionals who deliver emergency treatment in a hospital or medical facility. Rather than excluding the medical professional from the benefit of immunity, it specifically states that there is immunity under certain circumstances in the hospital. It extends immunity to "any health care practitioner . . . who is in a hospital attending to a patient of his or her practice or for business or personal reasons unrelated to direct patient care, and who *voluntarily* responds to provide care or treatment *to a patient with whom at that time the practitioner does not have a then-existing health care patient-practitioner relationship*, and when such care or treatment is necessitated by a sudden or unexpected situation or by an occurrence that demands immediate medical attention. . . ."

It is noteworthy that the Florida law does not refer to compensation or to the scope of the medical professional's employment. Whether "voluntarily responds" necessarily requires the care to be without compensation or outside the caregiver's scope of employment is unclear.

CONCLUSION

This comparison of the statutes of California, New York, Wisconsin, and Florida on civil immunity for physicians who respond to an emergency in the hospital or medical setting reifies the variation in Good Samaritan statutes. In general, these Good Samaritan cases are fact-specific, but the statutes are expansive in the legislators' attempt to create civil immunity for healthcare providers responding to an emergency care situation.

It is important for physicians to read and understand the Good Samaritan statute in their state. They should understand its language and the elements that identify circumstances in which immunity from civil liability applies to their actions when emergency care must be rendered at the scene of an unanticipated medical emergency. Physicians also should know what defines both the scene of an emergency and emergency care and what it means to provide care in good faith. By understanding the Good Samaritan statute in their state, they are prepared to handle emergency situations in a manner that aids the person in need of care and limits liability. Also, they will be enabled to teach coworkers about the risks associated with emergency aid and assistance.

CHAPTER 22

The Sunshine Act—What Every Physician Needs to Know

The Open Payment Program database, which the Centers for Medicare & Medicaid Services (CMS) released in September 2014, made available to the public information about payments made to physicians and teaching hospitals by manufacturers of federally covered drugs, devices, biologics, or medical supplies. Physician ownership or investment interests in manufacturer or group purchasing organizations were also included in the database.

In making this information available, the CMS complied with Section 6002 (Transparency Reports and Reporting of Physician Ownership or Investment Interests) of the Affordable Care Act, while adding another layer to its National Physician Transparency Program.

THE SUNSHINE ACT

The Physician Payments Sunshine Act (*42 U.S.C. & 1320a -7b*) requires manufacturers of drugs, medical devices, biologics, and medical supplies and group purchasing organizations (GPOs) to report to the CMS services payments made and investment interests given to physicians and teaching hospitals.

The Sunshine Act (SA) was enacted by the Obama administration as part of the Patient Protection and Affordable Care Act (PPACA) with a goal of promoting transparency in relationship to the monetary connections made by medical device manufacturers and pharmaceutical companies to physicians and teaching hospitals.

The SA decrees that physicians, teaching hospitals, and GPOs must account for any financial or investment relationships *(42 C.F.*R. & 403.902). Manufacturers and GPOs are mandated to report any ownership or investment benefits in those companies held by physicians or their immediate family members as stated in the Stark Law *(42 USC & 1320a – 7h(a)(2)*. These mandated reporting requirements are intended to provide a policy goal of preventing inappropriate financial influence on education, research, and patient clinical decision-making.

WHO IS AFFECTED?

All physicians, excluding resident physicians, who are not contractual employees of the manufacturers must report payments. Teaching hospitals that receive financial compensation for medical education programs must report the pecuniary amounts. Teaching hospitals are those that receive payment for Medicare direct medical education, indirect medical education, inpatient prospective payment system, or psychiatric hospitals programs *(42 CFR & 403.902)*.

In 2018 the number of healthcare providers impacted by the SA was expanded to include physician assistants (PAs), nurse practitioners (NPs), clinical nurse specialists, nurse anesthetists (NAs), and certified clinical nurse midwives. The transfer of monetary value from manufactures and GPOs to this expanded group of clinical providers will be reportable to CMS starting in calendar year 2020.

Thus, all teaching hospitals and physician group practices must review and comprehend how the expansion of impacted clinical practitioners will affect their relationship with manufacturers and GPOs. This understanding will mandate due diligence by the organizations to ensure comprehensive and accurate information is reported on all covered beneficiaries of payments.

REPORTABLE TRANSACTIONS

Transfer of monetary value, referred to as "payments," falls into several classifications. It is essential physicians and healthcare providers cited under the expanded categories understand the transactions that are considered payments and report to CMS within the defined time regulations.

Broadly the major categories of payments that are reportable under the SA include consulting fees, travel and lodging, food and beverages, honoraria, research, and current or prospective ownership or investment interests. This listing is not all-inclusive; the "nature of payments" *(42 USC & 403.904 (e) (2))* provides a complete listing.

Consulting Fees

Consulting fees are the monies paid to the consultant by the manufacturer or GPO. The consulting fees paid to the physician or other covered categories are reportable under the SA. The following examples help illustrate the concept:

- A payment made by a manufacturer to a physician for designing a research protocol.
- A payment made by a manufacturer to a physician to use a new product and to opine on the product.
- A payment made by a manufacturer to a clinic whereby a specific physician is requested for a consultative opinion.

Travel and Lodging

Travel expenses are the costs associated with traveling for the purpose of conducting business-related activities. Lodging expenses include costs associated with traveling away from residence or place of business to engage in trade or serve as an employee. Physicians who are provided payment for travel and lodging must report the payment; it is often reported in conjunction with the food and beverage reimbursements *(42 CFR & 403.904(e) (1)*.

Food and Beverages

Payment and transfer of monetary value related to food and beverages are subject to explicit rules *(42 CFR & 403.904 (g))*. For example, a manufacturer supplies food/drink to a physician group. The individual's financial reporting responsibility is calculated by dividing the entire cost by the number of individuals participating in the food serving. If a manufacturer offers a buffet meal with drinks and coffee, the conference attendants do not need to report.

Honoraria

Honoraria are defined as payments given to a professional person for services for which fees are not legally or traditionally required, such as speaking engagements that include promotional speaking on behalf of a manufacturer. Honoraria payments must be reported.

Research

Research is considered the systematic investigation into the study of materials and sources in order to establish facts and reach new conclusions. A payment or transfer of monetary value in connection with research activities is subject to reporting rules. Reported research payments must include a list of drugs, biological devices, or medical devices evaluated in the research study, as well as the total amount of the research payment as outlined in a written agreement, research protocol, or both *(42 CFR & 403.904 (f))*.

Ownership/Investment

Physicians or other included healthcare providers under the SA must report current or prospective ownership or investment interests. For example, a physician believes a new drug in development will be transformational and asks the drug company to be an investor and allow the physician to eventually own a percentage of the drug company. This investment and ownership interest must be reported. This also applies to a physician's family members.

Exceptions to Reporting Payments

The following are exceptions to reporting payments:

- Manufacturers and GPOs do not need to report transfers of value of \$107.91 each but must report transfers of \$107.91 in the aggregate within the calendar year. These threshold payments are tired to the consumer price index *(42 USC & 1320a-7h (e) (01)(B)(i))*.
- Product samples that are not intended to be sold do not need to be reported.
- Educational materials that directly benefit patients do not need to be reported.
- Discounts, including rebates and in-kind items used for the provision of charity care are exceptions as well *(42 USC & 1320a-7h (e) (01)(B) (ii)-9xii))*.

ACTING WITHIN THE REPORTING AND DISPUTE PERIODS

Manufacturers and GPOs must complete their reporting by the 90th day of the following calendar year, which is March 31(March 30 in a leap year). On April 1, the review and dispute process begins and lasts 45 days until May 15.

During this 45-day period, physicians and teaching hospitals my use the CMS online National Physicians Payment Transparency Program (Open Payment System) to formally dispute any information they believe is inaccurate. If the physicians or teaching institutions do not lodge a formal grievance in the 45-day period and the dispute is not resolved within 15 days, the information will be published on June 30 as originally reported and will be made available to the general public without indicating that the physician or teaching institution believes the information is inaccurate.

If the physicians or teaching institutions create a formal grievance within the 45-day period, the information will be published on June 30 as originally reported and made available to the general public with an indication that the physician or teaching institution believes the information is mistaken.

The singular way the information will be published correctly is if the dispute is resolved in the 15-day period and the manufacture or GPO corrects the submission. Physicians and teaching hospitals can file a dispute with CMS but cannot report any corrections to the reported information.

How to Make a Formal Complaint

To make formal complaint, physicians and teaching hospitals must be registered on the OPS. Reporters, regulators, patients, hospital systems, and other employers have increasing used the OPS to research physician relationships with manufacturers and GPOs. Therefore, physicians who fail to verify the accuracy of the information submitted by manufacturers and GPOs and formally dispute any incorrect information may be subject to unintended personal and professional consequences.

PRAGMATIC PROCESSES FOR PHYSICIANS AND TEACHING HOSPITALS

Physicians and teaching hospitals must register with CMS Enterprise Identity Management System (EIDM) to request access to the Open Payment System, then complete the registration process. Any account inactive for 180 days may be locked.

Physicians and teaching hospitals must have a surveillance system in place to track all payments or transfer of monetary value to ensure the accuracy of reported data in the Open Payments System. In the case of inaccurate data, physicians and teaching hospitals must submit a dispute to CMS within the 45-day review and dispute period, or no later than December 31 of the year reported, negotiate the dispute, and make clear any errors are corrected by resubmitting a report to CMS.

It is also mandatory that physician groups and teaching hospitals prepare for the expansion of covered recipients under the SA that become effective in 2021. Educational programs must be developed for PAs, NPs, certified NAs, and certified midwives.

SECTION 4

Why All Physicians Must Understand Informed Consent in a Liability World

CHAPTER 23

Medical Informed Consent: General Considerations for Physicians

Consent is ethically, morally, and legally mandated by the fiduciary responsibilities flowing from the patient–physician relationship. Negligence *per se* occurs when an actor's violation of a statute or regulation causes the kind of harm the statute was intending to prevent.

Ethically, physicians engaged in patient–physician relationships involving medical informed consent have a moral responsibility to identify the best treatments for each patient on the basis of available medical evidence and to discuss with patients the hoped-for benefits and the potential risks.

Physicians must allow for patients' questions about the proposed treatments, benefits, and risks and must answer those questions from the available medical literature and their professional experience. This exchange of information and ideas is the foundation of the patient-physician partnership and promotes informed decision-making in the most complex medical situations.

Legally, a physician must understand that many states have codified medical informed consent into statutory law, and lack of adherence to the statute can lead to *per se* negligence for the physician. The jurisdictions vary, and violation of the statute can be considered intrinsically negligent or merely a rebuttable presumption of negligence.

Ethically and legally, all physicians have a mandatory obligation to understand the medical informed consent process. Understanding this process allows for the exchange of ideas in medical practice that will yield informed decisions and will lead to the best outcomes on the basis of shared information. Further, informed consent limits the potential for negligence cases brought for lack of informed consent.

GENERAL CONSIDERATIONS IN INFORMED CONSENT

Informed consent is the legal embodiment of the concept that each individual has the right to make decisions affecting his or her health. It is generally accepted that patients should consider the potential risks and benefits flowing from their medical decisions. Patients must acknowledge those potential risks and benefits to make informed decisions.

Generally, the law protects the patient's right to informed consent by requiring physicians to disclose all pertinent information about risks and benefits of the procedure to the patient. Medical informed consent law requires disclosure of the risks of the suggested medical procedure and the risks of the alternatives to enable patients to make knowledgeable decisions.

All physicians would be prudent to educate themselves regarding their states' statutory laws concerning medical informed consent. Further, every practicing physician should understand the underpinnings of the common-law analysis of medical informed consent and negligence. The common law and statutory law create a burden on physicians that varies in different jurisdictions.

Risk can be defined as exposure to a chance of injury or loss. This definition has two distinct components: (1) chance related to uncertain events—those that are unpredictable in any single case, but for which a probability that an event will occur in any one case can be estimated through statistical pooling of large databases; and (2) injury or loss, including any consequences for which the patient sustains a disability.

The law places a positive obligation on physicians to disclose information about the risks to any patient who is at risk of an adverse event, that is, who will suffer injury if a chance event occurs.

DEVELOPMENT OF INFORMED CONSENT LAW

Medical informed consent law developed from the intentional tort of battery, which protects individuals from an unwanted physical touching of the body by others having neither express nor implied consent of the person touched. Battery occurs in medicine when a physician performs a treatment without the patient's consent, performs a substantially different procedure than the one for which consent was given, or exceeds the scope of the consent, or when a physician other than the one to whom consent was given carries out the procedure.

Prudent Behaviors of Physicians Engaged in the Process of Medical Informed Consent

- The physician directly involved in the proposed treatment should conduct the informed consent discussion. The discussion should include the treatment, the risks and benefits of treatment, and alternative therapies with associated risks and benefits.
- The physician directly involved in the proposed treatment should discuss the most likely outcome with no treatment, on the basis of the best available medical or surgical evidence.
- The physician directly involved in the proposed treatment should always discuss the severe risks, such as death, paralysis, loss of cognition, or loss of a limb, even if the probability of occurrences is negligible.
- The physician directly involved in the proposed treatment should always disclose less-severe risks that occur frequently. Courts do not place emphasis solely on consequences; they recognize frequency as an important component of risk.
- The physician directly involved in the proposed treatment should discuss informed consent in language the patient can understand, and treatment should not proceed until the physician believes the patient understands the risks and benefits and has made a rational decision.
- The physician directly involved in the proposed treatment must understand that the medical consent form is not medical consent; it represents evidence that the consent process occurred. The dialogue between the patient and physician is the essence of the consent process.
- The physician directly involved in the proposed treatment should document all patient-imposed restrictions in the medical record and the discussion with the patient about how the restrictions limit the physician's ability to provide standard medical care.

- The physician directly involved in the proposed treatment may advise the patient to seek care with an alternative healthcare provider if the restrictions imposed by the patient seem to inhibit good medical practice and seem likely to lead to a suboptimal medical outcome.
- The physician directly involved in the proposed treatment must understand the informed consent can be withdrawn at any time. When physicians allow 24 to 48 hours for patients to reflect after consent to a treatment strategy, the period of reflection validates the notion of informed consent.
- Withdrawal of consent should include a discussion and documentation through a withdrawal of consent form on which time and date are noted.

When physicians and patients take medical informed consent seriously, the patient–physician relationship becomes a partnership, with shared authority, decision-making, and responsibility for outcomes.

The physician directly involved in the proposed treatment can enhance the informed consent process through appropriate use of additional learning materials, such as pamphlets and video, and through involvement of support staff, such as physician assistants, in providing information that can be discussed by the responsible physician

The legal analysis of medical informed consent has evolved over the years from an allegation of battery to an allegation of negligence. Currently, the courts nearly unanimously characterize lack of informed consent as a matter of negligence of the physician to disclose necessary information to patients.

Negligence requires that four elements be established for liability of the physician-defendant: (1) a duty of the physician to meet a particular standard of care, (2) the physician's failure to perform that duty, (3) a causal connection (proximate cause) between the physician's failure and the patient's injury, and (4) an injury for which monetary compensation is due

A TYPICAL MEDICAL INFORMED CONSENT CASE

A typical medical informed consent case usually arises in conjunction with an underlying medical procedure. For example, if a patient suffers a stroke during an invasive vascular procedure, the patient might allege—in addition to and separate from any medical malpractice claim—that, because the physician did not discuss the risks and benefits of the procedure and reasonable alternatives to it, the patient could not make an informed decision whether to proceed.

As previously noted, to establish a lack of informed consent case, a patient must first show that the physician had a duty to discuss the risks and benefits of the procedure and reasonable alternatives to it with the patient, and that discussion should have been in accordance with an accepted standard within the medical community. That is, the physician is expected only to disclose risks that might reasonably be known to occur with the particular procedure. Therefore, the discussion might vary depending on the nature of the procedure and the patient's relevant comorbidities.

States have applied different approaches in articulating the standard regarding the physician's duty to disclose.

DEFINING THE STANDARD OF DISCLOSURE

Two dominant approaches, the "professional" standard and the "materiality" standard, define the standard of disclosure of information by which a physician's duty to the patient is measured.

The professional standard requires the physician to disclose information that other physicians possessing the same skills and practicing in the same or a similar community disclose in a similar situation. The second approach by courts is the materiality or "prudent patient" approach, allowing the jury to decide whether other information would have been considered important by a reasonable patient in making a decision and therefore requiring disclosure.

The courts recognize situations when a physician's non-disclosure will be excused, including cases of the patient's mental incompetence, medical emergencies, and the therapeutic privilege exception. If a patient is incompetent to make a reasoned decision, then disclosure to the patient might not be required. The physician can also withhold information under the therapeutic privilege if disclosure would interfere with treatment or would adversely affect the condition or recovery of the patient.

The emergency exception to disclosure applies in situations where attempting to secure consent would delay necessary and proper treatment. Last, physicians need not disclose risks of which the patient is already aware or risks that are commonly known. Individual state law and court decisions determine which approaches and exceptions apply in an individual physician's practice.

PHYSICIAN'S DUTY TO DISCLOSE RISK INFORMATION

Materiality jurisdiction courts have attempted to provide some guidance for physicians by suggesting that the physician's duty to disclose risk increases as the magnitude of the risk increases. These courts uniformly fail to give explicit guidelines or to identify on what scale risks are to be measured.

All severe risks (death, paralysis, loss of cognition, loss of a limb) should always be disclosed, even if the probability of occurrence is negligible. Further, even less-severe risks, if frequent, should always be disclosed. Nominal risks with low probability of occurrence need not be disclosed. Courts do not place emphasis solely on consequences, recognizing frequency as an important component of risk. The professional standard asserts the doctor's duty to disclose is what a reasonably prudent physician with the same background, training, and experience would have disclosed to the patient in the same or similar circumstances. The professional standard does not give explicit guidelines regarding the disclosure of risks.

The courts stress that full disclosure is not required. Full disclosure is a slippery slope for physicians involved in medical informed consent. There is reasons full disclosure, as a standard of practice should not be expected. First, the number of risks possible from even a routine procedure is large, and potential risks can span a range of consequences. For example, in a footnote, the California Supreme Court listed some of the risks of having blood drawn: "[T]he risks . . . are said to include hematoma, dermatitis, cellulitis, abscess, osteomyelitis, and death, to mention a few."

Second, the burden of identifying small consequences in extremely unlikely risks is too great a burden on the physician, and the resulting choice by the patient will be impaired by a litany of consequences. Despite the courts' pronouncements that full disclosure is not required, they have failed to delineate any clear limits on what must be disclosed. The California Supreme Court articulated this uncertainty: "One cannot know with certainty which medical consent is valid until a lawsuit is filed and resolved." There does not appear to be a standard of disclosure to which physicians can adhere to avoid liability with certitude.

DOCTRINE OF MEDICAL INFORMED CONSENT

The doctrine of medical informed consent states that, before a patient elects to proceed with a treatment that has risk, there must be a balanced discussion of the treatment strategy, including the potential risks and hoped-for benefits.

The magnitude of the risks and their frequency should receive special emphasis. Also considered are alternative treatments and their benefits, risks, and measured utility; the likely results of no treatment; and the probability of a good outcome with the proposed strategy. A good outcome and the major anticipated problems during recovery are described as well as the estimated time to resume normal life activities.

This information must be presented in language the patient can understand, and treatment should not proceed until the physician believes the patient understands the risks and benefits and decides to proceed on the foundation of that understanding.

The legal foundation for adopting the doctrine of medical informed consent is two-fold: (1) to establish and promote patient autonomy and (2) to promote informed, rational decisions. The courts hold that it is reasonable to require physicians to inform, educate, and partner with patients because patients are generally unable to dissect the details of medical science needed to make an educated decision about treatment. This educational process should inform the patient enough to allow for an informed decision. Information disclosure will not necessarily lead to an ideal patient–physician partnership, but it should promote patient autonomy in the decision-making process and achieve a foundation for an ethical and trusting relationship between a physician and patient.

To give valid informed consent, the patient must be competent and the patient's actions must be voluntary. *Voluntary* means "of free mind and free will." The patient must not be cognitively impaired by medication, personal emotional stress, or external stress by family members or physicians.

For example, one case involved a patient who was given a sedative to sleep and subsequently awakened in the middle of the night to give consent for a hernia operation. The court held that the medical consent was invalid because the patient was unlikely to understand what permission he had granted after being awakened from sleep and after taking a sedative.

Determining incompetence and competence is a matter for the court and not a question of fact for the layperson. In medical informed consent the focus should be on the capacity of the patient. Capacity means the ability to process information received and to communicate a meaningful response. An element of capacity is that the person making the decision is an adult and has not been judged incompetent or is not otherwise prohibited by law from exercising that decision-making capacity. *Decision-making capacity* means the ability to understand the significant benefits, risks, and alternative to proposed healthcare and to make and communicate a healthcare decision.

MEDICAL CONSENT

The purpose of medical consent, through medical consent forms and through documentation of the informed consent discussion in the medical record, is to have evidence of the exact terms of the medical consent in case of future disagreement. If a patient sues a physician, an outpatient surgery center, a medical group, or a hospital and alleges lack of informed consent, the defendant will be able to present the written consent form or the documentation of the discussion in court as evidence that medical consent was in fact secured.

If the medical consent form or documentation of the discussion in the medical record is comprehensive and specific in terms of risks and benefits, and if the medical consent was granted voluntarily by a competent patient who understood the information presented, the probability of a successful lawsuit is low.

However, the medical consent form does not equate to medical consent. Rather, it represents evidence that the medical consent process occurred. A patient could present evidence that medical informed consent did not occur, despite a signed form, for example, when a nurse presented the risks to the patient and the physician signed the form as if consent had been obtained.

What should a medical consent form contain? First, a consent form is not necessary to achieve valid medically informed consent. If an entity, such as a hospital, an outpatient surgery center, or other healthcare organization, chooses to honor a medical informed consent form, the form should contain all the information needed to comply with the elements of medical informed consent.

The form should contain an accurate description of the proposed procedure, the risks and benefits of the proposed procedure, the potential advantages and disadvantages of no treatment, alternative treatment strategies and their risks and benefits, the potential for a successful outcome, the estimated recuperation time, and the estimated time required for returning to normal activity.

The consent form should contain the name of the physician involved and clauses dealing with photography, disposition, and use of removed tissues, organs, and body parts. Patients should be made aware that they are allowed to strike out any part of the medical consent form with which they do not agree or to which they do not consent. If a patient does not understand details of the treatment, the patient and physician should discuss treatment and risks to reach mutual understanding.

If a physician believes the limits placed on the medical informed consent hamper standard medical practice, he or she should document all the patient-imposed restrictions in the record, with a discussion of how the limits placed on the physician limit his or her ability to proceed in a standard fashion, and that the limits were described to the patient.

Alternatively, if a physician believes the restrictions seriously inhibit good medical practice and might lead to a suboptimal clinical outcome, he or she may advise the patient to seek care with another physician.

WITHDRAWING CONSENT OR REFUSING TREATMENT

May a patient withdraw consent after signing a medical consent form? Consent must be freely given and can be freely withdrawn at any time. Whether consent was given orally or in writing does not affect the patient's ability to change or withdraw consent.

Physicians may choose to allow 24 to 48 hours for patients to reflect after consent to a treatment strategy. During this time, patients can weigh the alternatives and come to an independent conclusion either to proceed with or to withdraw from the proposed treatment. A time for patients to appraise the risks and benefits reinforces the validity of medical informed consent.

If a patient orally indicates a desire to withdraw medical consent, the physician would be wise to execute a withdrawal of consent form, noting time of day and date consent was withdrawn, or to carefully document in the medical record the details of consent withdrawal including a time and date.

May a patient refuse treatment? A competent patient may decline any and all treatment. Even mentally ill patients are generally considered competent to refuse treatment. Physicians would be prudent to have a patient who has been diagnosed with mental illness and who refuses an apparently beneficial treatment evaluated by a psychiatrist. In some situations, patients can be compelled to receive treatment. For example, a mentally ill patient could be considered a danger to society and institutionalized against his or her will.

Competent individuals with contagious diseases may refuse treatment, but public health officials may quarantine or involuntarily hospitalize and isolate them if they are dangerous to other people. This policy is based on broad "police power" that states have (and can exercise through their departments of health) to protect the health and safety of the public.

The reason for refusal of treatment can be rational or irrational. Whether rational or irrational, decisions are legally binding on the physician and the hospital. Individual freedom is guaranteed only if people are given the right to make choices that would generally be regarded as irrational behavior.

Some states also require hospitals to ensure proper consent is obtained for no treatment. This consent for no treatment should contain a release of medical responsibility and any associated liability for the hospital, nurses, and employees, together with all physicians connected in any way to the patient.

GOOD CLINICAL PRACTICE AND INFORMED CONSENT

Are good clinical practice and informed consent inseparable? Respect for patient autonomy in clinical practice is of great moral importance in our society. The moral and legal responsibility of medical informed consent depends on the transmission of appropriate information to patients. We believe patients' choices must not be coerced by members of the healthcare team or by other third parties, such as friends, family, or payers. Equally, we believe patients must be competent to consent; they must understand, remember, consider, and believe clinical information given to them about the specific treatments.

The moral foundation for the requirement of medical informed consent in general is not disputed. The question arises whether in certain situations exceptions from the general requirement of medical informed consent would be acceptable.

An exception to medical informed consent could be motivated by the idea that an exception is reasonable if insistence on the requirement of medical informed consent causes more harm than good.

INFORMED CONSENT IN EMERGENCIES

Is medical informed consent always necessary in emergency medical situations? Is a patient who is having an acute myocardial infarction sufficiently competent to understand what he or she is being told?

In a survey of Swedish cardiologists about their perceptions of medical informed consent during acute myocardial infarction, 86% thought that patients were unable to comprehend all the information provided and so, by definition, were unable to give fully informed consent.

What evidence is there that patients with acute illnesses themselves fail to understand all the issues in the medical informed consent process? A report from the Fourth International Study of Infarct Survival revealed that only 31% of 129 patients perceived that they had full comprehension of the trial, and 19% thought they did not understand the trial. A review of patients with subarachnoid hemorrhage revealed only 19% of those who had given medical informed consent themselves could remember the consent process.

The studies suggest that during a medical emergency many of the patients were too ill to give fully informed consent. Does this mean that patients with an acute myocardial infarction or subarachnoid hemorrhage are unable to engage in the decision-making process of medical informed consent? The answer is no. Although acute myocardial infarction is a medical emergency and there is evidence that some patients do not fully comprehend all the information to make a fully informed decision, some patients do comprehend and are capable of doing so.

Ideal Statute Outlining Physicians' Duty to Disclose

Information shall be supplied to the patient or the patient's guardian or legal surrogate before obtaining consent to a proposed medical or surgical treatment or a diagnostic or therapeutic procedure as follows

- Describe condition to be treated.
- Describe proposed treatment or procedure.
- Outline intended and anticipated results of proposed treatment or procedure.
- Describe recognized alternative treatments or procedures, including the option of not using these treatments or procedures.
- Describe recognized material risks of serious complications or mortality associated with the following Proposed treatment or procedure.
- Recognized alternative treatments or procedures No treatment or procedure.
- Outline recognized benefits of alternative treatments or procedures and risks of alternative treatments.
- Disclosure of information and consent provided for in this statute shall not be required in certain conditions.
- Emergencies as defined by statute.

When the surgical or diagnostic procedure is unforeseen or is not known to be needed at the time consent is obtained, and the patient has consented to allow the responsible physician to make the decision concerning such procedure, trust between the physician and patient is essential. This is a unique opportunity to involve appropriate family members or healthcare surrogates in decision-making during emergencies. Patients do not need to stand alone in the patient–physician partnership.

THE PARADOX OF CHOICE

Responsibility for medical care has landed on the shoulders of patients with a resounding thud. Patients have the choice of telling physicians what to do in relation to healthcare decisions. The tone of medical practice has shifted from paternalistic to consultative, in which the physician lays the possibilities before the patient, with the potential pluses and minuses of each, and the patient makes a choice. This attitude was well described by Atul Gawande: "Only a decade ago, doctors made the decisions, patients did what they were told. Doctors did not consult patients about their desires and priorities. . . . They were regarded as children: too fragile and simple minded to handle the truth, let alone make decisions."

According to Gawande, *The Silent World of Doctor and Patient*, by physician and ethicist Jay Katz, launched us into the era of autonomous patient choice. There is little doubt that this change in the decision-making paradigm has improved the quality of medical care generally. Yet no single paradigm fits all patients. Gawande suggests the shift in responsibility has gone too far: "The new orthodoxy about patient autonomy has a hard time acknowledging an awkward truth: patients frequently don't want the freedom that we've given them. That is, they're glad to have their autonomy respected, but the exercise of that autonomy means choosing sometimes to relinquish it."

Gawande describes a family medical emergency where his newborn daughter stopped breathing, and the family rushed her to the emergency department. The physicians on duty asked Gawande if he wanted his daughter intubated. He said that he wanted the physicians to make that decision for him: The uncertainties were savage, and he did not want to bear the responsibility of making the wrong call. Gawande did not want to have to live with the guilt of making the wrong call.

When it comes to medical treatment, patients see choice as a burden and a blessing. Physicians must evaluate each patient–physician relationship individually and identify the level of responsibility each party wants to assume in the decision-making process. This process must be documented in the medical record and must detail the assumed responsibilities of each partner in the patient–physician relationship.

The art of medicine demands an ability to apply multiple paradigms to the decision-making process when guiding patients through complex medical decisions. This process requires empathy, time, mutual understanding, and courage.

CONCLUSION

Medical informed consent is essential to a true patient–physician relationship. Patients need to participate in the informed consent process to understand the risk–benefit relationship for the proposed treatment strategy. This understanding is essential because patients are often psychologically regressed secondary to the realization that they are confronting a life-preserving procedure.

Physicians need to participate in the informed consent process to provide patients with the best treatment available by sharing decision-making and limiting any potential for liability.

Medical ethics, common law, and, in many states, codified statutory law mandate the informed consent process. Physicians would be prudent to be knowledgeable in these areas of medical ethics, common law, and statutory law. Physicians would be prudent also to understand that the consent process is vital to the physician–patient relationship and that no single paradigm can define the ethical, medical, and legal approach a physician should undertake to achieve informed consent. The process should be individualized within the boundaries of the patient's desires for autonomy, thus reflecting true patient autonomy.

Reprinted with permission, Timothy J. Paterick, Geoff V. Carson, Marjorie C. Allen, Timothy E. Paterick, Medical Informed Consent: General Considerations for Physicians, *Mayo Clinic Proceedings*, 83(3): 313–319, ISSN 0025-6196, https://doi.org/10.4065/83.3.313.

CHAPTER 24

The Standard of Care: Medical Errors, Violations and the Law

In medical negligence cases, a medical expert must explain to a trier of fact whether a defendant physician's conduct constitutes a breach of duty—a component of a negligence cause of action. The parameters of the physician's fiduciary duty are delineated by the standard of care.

Physicians have a fiduciary duty to act in the best interests of patients. Many features of the standard of care have been well investigated, but there remains an incomplete understanding of this concept.

This chapter examines the standard of care, defining its theoretical underpinnings, the inherent human factors that lead to medical errors and violations, and the real world of medical negligence today. Additionally, I reflect upon state and national standards of care. The locality rule requires a defendant physician to provide the same degree of skill and care that is required of a physician practicing in the same or similar community. Last, I address the relationship between the standard of care and clinical practice guidelines.

A medical negligence case is the result of a clinical situation that has had an adverse outcome alleged to be due to a medical error or rule violation. The task of the medical expert is to determine what actions a defendant physician should have taken, or not taken, and whether a breach of duty has occurred, in accordance with the parameters set forth by the standard of care. Thus, the medical expert must understand elements of the standard of care and determine whether that standard was met. This article explains why understanding the standard of care can be challenging.

DEFINING THE STANDARD OF DISCLOSURE

Two dominant approaches, the "professional" standard and the "materiality" standard, define the standard of disclosure of information by which a physician's duty to the patient is measured. The professional standard requires the physician to disclose information that other physicians possessing the same skills and practicing in the same or a similar community disclose in a similar situation.

The second approach is the "materiality" or "prudent patient" approach, allowing the jury to decide whether other information would have been considered important by a reasonable patient in making a decision, therefore requiring disclosure.

The courts recognize situations when a physician's nondisclosure will be excused, including cases of the patient's mental incompetence, medical emergencies, and the therapeutic privilege exception. If a patient is incompetent to make a reasoned decision, then disclosure to the patient might not be required.

The physician can also withhold information under the therapeutic privilege if disclosure would interfere with treatment, or would adversely affect the condition or recovery of the patient. The emergency exception to disclosure applies in situations where attempting to secure consent would delay necessary and proper treatment. Last, physicians need not disclose risks of which the patient is already aware, or risks that are commonly known. Individual state law and court decisions determine which approaches and exceptions apply in an individual physician's practice.

PHYSICIAN'S DUTY TO DISCLOSE RISK INFORMATION

"Materiality" jurisdiction courts have attempted to provide some guidance for physicians by suggesting that the physician's duty to disclose risk increases as the magnitude of the risk increases. These courts uniformly fail to give explicit guidelines or to identify on what scale risks are to be measured.

All severe risks (e.g., death, paralysis, loss of cognition, loss of a limb) should always be disclosed, even if the probability of occurrence is negligible. Further, even less-severe risks, if they occur frequently, should always be disclosed. Nominal risks with low probability of occurrence need not be disclosed. Courts do not place emphasis solely on consequences, recognizing frequency as an important component of risk.

The "professional" standard asserts that the doctor's duty to disclose is what a reasonably prudent physician with the same background, training, and experience would have disclosed to the patient in the same or similar circumstances. The professional standard does not give explicit guidelines regarding the disclosure of risks, but would be established by medical expert testimony.

The courts stress that full disclosure is not required. Full disclosure is a slippery slope for physicians involved in medical informed consent. There are reasons why full disclosures, as a standard of practice, should not be expected.

First, the number of risks possible from even a routine procedure is large, and potential risks can span a range of consequences. For example, in a footnote, the California Supreme Court listed some of the risks of having blood drawn: "[T]he risks . . . are said to include hematoma, dermatitis, cellulitis, abscess, osteomyelitis, and death, to mention a few." Second, the burden of identifying small consequences in extremely unlikely risks is too great a burden on the physician, and the resulting choice by the patient will be impaired by a litany of consequences.

Despite the courts' pronouncements that full disclosure is not required, they have failed to delineate any clear limits on what must be disclosed. The California Supreme Court articulated this uncertainty: "One cannot know with certainty which medical consent is valid until a lawsuit is filed and resolved." There does not appear to be a standard of disclosure to which physicians can adhere to avoid liability with any certainty (see Table 1).

The Standard of Care Remains Obscure

Clinical experiences and review of expert witness testimony suggest that a complete understanding of the standard of care is still ambiguous. What is a "standard of care"? Who determines the prevailing standard of care?

TABLE 1. Ideal Statute Outlining Physicians' Duty to Disclose

Information shall be supplied to the patient or the patient's guardian or legal surrogate before obtaining consent to a proposed medical or surgical treatment or a diagnostic or therapeutic procedure as follows:
Describe the condition to be treated.
Describe the proposed treatment or procedure.
Outline intended and anticipated results of the proposed treatment or procedure.
Describe recognized alternative treatments or procedures, including the option of not using these treatments or procedures.
Describe recognized material risks of serious complications or mortality associated with the following proposed treatment or procedure: • Recognized alternative treatments or procedures • No treatment or procedure
Outline recognized benefits of alternative treatments or procedures and risks of alternative treatments
Disclosure of information and consent provided for in this statute shall not be required in certain conditions
Emergencies as defined by statute
When the surgical or diagnostic procedure is generally recognized by reasonably prudent physicians not to involve a material risk to the patient
When the patient, another person, or people authorized to give consent pursuant to this chapter make a request in writing that the information provided for in this Code section not be disclosed
When prior consent has been obtained within 30 days of the surgical or diagnostic procedure as a part of a course of treatment for the patient's condition, complying with the requirements of this statute for the surgical or diagnostic procedure; provided, however, that if such consent is obtained in conjunction with the patient's admission to a hospital for the performance of such procedure, the consent shall be valid for 30 days from the date of admission or for the period the person is confined in the hospital for that purpose, whichever is greater
When the surgical or diagnostic procedure is unforeseen or is not known to be needed at the time consent is obtained, and the patient has consented to allow the responsible physician to make the decision concerning such procedure

This chapter examines these questions, beginning with an overview of the history of the standard of care and using case law to trace its evolution from a local standard to a national standard. I probe the waning of the locality rule and consider the entry of national standards of care. Finally, I address the relationship between the standard of care and concepts with which it is often conflated, such as best practices, expert opinions, and the now pervasive clinical practice guidelines.

Conceptual Underpinnings of "Standard of Care"

The "standard of care" is best perceived as a fluid and changing standard by which the law measures liability. The moral climate against which it is defined dictates that the prevailing standard should be viewed as what can be reasonably expected of people. The standard is embedded in the language of culpable failure. Culpable failure implies responsibility and the deserving of blame for having done something wrong.

Often, in summation, the question before the court is whether the conduct of the actor being considered is below the standard that can be expected by the plaintiff in the circumstances in question, and that expectation is different for professionals as opposed to laypeople.

Ultimately, the law imposes civil liability in those cases where the defendant risked unacceptable harm, whether or not he or she intended to place others at risk, and whether or not she was capable of acting to a higher standard. The court at such a level defines the standard that most people in the profession might reasonably meet it. The standard is pegged to a sense of the possible and reasonable.

The principal judicial foundation for the attribution of liability includes a consideration of justice and equity. A standard of care must galvanize an understanding of reasonableness and foreseeability, and overcome the inherent biases of hindsight and outcome.

It is easy today to say the Challenger space shuttle should not have been launched, because we know in hindsight that the O-rings failed. This is the wisdom of hindsight, wisdom that often compels the reviewer to conclude that we should have seen a disaster coming, even if those who acted did not foresee it. Outcome blame causes us to attribute blame more readily with a seriously adverse outcome than when the outcome is comparatively minor.

The significance of outcome bias is that if the harm is great (e.g., death), the desire to find wrongdoing is intense, whereas if evaluated dispassionately, there may be no negligence found. The variables of reasonableness, foreseeability, hindsight, and outcome bias must be inserted into the calculation that defines our standard of care.

The Human Factor—Understanding Errors, Violations, and Recklessness

Misfortune invites explanation. When things go wrong in human affairs, the inevitable response is to seek an explanation for the mishap. Human curiosity compels us to try to understand the events that touch our lives and the lives of our loved ones. Mishaps in medicine are no different, and when there is a tragic outcome, the search for an answer may become all-consuming.

This mandates a discussion and understanding of human errors, violations, and acts of malice in relation to the standard of care. When we are evaluating events for the purpose of attributing blame we must focus on the actions and thought processes, not on the results or outcome. This makes it important for us to define errors, violations and acts of malice.

Reason defines *error* as an *unintended* failure in the formulation of a plan intended to achieve a goal, or an unintentional departure of a sequence of mental or physical activities from the sequence planned.

This definition retains the principle that errors are not associated with automatic actions, and that there must be some intended aspect of the act or plan that goes awry. The error itself is unintentional; the error shifts focus from the outcome of an act to a failure in the act or plan itself. There are skill-based, rule-based, and knowledge-based errors. It is imperative to understand the distinctions among these types of errors and how they relate to attribution of fault.

- Skill-based errors involve actions and usually are the result of distraction. Human are prone to distraction. For example, the distribution of medication to the wrong patient often results from a lapse in attentiveness to the task at hand.
- Rule-based and knowledge-based errors are problem-solving failures or planning failures and are grouped under the heading of mistakes. Rule-based errors involve some failure in the process by which a set of circumstances is recognized and an appropriate rule is applied. In medicine, physicians use a mental schema called *frequency gambling.* Physicians tend to choose an algorithm known to have worked on previous occasions in similar circumstances without establishing

beyond a doubt that the clinical situation is equivalent. The problems that evolve from a rule-based approach are that the rule selected may be inadequate or it may simply be wrong.

- Additionally, in medical practice we may have technical errors and errors in judgment. Technical errors are a type of skill-based error distinct from lapses. In technical errors there is a failure to carry out the intended procedure successfully. This may be related to patient variability, or variation in the skill and knowledge of the practitioner. Technical errors are an important category of error in medical practice, because specialists are being called upon to do increasingly difficult and hazardous procedures on sicker and sicker patients. These errors may be an inherent risk of the procedure that requires disclosure.

Trial-and-error deliberation (i.e., thoughtful due diligence to the issues inherent to the treatment/procedure) is a slow, planned process of reasoning with constant feedback. This is a powerful, but slow, tool. There must be adequate time, and it is only reasonable if a trial-and-error approach can be tolerated. Because it is an error driven process, it follows that deliberative reasoning will be inevitably prone to errors, especially at an early stage of the iterative process. The implications of this for a medical emergency are obvious. The common allegation physicians face is an error in judgment, which falls into the category of an error in deliberation.

The element of choice in relation to an action, but not related to the outcome, defines an action, which, falling short of some identifiable standard, is a violation, rather than an error. A violation is a *deliberate*—but not necessarily culpable—deviation from those practices appreciated by the individual as being required by regulation, or necessary, or advisable to achieve an appropriate objective, while maintaining the safety of patients and the ongoing operation.

Violations are defined in relation to established rules. The existence of the rule makes the violation crystal clear. The rule need not be formalized in writing; it is enough to know some identifiable rule has been knowingly breached. This principle may involve foreseeability or variation from scientific fact. Take the case of the surgeon who goes from room to room without washing hands in between examining different patients.

The well-established rule being violated is that hand washing between examining patients reduces the risk of infection.

The fact that a course of action constitutes a violation does not necessarily mean that it amounts to recklessness. Recklessness carries a considerable amount of moral opprobrium. Recklessness implies knowing that an action or omission will involve an unacceptable level of risk to someone, and deciding nevertheless to take that risk. Violations involve a decision to do something with the knowledge that the given action or decision will place at risk some aspect of safety.

Writing in *The New Yorker*, Atul Gawande observed, "The real problem isn't how to stop bad doctors from harming, even killing their patients. It's how to prevent good doctors from doing so." In 1984, the Libby Zion case highlighted the role fatigue was playing in medical errors and violations. The natural inference is that a good physician who is fatigued will be prone to medical errors and violations.

The commission of a violation is a clear wrong in respect to the rights of those affected. We have distinguished errors that should be accepted as an inevitable consequence of complex human undertakings; the same does not necessarily apply to violations. It is complicated because certain necessary violations (e.g., meeting a workload that results in fatigue) may be imposed upon the practitioner by the system.

The gray area surrounding definitions of medical errors, violations, and reckless behavior must be appreciated to perceive the complexity of assigning blame when there is alleged negligence. The standard of care must reflect the threshold where medical errors and violations will invoke the charge of negligence.

FROM THEORY TO REAL-WORLD NEGLIGENCE

What is medical negligence? Medical negligence is an act, or omission, by a medical professional that deviates from the accepted medical standard of care. This begs the question: what is the standard of care? *Standard of care* refers to the degree of attentiveness, caution, and prudence that a reasonable physician in the existing circumstances would exercise. Failure to meet the standard is negligence, and the person who fails to meet the standard is liable for any damages caused by such negligence. The relation between the standard of care and negligence is similar to a lock and key "fit" that opens the door.

In medical negligence cases, the medical expert must explain to a trier of fact what a defendant physician should have done, or not done, in a specific set of circumstances, and whether the physician's conduct constitutes a breach of duty. The parameters of that duty are delineated by the standard of care. Many facets of the standard of care have been well explored in the literature, but gaps remain in establishing a wide-ranging understanding of this concept.

The standard of care changes through time. We examine those changes and adaptations in the understanding of the standard of care, including the locality rule and the now well-recognized national standard of care. The locality rule required a defendant physician to provide the same degree of skill and care that is required of a physician practicing in the same or similar community.

This rule remains alive in a few jurisdictions in the United States, but the locality rule has been largely abandoned in favor of a national standard of care. This has been justified by the fact that the impact of telecommunications allows physicians equal access to information. Lastly, we address the relationship between the standard of care and clinical practice guidelines.

The Locality Rule

As malpractice law evolved, courts began comparing a physician's practice with those of similarly situated physicians in their community. The applicable standard of care in medical malpractice lawsuits varies somewhat among jurisdictions in the United States. The locality rule requires defendant physicians to provide the same degree of skill and care that is required of other doctors practicing in the same or similar community. It places a geographical dimension on the professional standard of care in medical negligence litigation. The strictest form of the locality rule would require expert witnesses to practice in the same or a similar community of the case in which they are offering opinions.

Once widely adopted in the United States, the locality rule was originally designed to protect rural physicians from having to uphold the same standard of care as that provided in the academic health science centers and modern clinics of the city. It was believed that rural practitioners lacked equipment comparable to that of urban health centers and did not benefit from the latest advances in science and practice that emanated from medical research conducted at urban hospitals. The origin of the locality rule is often attributed to *Small v. Howard.*

The Supreme Judicial Court of Massachusetts offered the following, which is often credited as the origin of the *locality rule*:

> The defendant . . . being the practitioner in a small village . . . was bound to possess that skill only which physicians and surgeons of ordinary ability and skill, practicing in similar localities, with opportunities for no larger experience, ordinarily possess; and he was not bound to possess that high degree of art and skill possessed by eminent surgeons practicing in large cities, and making a specialty of the practice of surgery.

In *Brune v Belinkoff*, the Supreme Judicial Court of Massachusetts overturned their prior locality ruling in *Small v Howard.* The Supreme Judicial Court of Massachusetts offered:

> A general medical practitioner is to be held to the standard of care and skill of the average qualified practitioner, and a medical specialist is to be held to the standard of care and skill of the average practitioner of the specialty, taking into account with respect to either the general practitioner or the specialist the advances in the profession and the medical resources available to him.

Thus, *Brune* ruled a specialist should be held to the standard of care and skill of the average member of the profession practicing the specialty, taking into account the advances in the profession.

Emergence of a National Standard of Care

The locality rule was established before the standardization of medical training and certification, which, critics argue, eliminated the need for a locality rule. The Liaison Committee on Medical Education (LCME) grants the accreditation of allopathic medicals schools in the United States through compliance with *national*, not local, standards. The LCME is recognized by the U. S. Department of Education as the reliable authority for the accreditation of medical education programs leading to a Doctor of Medicine degree. The locality rule is now difficult to justify, because medical education has become more standardized, and modern technology provides rural physicians with the same access to information for patient care as is available to urban physicians.

The Accreditation Council for Graduate Medical Education (ACGME), founded in 1981, accredits all U. S. clinical residencies and fellowship programs. The ACGME accredits organizations that provide continuing medical education that has a national focus. Medical board certification examinations, administered by the member boards of the American Board of Medical Specialties since 1933, are national in scope. Although medical school training, medical licensing requirements, and board certification requirements are based on national standards, some states continue to rely on local practice standards to determine the applicable standard of care in medical malpractice lawsuits.

Brune overturned *Small* based on the reasoning that there is an established national basis to the training and certification of medical education. A national standard of care presupposes that rural physicians will have the same training, and exercise the same level of judgment and diligence, as urban practitioners. It does not require that rural physicians have the same available medical facilities.

For example, if the community does not have facilities for emergency surgery, physicians cannot be found negligent for failing to perform this surgery within the amount of time that might constitute the standard in a well-equipped urban hospital. Because there would still be differences in available resources, physicians practicing under a national standard would need to alert patients to the lack of necessary facilities or resources. Advances in modern medicine and the ease of access to those advances regardless of practice location give further support for the eradication of the last vestiges of the locality rule in United States.

THE FAILURE OF CLINICAL PRACTICE GUIDELINES TO SERVE AS A STANDARD OF CARE

In the 1970s and 1980s, the literature regarding healthcare costs, common practices, and outcomes exploded. Research demonstrated that medicine was practiced differently depending on location. For example, patients in Miami spent twice as much time in the hospital and intensive care units as similar patients in Minneapolis. In addition, costs for comparable populations differed markedly across the United States.

Gawande reported that, in 2006, the average Medicare enrollee in McAllen, Texas, received approximately $15,000 per year in medical services, twice as much as comparable patients in the nearby and socio-demographically similar El Paso. Such disparities represent, in part, local differences in medical culture, including the degree to which communities practice defensively, especially if the science is imprecise.

Because of these marked healthcare delivery inconsistencies, the United States Congress heeded the call for improvements in 1989 by creating the Agency for Healthcare Research and Quality (AHRQ). This organization was charged with creating specialty-specific clinical practice guidelines to align the fragmented practice of medicine in America. The AHRQ defined practice guidelines as "systematically developed statements [to] assist health care practitioners and patients to make decisions about appropriate health care for specific clinical circumstances."

Professional medical societies, state governments, liability insurers, and health insurance companies followed suit and created their own guidelines. The AHRQ hoped that practice guidelines would result in a more uniform practice of medicine. In addition, the guidelines would provide a host of other benefits, including effective dissemination of research findings into clinical practice, promotion of patient safety, and reduction in the rising cost of healthcare.

Regarding healthcare costs, the goal was to diminish the practice of both defensive and offensive medicine. The latter refers to reducing the frequency of unnecessary interventions performed by physicians purely for financial gain. In establishing these guidelines, the intent was not to establish the standard of care for medical practice. Nonetheless, many states hoped that, through the creation of these guidelines, adherent practitioners could be shielded from frivolous litigation, eventually reducing the practice of defensive medicine. According to the AHRQ, as of 2017, there were more than 8,000 individual guideline summaries for all medical specialties. It is easy to conclude that, at best, many provide redundant information and, at worst, they provide conflicting information, thus undermining their primary intent.

These guidelines have several pitfalls that limit their usefulness in unifying the practice of medicine and providing a concise summary of appropriate medical care for specific clinical circumstances.

First, many guidelines become outdated because of new research and practices. After approximately six years, only half of all practice guidelines on the AHRQ website were valid. The rapid expiration of guidelines requires large expenditures of time and money that can hamper effective dissemination of concise recommendations. Second, many of the guidelines conflict with each other, even when created contemporaneously. Third, many of the guidelines lacked the requisite scientific evidence to support their recommendations.

Furthermore, some guidelines note that relevant older literature was explicitly excluded from the guidelines for practical purposes, to streamline literature review. Finally, guidelines established by private health insurance companies, liability insurers, and the pharmaceutical industry, groups without fiduciary responsibilities to patients, often are biased.

Guidelines created by these entities should be viewed with some skepticism because of inherent financial conflicts. Nor are guidelines that are issued by professional medical societies immune from bias, because many authors have significant relationships with industry. Many physicians surveyed did not know that guidelines existed online. Even those aware of the guidelines objected to following them, for various reasons, including an aversion to practicing "cookbook" medicine, the wish to adhere to non–evidence-based recommendations, and the desire to maintain autonomy.

Even though the creation of practice guidelines was not intended to set the standard of care, artful attorneys have found that these widely published standards, despite their many pitfalls, could be persuasive to juries in malpractice litigation, especially those guidelines created by professional medical societies. The Federal Rules of Evidence and the landmark case of *Daubert v. Merrell Dow Pharmaceuticals, Inc.* paved the way for entering medical treatises as evidence. Plaintiff attorneys attempt to use clinical practice guidelines as a "sword," or as inculpatory evidence. Defense attorneys attempt to use clinical practice guidelines as a "shield," or as exculpatory evidence.

THE MEDICAL ORGANIZATION AND MEDICAL ERRORS/VIOLATIONS AND NEGLIGENCE

Most physicians practicing medicine today are employed by an organization. Inherent to that employment are relative value unit (RVU) quotas and other metrics that grade the physician's performance. These quotas and metrics mandate that physicians must see many patients and work long hours, often resulting in fatigue.

Emanating from this employment relationship is an increased risk for medical errors and violations. It seems logical, therefore, that organizations should shoulder some of this risk and develop systematic approaches to prevent medical errors (skill-based, rules-based, technical, and knowledge-based) and violations in an attempt to provide the highest quality and safest approach to patient care. It will take a focused, coordinated effort among physicians, administrators, and the available technology to reduce the likelihood of adverse events and outcomes.

DISCUSSION

This review of the standard of care and medical errors/violations and their relation to medical negligence law highlights the complexity of evaluating the standard of care physicians must meet in this fast-paced, exponential, corporate, and digital medical world. There does not appear to be a standard of disclosure to which physicians can adhere to avoid liability with any certitude.

The standard of care has been and remains obscure, dependent on the circumstances presented in each individual case. The key to improving clarity for physicians is to develop an understanding of the underpinnings of potential negligence (e.g., were the actions taken reasonable and foreseeable?). Additionally, there must be an understanding that the insights gleaned from hindsight and outcomes should not be construed to be necessary components of the physician's deliberation prior to medical and surgical decisions.

Hindsight is always 20/20. These concepts are central to how the courts determine whether blame is to be attributed to a physician's actions. Physicians also must be aware that they live in a world generally governed by a national standard that may impose national guidelines and expert opinion to judge their actions.

Organizations must understand the importance of human factors in medical errors and violation and respond with system approaches that take into account the fact that to be human is to err. There must be systematic approaches that reduce the potential for skill-based, rule-based, knowledge-based, and technical errors, as well as rule violations. If the system has not acted to counteract these well-known precipitants of medical errors, it should shoulder a significant degree of the burden for alleged negligence.

Finally, experts who are retained in medical malpractice cases must remember that the standard of care may vary among jurisdictions in the United States. Practice guidelines, although intended to unify and improve the practice of medicine, often fail to provide sufficient clarity because of age, conflicting recommendations, various levels of evidential support, and underutilization by practitioners. In many cases, the standard of care is determined de novo and is a moving target. This is one reason why static documents, guidelines, and algorithms are not quite coextensive with the requirements of the legal system. Furthermore, learned medical treatises do not constitute evidence per se. Rather, they are elements of the experts' opinions that may be introduced into evidence at trial.

CHAPTER 25

Medical Informed Choice: Understanding the Element of Time to Meet the Standard of Care for Valid Informed Consent

Medical informed choice is essential for physicians meeting their fiduciary duty when proposing medical and surgical actions, and necessary for a patient to consent or cull the outlined therapeutic approaches. Informed choice, as part of a shared decision-making model, allows a wide-ranging give-and-take of ideas between the patient and physician.

This sharing of ideas produces a partnership for decision-making and a shared responsibility for medical and surgical outcomes. Informed choice is indispensable to the patient education process that meets the desired outcome of any covenant—an offer of and acceptance of the proposed treatment. The covenant anchors a true patient–physician partnership with parity and equality in decision-making and medical/surgical outcomes.

Medical informed choice flows from ethical and legal principles necessary to meet the acknowledged standard of care. This is codified by statute and fortified in general common law. This espouses a fiduciary relationship where the patient and physician understand and accede to the degree of autonomy the patient requests.

In today's medical marketplace, physicians are working at a feverish pace to meet the demands of the business model decreed by their employer.

That business model has physicians seeing more patients in less time. The operative word is "time," because quality work requires time and meeting the medical professional standard of care also requires time.

The medical standard of care is the ethical and legal duty of a professional to exercise the level of care, diligence, and skill prescribed in the "code of practice" of his or her profession, or as other professionals in the same discipline would in the same or similar circumstances. This is the standard physicians face as they practice in a fast-paced medical marketplace where reimbursements are shrinking and increased patient volume is the prevailing mechanism to increase revenues.

That creates a dilemma for physicians, because that faster pace means less time per patient, and less time means less deliberation and diligence in taking a medical history, performing a physical examination, developing a differential diagnosis, and educating patients about the elements of medical choice so they can then make an informed, knowledgeable, and voluntary decision about the healthcare they want or don't want. That shared, informed decision-making process is time dependent.

Time is the dependent variable in the informed choice function of meeting the standard of care. The new healthcare business equations are creating a shrinking time variable. This disconnect between patient care and business models of medicine puts physicians at risk for failing to meet the threshold for the informed consent standard of care. This failure may place physicians at risk for allegations of negligence. The disconnect weighs heavily on physicians' minds, because they constantly face the potential of alleged liability. Shrinking time with patients can never lead to increased quality or a trusting physician–patient relationship.

Physicians have a moral, legal, and ethical responsibility to understand medical informed choice. This responsibility emanates from the fiduciary duty physicians owe patients. Furthermore, true informed choice results in a meeting of the elements of the standard of care and limits any potential for alleged negligence.

This chapter addresses the patient and physician criteria for medical choice to be valid, the exceptions to obtaining medical informed choice, the ethical and legal foundations to medical informed choice, the different standards that are adequate to meet the standard of care, and the fact that no single paradigm fits all patient situations.

MEDICAL INFORMED CHOICE: PATIENT CRITERIA FOR VALID INFORMED CHOICE

What considerations define whether patients are capable of participating in the informed choice/shared decision-making process? That determination is based on deciding whether the patient is mentally capable and has decision-making capability. *Capacity* is a person's ability to make an informed decision. Succinctly stated, the patient must be able to comprehend the information presented and the associated potential benefits, risks, and alternative choices in their medical care.

Every part of a patient's decision must be intentional. Family members, other interested parties, or healthcare professionals should not affect the patient's decisions. It is imperative that medications or life stressors not compromise patients involved in informed choice/shared decision-making. A patient with intact cognitive capacity and intact decision-making capacity may reverse a medical/surgical decision at any time. The competent patient may reject any proposed treatment, despite the consequences of that decision.

PHYSICIAN CRITERIA FOR INFORMED CHOICE TO BE VALID

What subjects must a physician share with a patient to meet the threshold for valid informed choice/shared decision-making? Physicians must divulge to patients the diagnosis; the nature and purpose of the proposed treatment or procedure; reasonable available alternative approaches; relevant risks, benefits, and uncertainties of each alternative; and the risks and benefits of choosing not to have a treatment or procedure. Additionally, physicians should take the time to ensure that the patient understands the diagnosis, treatment choices, and the risks and benefits of treatment versus no treatment.

THE EXCEPTIONS TO OBTAINING INFORMED CHOICE

Exceptions to medical informed choice occur when physicians are confronted with medical emergencies that would result in permanent injury or death without immediate intervention. In these unique circumstances, even though the patient's preferences and desires are unknown, informed consent is presumed.

Additional exceptions to informed choice include a patient foregoing a right of informed choice and therapeutic privilege. By signing a waiver, a patient freely and willfully relinquishes a legal right. Patients may elect to sign a medical waiver when considering medical informed choice/shared decision-making. The patient may choose a surrogate decision maker or adopt the physician as the decision maker. Caution should be abundant when using a waiver for informed choice. Legally, waivers can be a slippery slope, and it is in the best interest of physicians to involve the risk management or legal team to develop an exhaustive legal covenant in such a situation.

The *therapeutic privilege* is a doctrine that allows the physician to withhold information if disclosure of the knowledge would actually harm the patient. The therapeutic privilege should be used on rare occasion, because it is dicey, both ethically and legally. State precedent governs the interpretation of the therapeutic privilege, and the court's analysis is variable from state to state. In these circumstances, it is imperative for the physician to document in detail the rationale for invoking the therapeutic privilege, and the ethics and risk management teams should be involved.

ETHICS AND INFORMED CHOICE: BENEFICENCE AND NON-MALEFICENCE

Beneficence (doing good) and non-maleficence (do not harm) underlie the physician's moral imperative. This moral imperative infers there are times or circumstances when partial disclosure or no disclosures are concordant with meeting the standard of care and fiduciary duties.

This flows from the fact that some patients are emotionally incapable of handling discussions that entail life-and-death issues or consequences when they are in a regressed state of mind. It permits physicians the opportunity to modify the medical information they deliver to patients in an empathic manner that meets the moral imperative of beneficence and non-maleficence.

The ultimate goal of informed choice should be respect for a patient's autonomy combined with tactful application of beneficence and non-maleficence. This requires ongoing conversations over time and a trusting partnership.

THE LEGAL FOUNDATION FOR INFORMED CHOICE

The legal basis for mandating informed choice dates back to the 1700s. In *Slater v Baker and Stapleton* in 1767, the court established that physicians should obtain consent from patients before surgery and could be held legally liable if they proceeded without informed consent.

In *Schloendorff v Society of New York Hospital* in 1914, a physician removed a tumor from a patient who had consented only to an examination and had refused an operation. Justice Cardozo wrote: "Every human being of adult years and sound mind has a right to determine what shall be done with his own body; and a surgeon who performs an operation without his patient's consent commits an assault, for which he is liable in damages."

Schloendorff established the necessity of voluntary agreement for each specific proposed procedure (*Schloendorff v. Society of N.Y. Hosp.*, 211 N.Y. 125, 129-30).

The phrase "informed consent" was born in the California Court of Appeals case *Salgo v Leland Stanford Jr. University Board of Trustees.* The court held that a physician could be held liable for failing to provide facts about a proposed treatment that are necessary for a patient to make an informed decision.

Additionally, the decision stated that physicians must exercise discretion when deciding what risks to disclose in order to protect a patient's well-being *(Salgo v Leland Stanford Jr. University Board of Trustees.* Pacific Reporter, 2d Series 1957; 317: 170-182). This decision failed to delineate any clear limits on what must be disclosed. The California Supreme Court articulated this uncertainty: "One cannot know with certainty which medical consent is valid until a lawsuit is filed and resolved" (*Moore v Regents of the University of California*, 51 Cal 3d D20 165 793. P 2d 479 291 Cal Rptr. note 41(1990)).

There does not appear to be a standard of disclosure to which physicians can adhere to avoid liability with certainty.

WHAT DOES THE COURT REVIEW WHEN PRESENTED WITH AN INFORMED CONSENT CASE?

When a case advances to court, appropriate documentation of the informed choice process can be used as a defense that the physician properly informed a patient about a treatment or procedure. That documentation should be stored in the medical record. Physicians should document the details of the discussion and the time devoted to educating the patient and answering the patient's questions.

Informed consent forms may be helpful to satisfy legal requirements and make documentation more efficient, but they are not an acceptable replacement for time spent with the patient. Consent forms used to replace physician time negatively impact the physician–patient relationship.

The use of informed consent forms has evolved into a legalistic process attempting to limit liability rather than facilitating comprehension and understanding of the treatment or proposed procedure. There is a feeling that the focus of physicians is on risk communication and not on informed medical decision-making.

Sensibly, if more time were spent educating and building a trusting partnership with the patient, there would be less need to have consent forms and a lower likelihood of ending up in court facing an allegation of negligent informed consent. Ultimately, upon review of the medical record the court evaluates the time dedicated to information sharing and shared decision-making between the physician and the patient to determine whether a physician met the standard of care for informed consent.

DEFINING THE STANDARDS OF DISCLOSURE

Two dominant approaches, the "professional" standard and the "materiality" standard, define the standard of disclosure of information by which a physician's duty to the patient is measured (*Madare v Oschner Foundation Hospital*, 505 So 2d 146 (La Ct App 1987)).

The professional standard requires the physician to disclose information that other physicians possessing the same skills and practicing in the same or a similar community disclose in a similar situation (Canterbury v Spence, 446 F2d 772 (CADC 1972)).

The materiality, or "prudent patient," approach allows the jury to decide whether other information would have been considered important by a reasonable patient in making a decision and therefore requiring disclosure (*Cowman v Hornaday*, 329, NW 2d 422 (Iowa 1983)).

The courts recognize situations when a physician's nondisclosure will be excused, including cases of the patient's mental incompetence, medical emergencies, and the therapeutic privilege exception. If a patient is incompetent to make a reasoned decision, then disclosure to the patient might not be required (*Banks v Wittenberg*, 266 NW 2d 788 82 Mich App 274 (Mich. App 1978)).

The physician also can withhold information under the therapeutic privilege if disclosure would interfere with treatment or would adversely affect the condition or recovery of the patient. The emergency exception to disclosure applies in situations where attempting to secure consent would delay necessary and proper treatment *(Shafford v Louisiana State University*, 448 So 2d 852 (La Ct App 1984)).

Last, physicians need not disclose risks of which the patient is already aware, or risks that are commonly known *(Kissinger v Lofgren*, 836 F 2d 678 (CA 1 [Mass] 1987)). Individual state law and court decisions determine which approaches and exceptions apply in an individual physician's practice.

In order to facilitate true informed consent, some states have initiated shared decision-making legislation. Shared decision-making requires intense education of the patient. Pamphlets, videos, and a vast array of telecommunication infomercials often are provided to patients, allowing them to more fully understand the proposed treatment or procedure and then incorporate their own values and preferences into the decision-making process. Providing additional written material; audiovisual, multimedia and test and feedback techniques; in addition to adequate time for education and shared decision-making all improve patient comprehension, especially regarding risks and general knowledge about the procedure.

CONCLUSION

There is no single prototype that meets the elements of the standard of care for informed consent and applies to all patients. Medical informed consent is essential to a true patient–physician relationship. Patients need to participate in the informed consent process to understand the risk–benefit relationship for the proposed treatment strategy. This understanding is essential because patients often are psychologically regressed secondary to the realization that they are confronting a life-preserving procedure that carries significant risk.

Physicians need to participate in the informed consent process to provide patients with the best treatment available by sharing decision-making and limiting any potential for liability. Medical ethics, common law, and, in many states, codified statutory law mandate the informed consent process. Physicians would be prudent to be knowledgeable in these areas of medical ethics, common law, and statutory law.

Physicians would be judicious also to understand that the consent process is vital to the physician–patient relationship and that no single archetype can define the ethical, medical, and legal approach a physician should undertake to achieve informed consent. The process should be individualized within the boundaries of the patient's desires for self-determination, thus reflecting true patient autonomy.

The overarching principle is meeting the elements of true informed choice/consent, and informed consent requires time. Despite the evolving business model of medicine, physicians must demand abundant time to educate, counsel, and share decisions with patients. The constellation of abundant time, true partnership, and sharing in decisions is the panacea to preventing allegations of negligence.

Time cannot and must not be shorted. Adjuncts such as pamphlets and videos are helpful, but cannot replace a physician taking time with a patient. All true relationships are time dependent. Meaningful shared decisions require time, and taking that time will result in better clinical decisions and outcomes and less potential for liability.

Informed consent ideally results in patient autonomy and rational healthcare decisions. Frequently, patients face complex medical decisions that require a delicate balancing of anticipated benefits and potential risks, which is the concept of informed consent. This balancing process requires an understanding of available medical evidence and alternative medical options, and input from experienced physicians.

SECTION 5

The Electronic Medical Record and Physician Liability

CHAPTER 26

Medical Liability in the Electronic Medical Records Era

Physicians may encounter new medical liability risks in a medical milieu dominated by electronic health information exchange. The budding electronic medical record systems have revolutionized how healthcare is dispensed. The electronic medical record alters the doctor–patient relationship in many uncertain and evolving ways. The shifting landscape of electronic information and potential medical liability risk is important for every practicing physician to understand.

The historical changes of the electronic medical record and the emerging changes of the maturing electronic medical record are reviewed, as well as the potential medical liability risk for physicians using the emerging electronic medical record systems. Since the electronic medical record appears to be here to stay, it is imperative physicians adapt to efficient and effective use of electronic information highway ushered in by the federal government.

Physicians, patients, policy gurus, and financiers have watched a healthcare system evolve into an information technology highway denied a speed limit. The HITECH ACT of 2009 endorsed grants and incentives totaling billions of dollars to stimulate "meaningful use" of electronic medical records (EMRs) by healthcare professionals. The stimulus for meaningful use highlighted the benefits but gave the potential associated risks minimal verbal or penned space. The potential risks associated with the information technology highway include the risk of medical malpractice liability.

Additionally, the legal repercussions of EMRs extend beyond malpractice liability and include liability linked to privacy and confidentiality laws, debates over ownership of healthcare data, and susceptibility to

Medicare and Medicaid fraud claims resulting from improved information between services rendered and services billed.

These are broad and complex topics beyond the discussion of this chapter, whose range of analysis will include only potential malpractice issues associated with this new and evolving health information highway. This chapter is limited in scope to the implications for potential malpractice liability of the core features of today's EMR systems. Attention will focus on features pertinent to healthcare teams on a daily basis, including the documentation of clinical findings, recording of testing and imaging results, computerized health professional order and data entry, and clinical-decision support.

BRIEF HISTORICAL PERSPECTIVE

A rearview mirror analysis allows one to see how we survived the initial implementation of the EMR and the potential medical-liability risks of electronic technologies.

The adversities encountered have included the transition from paper to electronic records, which created documentation breaches; the failure to implement policies and procedures a reasonable and prudent healthcare professional would implement during the transition to electronic records; the failure to provide ample and sufficient training on the EMR; and a lack of surveillance of errors by new electronic system users that inserted incorrect or missing data entries.

PRESENT DAY PERSPECTIVE

In today's healthcare world, the electronic technologies have become robust and widespread. The EMRs have matured and almost all healthcare entities have implemented electronic technologies across all spectrums of their clinical practices to enhance health information exchange. This maturation and robust use of the electronic technologies may create an army of new liability risks. The new potential risks include, but are not limited to:

- Clinical decisions are extensively documented, potentially creating more discoverable evidence, including metadata.

- The temptation exists to copy and paste patient information and data instead of taking a new history and physical examination. This risks missing new or changing information and allows the perpetuation of prior inaccuracies.
- E-mail advice is expanding with meaningful use requiring use of patient portals, where patients and physicians exchange e-mail correspondence, this mandate multiplies the number of patient encounters many fold, and that may give rise to patient accusations of negligence.
- The increasing telecommunication encounters heighten the risk if medical advice is offered without comprehensive investigation of the patient complaints and the absence of a recorded physical examination.
- Failure to respond to e-mail in a timely fashion could constitute negligence, even when there are physician disclaimers.
- Information overload may lead to physicians missing important clinical information among "the noise and chaos" of an information-overloaded medical world.
- Physicians departing from clinical-decision support guidelines may represent a risk for potential malpractice liability. The widespread use of clinical-decision support may alter the standard of care.
- Better access to clinical information through EMRs may create legal duties to act on the information.
- The widespread use of health information exchange may increase physician duty to search the extensive data generated by healthcare providers.
- The failure to adopt and use electronic technologies may establish a deviation from the standard of care.

PERCEIVED POTENTIAL BENEFITS AS HEALTH INFORMATION SYSTEMS MATURE

EMRs are believed to have the potential to reduce gaps and errors in medical care. This benefit is expected to reduce adverse events and therefore allegations of negligence. The presumed better documentation of clinical decisions through both clinician-entered data and metadata may improve the ability of a physician to defend against malpractice claims when medical/surgical care was within the standard of care.

EMRs that include integrated clinical-decision support systems may improve clinical decisions, thus, reducing medical adverse events and potential for malpractice claims. Compliance with clinical-decision support care guidelines may provide evidence that the standard of care was met. This will be determined when the courts confront these medical–legal issues.

The secure messaging systems built into EMRs may improve communication with patients, allowing for better understanding of clinically significant information. This will result in patient satisfaction, a higher likelihood of compliance with medical recommendations, and a lower likelihood of allegations of negligence. Advocates for EMRs believe an increase in health information exchange will lead to better care and better outcomes. EMRs hold promise for preventing harmful medical errors and attendant medical malpractice claims. They promote comprehensive documentation and timely access to patient data facilitating precise and accurate medical decision-making. The use of electronic technology may decrease transcription errors, improve the speed and accuracy of communication between healthcare professionals, and reduce the duplication of testing.

The goal of clinical-decision support systems is to offer a safety net by reminding busy physicians of clinical guidelines so they identify errors before they cause harm. Evidence suggests far-reaching EMR systems may improve compliance to clinical guidelines and reduce rates of medication errors.

POTENTIAL HAZARDS AS HEALTH INFORMATION SYSTEMS MATURE

Despite this optimism surrounding the electronic records, there is no current evidence that the use of EMRs reduces diagnostic errors. Computerized provider-entry systems can increase some kinds of medication-ordering errors. Gaps between information systems may cause life-sustaining prescribed medications to be automatically canceled. Information technology systems that default to a hazardous drug dose due to failure to input changes in hepatic or renal function may lead to patient harm if physicians fail to recalculate doses based upon

EMR Functionality and Potential Liability Risk

EMR function	Potential liability risk
Document clinical findings	Copy and paste function may prevent addition of new and evolving historical and physical examination changes.
Record testing and imaging	Electronic transfer of lab and imaging data may allow for the wrong information to be charted in a patient's chart and acted upon.
Data entry	Over-dependence of copy-and-paste functions may document and disseminate earlier inaccuracies. Insert incorrect data and ignore missing data.
Order entry	Gaps between information systems may allow life sustain medications to be automatically canceled.
Clinical decision-support	Information systems that automatically default to a hazardous drug dose because of failure to entry changes in hepatic or renal function. Eliminate drug that is beneficial in clinical practice but falls outside the algorithm of the support system.
Messaging systems	HIPPA violation or treatment for the wrong patient because of transport of data to the wrong recipient.
Electronic communication	Providing medical advice over the patient portal without a comprehensive history and physical examination may lead to allegations of negligence.

new clinical information. Over-dependence on the copying-and-pasting function of many documentation systems appears to disseminate earlier inaccuracies and oversights.

Secure messaging systems and electronic communications may have liability risks. Proposing medical advice without a comprehensive history and physical examination escalates the risk of an inaccurate diagnosis and erroneous treatment decisions.

Courts have held that telephone communications between a physician and a patient can be sufficient to establish the doctor–patient relationship necessary for malpractice liability. The corollary to the court-held telephone communication decision is a slippery slope to applying electronic communications as establishing a sufficient doctor–patient relationship to impose potential liability. The inference is that once a doctor–patient relationship is established, a failure to respond to e-mail in a timely manner may constitute a violation of the standard of care. The physician e-mail disclaimers have not been tested in a court of law to date.

The secure messaging systems shape patient perception of physicians and their staffs. The American Medical Association (AMA) has promulgated ethics policies and guidelines on the use of electronic communications in clinical practice, stating that physicians should not establish doctor–patient relationships through electronic communications, but rather use secure messaging as a supplement to prior personal encounters.

Physicians are encouraged to develop guidelines for appropriate use and turnaround time for electronic communications. This should be discussed with patients and a contract established that outlines expectations of both parties. Furthermore, physicians should establish a procedure for terminating e-mail relationships with patients who repeatedly violate the rules of appropriate electronic communication. Physicians would be prudent to establish guidelines for e-mail communications and obtain informed consent for the use of secure messaging. Physicians should notify in writing the termination of e-mail privileges.

EMRS AND THE LAW

EMRs may affect the progression of malpractice litigation by increasing the availability of documentation with which to defend or prove a malpractice claim. The documentation can be a shield or a sword. The use of the EMR increases the entry of more extensive notes and includes physician notes, nursing notes, and e-mail communications.

EMRs record all electronic transactions, from the input of orders to the time stamps of clinical activity. These metadata provide a permanent electronic footprint that can be used to track physician activity. Under federal law, metadata are discoverable in civil trials, which means a defendant physician must surrender metadata to the plaintiff's lawyer.

State law, which administers most malpractice litigation, varies as to the discoverability and permissibility of metadata. Metadata can be used to validate that the EMR was modified when the treatment was administered, bolstering the defendant's ability to rely on the EMR when defending against a malpractice allegation. Alternatively, if the record was revised at an incongruous time to the treatment, metadata can raise a suspicion of falsification of the medical record, even in the absence of actual wrongdoing. Whereas in the pre-electronic era such a practice posed no risk of liability, the availability of metadata is a game changer.

THE STANDARD OF CARE IN AN ELECTRONIC ERA

Proving medical negligence, a plaintiff must establish the applicable standard of care and prove that the defendant caused injury by failing to meet the established standard. The maturation of the EMR may reshape medical liability by amending the way in which courts determine the standard of care and by shifting the standard of care that is accepted by the medical community.

Clinical-decision support systems have the potential to initiate the transformation of present-day standards of care. In malpractice proceedings each party presents expert testimony to delineate the applicable standard of care. Experts vary in their approach to defining the standard of care. They may rely on their clinical experience and judgment or they may summon clinical practice guidelines.

Courts have allowed the use of medical practice guidelines in malpractice proceedings. This raises the potential for a court to admit clinical-decision support protocols as evidence of the standard of care if an expert testifies that the clinical-decision support reflects reasonable and customary care. The logical inference being that departure from clinical-decision support may be evidence of negligence.

Clinical-decision support protocols could affect the standard of care; however, these protocols may not anticipate the myriad clinical scenarios physicians encounter in clinical practice. Superseding a system default that may represent a potential standard of care creates an electronic medical record that a physician may need to defend in a court of law.

A case in point would be when a physician-override of a clinical-decision support system is necessary for risk of excessive bleeding safety protocols when aspirin and Plavix are used in conjunction after myocardial infarction, where generally the combination of drugs is considered indicated. Juries' and courts' reliance on clinical-decision support systems may result in increased and potentially incorrect liability when physicians depart from clinical-decision support protocols.

The exponential development of health information exchange with access to voluminous outside medical records may also impact the standard of care for practicing physicians. Courts previously have not held physicians to a legal duty to obtain and review all outside medical records. The easy access through electronic technology makes it more likely a court may impose liability for not reviewing pertinent EMR records that would have potentially aborted an adverse outcome.

The important question that surfaces for physicians is whether the medical practice environment will evolve in concert with the information highway, allowing physicians to make use of the voluminous health information available in the electronic medical era. The present-day demanding physician schedule, often allowing only 15–20 minutes to take a history, examine a patient, and review the EMR and health exchange information, makes the review of volumes of data unreasonable. The legal standard of care in litigation is meant to reflect reasonable and customary medical care, but the reasonableness of care may differ when viewed from the eyes of the defendant or plaintiff.

MEDICAL MALPRACTICE LAWSUITS FOR EMR ERRORS

Until recently, lawsuits involving patient safety and EMRs have been conducted as malpractice cases, where it can be difficult to determine the nature of the alleged EMR errors or who exactly who has been named in the suit. These cases settle out of court and include nondisclosure clauses.

But the number of such malpractice suits will likely continue to rise. Medical malpractice insurer the Doctors Company closed 28 claims in 2013 involving EMRs, and nearly that many during the first two quarters of 2014. In all, the Doctors Company closed 97 claims involving EHRs from January 2007 to June 2014.

EMR-related issues contributed to less than 1% of all claims closed by the malpractice insurer during that time. In that limited sample, 64%,involved user errors and 42% involved issues with the EHR system itself; some of those claims involved more than one contributing factor. Of those overall EMR claims, 10% involved a failure of system design and 9% involved an electronic systems or technology failure.

The rate of paid malpractice claims has been declining and is temporally related to the implementation of EMRs — the caveat being that it takes time for medical-legal cases to go through the judicial system. We will not know the impact of the EMR on potential medical legal issues for years.

Physicians can expect a changing landscape of medical liability risks as the adoption of medical electronic systems continues. This mandates that physicians require electronic information systems that are so seamless and efficient that they swing the pendulum back to patient care with an eye on the patient and a compassionate listening ear.

When confronting EMRs, physicians must understand:

- Electronic documentation may bolster the ability of courts to determine liability in malpractice claims.
- EMRs may lead courts to alter the standard of care.
- Physicians must review the medical record carefully to prevent data entry errors and medication errors.
- Physicians must carefully document the rationale for overriding any clinical-decision support protocols.
- Although it is uncertain how the liability associated with EMRs will be allocated between physicians, EMR developers, and organizations that select and implement EMR systems, physicians should assume responsibility for their medical record.
- EMRs are here to stay so it is imperative to use them efficiently and effectively within the scope of your medical practice.
- The medical record is a professional responsibility that requires physician's utmost respect as it will either support or condemn their defense when negligence allegations occur.

Reprinted with permission, Paterick ZR, Patel NJ, Ngo E, Chandrasekaran K, Jamil Tajik A, Paterick TE. Medical Liability in the Electronic Medical Records Era. *Proc (Bayl Univ Med Cent)*. 2018;31(4):558–561. Published 2018 Sep 11. doi:10.1080/08998280.2018.1471899

CHAPTER 27

The Unintended Consequences of the Electronic Medical Record on Physicians in Training and Their Mentors

For physicians in training and their mentors, the process of learning and teaching clinical medicine has become challenging in the electronic medical record (EMR) era. Trainees and their mentors exist in a milieu of incessant box checking and laborious documentation that has no clinical educational value, limits the time for teaching, and curtails clinical cognitive skill development.

These unintended consequences of the EMR are juxtaposed against the EMR's intended benefits of improved patient care and safety with reduced medical errors, improved clinical support systems, reduced potential for negligence with clinical data and metadata data supporting compliance with the standard of care.

Although the mindset was that technology would be the solution to many healthcare issues, there was not an appreciation of the cumulative impact of the non-educational workload on physician time and education. The EMR was intended to improve the efficiency of medical care and time management. It appears that the unintended consequences of the EMR with numerous checkboxes, automatic filling of computer screens, pre-worded templates, and automatic history and physical examination functions with detailed administrative oversight and compliance monitoring were not appreciated, and many believe that burden has overwhelmed the intended benefits of the EMR.

This juxtaposition of the intended and unintended consequences of the EMR has left trainees and mentors struggling to optimize medical education and development of clinical skills while providing high-quality patient medical care. Physician educators must identify how to use the benefits of the EMR and overcome the unintended consequences.

A major unintended consequence of the EMR is time dedicated to automate functions that detract from the time spent with mentors and patients. This time loss has the potential to restrict the physician from meeting the essential canons of medical informed consent and interfere with a physician meeting her fiduciary duties to the patient. To raise awareness and stimulate a search for solutions that benefit medical education and patient care, we will explore the intended and unintended consequences of the EMR and potential solutions using the intelligent systems of the EMR.

Physicians in the United States encounter a daily workload that is challenging from a time perspective. The additional time constraints introduced by the EMR reduce the time for mentors to teach young physicians. This has the potential to diminish the learning curve of physician trainees.

Every new policy regarding the introduction of technology in the healthcare systems should be evaluated to determine the impact on the education of young physicians, the ability of mentors to educate, and the effects on patient care. Ensuring manageable opportunities for optimal education and patient care is a shared responsibility among all healthcare organizations.

THE EVOLUTION OF OUR PRESENT HEALTHCARE SYSTEM

Physicians have observed a healthcare system evolve into an information technology highway that defies the speed limit of most physicians' learning curves. The HITECH ACT of 2009 endorsed grants and incentives totaling billions of dollars to stimulate "meaningful use" of electronic medical records (EMRs) by healthcare professionals.

The intended benefits of the EMR created euphoria in the healthcare world. Health policy gurus promised the EMR would improve many aspects of healthcare including:

- Improved data analysis and management.
- Improved documentation.
- Improved clinical decisions with integrated clinical decision support systems.
- Clinical data and metadata establishing evidence of compliance with the standard of care.
- Meeting the standard of care would reduce allegations of negligence.
- Ultimately, improved patient care and safety.

These intended consequences have merit and have improved many aspects of clinical care.

THE UNINTENDED CONSEQUENCES OF THE EMR

Apparently the unintended consequences of the EMR were not appreciated before its introduction. Time has taught us that there were costs to trainees, mentors, and patients that were inherent to the "efficiencies" of the EMR. The EMR included panoply of "time saving" check boxes, automated history and physical examination functions, pre-worded templates, embedded problem lists, as well as EMR-sanctioned copy-and-paste functions.

The efficiency measures are appealing for technologically shrewd trainees to save time, as well as for staff physicians trying to meet the high RVU production quotas demanded by employers. The unintended cost of this technological efficiency is that training physicians may not learn how to appropriately perform a detailed history and physical examination, interact with the patient and family, and take the time to construct a broad differential thought process.

The time used by trainees and mentors to meet the demands of the automated functions of the EMR limits the time the mentors have to educate and mentor trainees. The time deficit interferes with the fiduciary duties of the mentor to the trainee. Time is necessary to educate trainees and what we have learned is there are no short cuts.

These concerns arise because, since the introduction of the EMR, many physicians in training often document their initial patient encounter by clicking required boxes and then "copy and paste" information that others had completed during prior encounters. The cost of this expediency in patient evaluations must be reevaluated comparing the elicitation of new health information against the technological efficiency.

This is a real concern because recent data suggests a high rate of copying and pasting of many elements of medical documentation. Recent surveys identify that 25% of notes contain copy and pasted physical examination. This defies the concept that young physicians should consider the medical note as a thoughtful description of the patient encounter where there is an integration of a comprehensive history, physical examination, and critical analysis of the differential diagnosis. In today's fast paced medical world clinicians are constantly facing time constraints, EMR unintended functions have the potential to impede the medical education of trainees and the medical care of patients.

THE UNINTENDED CONSEQUENCES OF COMPLIANCE/ UTILIZATION REVIEW/MAXIMAL BILLING

The EMR was envisioned with many potential advantages as discussed, but few disadvantages were penned or discussed. The HITECH ACT, which was ushered in by the federal government, envisioned a methodology of tracking every aspect of medical care from patient encounters to billing. The EMR is often believed to achieve optimal compliance with utilization reviews' recommendations for optimum billing practices. It is less optimal in promoting optimal discussion of patient care.

The EMR allows and facilitates tech savvy users to save time on notes by copying and pasting information from one day's note (or month's or year's) to the next, or by using templates that insert medication lists, labs, and vital signs without protections that actually ensure the material has been carefully read and critiqued. There is no check and balance system to guarantee the note accurately reflects the patient's condition and course of treatment.

It is common knowledge that in clinical practice imprecise, erroneous information has been copied and forwarded, or that incorrectly entered metrics infiltrates the medical record. These unintended consequences greatly impact trainee learning and patient care.

THE MEANING OF INFORMED CONSENT IN THE EMR ERA—COMPETENCIES IN PATIENT CARE AND PROFESSIONALISM

Medical informed consent is essential to the physician's ability to diagnose and treat patients, and to the patient's right to accept or reject clinical evaluation, treatment, or both. Medical informed consent should be an exchange of ideas that buttresses the patient-physician relationship.

The consent process should be the foundation of the fiduciary relationship between a patient and a physician. Physicians must recognize that informed medical choice is an educational process and has the potential to affect the patient-physician alliance to their mutual benefit. Physicians must give patients equality in the covenant by educating them to make informed choices. When physicians and patients take medical informed consent seriously, the patient-physician relationship becomes a true partnership with shared decision-making authority and responsibility for outcomes.

Physicians need to understand informed medical consent from an ethical foundation, as codified by statutory law in many states, and from a generalized common-law perspective requiring medical practice consistent with the standard of care. It is fundamental to the patient-physician relationship that each partner understands and accepts the degree of autonomy the patient desires in the decision-making process.

Informed consent as a component of the fiduciary responsibility can only be realized through a caring and trusting doctor-patient relationship dependent upon time spent engaging and connecting with the patient. The EMR may impact the time spent with patients.

A 2013 study suggested interns spend 40% of their time with the computer and approximately 10%-12% in direct patient engagement. This allotment of time does not foster the crucial goals of empathic communication and the development of strong clinical judgment based upon seeing and touching the patient. This appears to have the potential for downstream degradation of competencies in patient care and professionalism.

The minimal time allotted to direct patient engagement is concerning. Time is essential to clear, concise communication, informed shared decision-making, and meeting the duties of a fiduciary. The inevitable time constraints introduced by the EMR must not constrain the fiduciary relationship between mentor and trainee and between physician and patient.

Fortunately the EMR contains the seeds to the solutions for overcoming the unintended consequences of the EMR. The EMR is an intelligent system that has the potential through automated functions to prevent trainees from using copy/paste function, prevent automatic filling of computer screen fields, and monitor the time spent developing a thoughtful and deliberative integration and synthesis of patient information. Ultimately the mentor must address the trainee's assessment and understanding of the patient clinical conditions.

THE PHYSICIAN EDUCATOR

Mentoring physicians must consider the methods that can be employed when using the EMR to optimize the clinical experience for the patient and the training physician. Perhaps physicians in training should be required to update mandatory fields, create original physical examination notes after each encounter, and incorporate labs and imaging studies in a manner that ensures thought and consideration. There should be a prerequisite to produce a newly prioritized differential thought process, assessment, and strategy for each encounter. The question we must ponder is do the EMR's promised benefits come at the expense of the training physician's ability to identify nuanced details of the patient interaction, or a missed diagnosis because of the copy and pasted physical examination?

THE FUTURE OF MEDICAL TRAINING

There are many pressures confronting medical education and medical care in general. The existing healthcare cost conundrum is the nidus of many of the issues we encounter in medicine. Despite this reality, we as educators must accept the responsibility to eliminate poor practice patterns, develop alternative approaches and standards to optimize patient care, and create expectations that promote optimal patient care and physician training. The paradigm we develop must foster accountability and professionalism. The integration of EMRs into our daily medical practice cannot come at a loss of the fundamentals necessary to having a shared patient-physician partnership.

The goal of all physicians must be to take advantage of all benefits of the EMR and overcome the unintended consequences of our evolving technologies so we can maximize medical education and patient care. The first step is recognition of the unintended consequences we seek to surmount and the second step the development of practical solutions to the unintended consequences. We must utilize the smart systems embedded in the EMR to optimize trainee education and patient medical care.

The efficient use of the computer is important and should facilitate all the intended consequences of the EMR but not at the cost of having physician perform a detailed history and physical examination and then take the time to develop the cognitive skills for critical analysis of complex medical issues. The use of copy and paste and other technology derived automatic field filling is a slippery slope to inadequate medical education and patient care.

CHAPTER 28

The Physician Fiduciary in the New and Evolving Digital Age—What Young Physicians Need To Know

The doctor–patient relationship is a member of a special class of legal relationships called fiduciary relations. Arising from the physician's role as a fiduciary to the patient is a duty to always act in the best interest of the patient.

The physician–patient relationship has its foundation in the theory that the physician is knowledgeable, skilled, and experienced in health issues, a subject where the patient has limited insight. Thus the patient places confidence and trust in the professional advice of the physician. The dynamic relationship between the physician and the patient has been evolving to emphasize the rights of patients to share in the decision-making process and to have the autonomy to accept or decline recommended treatment.

The query we face is whether the fiduciary responsibilities of the physician have been altered by the patient's autonomous use of the Internet, social media, and direct-to-consumer medical testing in the new and evolving digital age of medicine. We will explore the impact upon the physician's duties as fiduciary in this changing doctor–patient relationship.

Prior to the beginning of the 20th century, the physician–patient relationship was governed by physician paternalism. The idea of patient autonomy in decision-making regarding healthcare preferences dates back to the early 1900s, as so eloquently coined by Justice Benjamin Cardozo, who said "*Every human being of adult years and sound mind has a right to determine what shall be done with his own body; and a surgeon who performs an operation without his patient's consent commits an assault, for which he is liable in damages."*

Since the 1950s, there has been an increasingly strong emphasis on the rights of patients to share in medical-decision making and to exercise the autonomy to accept or reject recommended medical and surgical treatments.

This change in the characterization of the physician–patient relationship did not overturn physician control of the relationship. In theory, physician paternalism was dead. Paternalism does not respect the rights of adults to self-determination, and patient autonomy does not respect the principle of beneficence that leads physicians to argue that acting on behalf of others is essential to their craft.

Late in the first decade of the 2000s, it was felt that fundamental to the patient–physician relationship was the fact that each partner understands and accepts the degree of autonomy the patient desires in the decision-making process. In fact, despite the rhetoric of shared decision-making, physicians still retained control over decision-making because they controlled medical information and medical resources.

Today's patients drive the information highway, becoming informed by the Internet and social media. Additionally, they have access to a large array of direct-to-consumer (DTC) testing modalities. This information highway and DTC testing raises a query as to whether patients are less dependent on physicians for access to medical information and services/resources. Germinating from this query is the next question of whether this changes the doctor–patient relationship and the fiduciary responsibilities of the physician.

THE CLAIM

Some claim there is a new characterization of the doctor–patient relationship in which patients drive the information highway and consume DTC testing so they are less dependent on physicians for access to medical information and medical services. I argue that this claim is false.

HISTORICAL PERSPECTIVE

The transition from physician paternalism—the idea that the doctor knows best and decides course of treatment—to an emphasis on informed patient choice with shared decision-making became mainstream in the 1980s and has remained a staple of patient–physician interactions.

Shared decision-making involves the physician and patient working cohesively together to make medical decisions that align with the patient's values and preferences. This typically involves a doctor–patient exchange wherein the physician provides information about all potential treatment options and the patient absorbs, digests, and reflects, ultimately questioning the physician in a quest for a treatment that allies with his or her values and preferences.

This dynamic interaction supports the notion that informed medical choice is an educational process that has the potential to work to the benefit of the patient and physician. This equality in the covenant allows for informed choice. Physicians must realize that they may need to help the patient clarify healthcare goals and values when decisions are difficult and patients feel regressed.

By the late 2000s, there was a general consensus that patients participate in and ultimately make their own decisions whenever feasible. The general consensus was that with shared decision-making, physicians have a key role because of knowledge, access to medical information, clinical wisdom through experience, and medical resources not available to patients. Therefore, the paradigm shift from medical paternalism to autonomous patient decision-making did not completely transform the physician's role and the fiduciary duties remained intact.

THE DIGITAL ERA

The Internet and the associated information highway introduced patients to unlimited health information, including how to access medical services, with a burgeoning of companies offering DTC testing and services without a physician's order. This has allowed patients to arrive at the physician's office with thoroughly researched information regarding their symptoms, assumed disease state, and DTC test results to be interpreted.

This expanding marketing of DTC services to the general populace complicates and may diminish the physician's role in deciding what testing is appropriate in light of clinical symptoms, personal family history, risk factors, and pre-test probabilities. Physicians must listen carefully to identify the patient's concerns and fears, and any misunderstanding generated by the ambiguity of the DTC testing.

The escalating availability of DTC tests and screening has augmented patients' access to medical resources. The Food and Drug Administration (FDA) approved genetic testing by companies like 23 and Me in 2017, giving consumers access to gene testing for Alzheimer disease, Parkinson disease, hereditary thrombophilia, and BRCA mutations that are associated with an increased incidence of breast and ovarian cancer to name a few. So now we are faced with the advantages and disadvantages of the DTC testing and how it impacts the fiduciary duties of physicians.

THE ADVANTAGES AND DISADVANTAGES OF DTC MEDICAL TESTING

This is a hotly contested topic that is presented here with equal attention to the advantages and disadvantages of DTC testing. When there is an intense negotiation between competing interests of polar opposite views, shared interests are the "elixir of negotiation," the salve that will appease the parties' passionate debate. After exploring the advantages and disadvantages, this chapter offers ways physicians may respond to the perturbations in the doctor–patient relationship and remain true to their fiduciary responsibilities.

The Advantages of DTC Health Marketing Services

There can be advantages to patients having the autonomy to access medical devices and medical testing such as blood pressure monitors, glucometers, pregnancy tests, and HIV testing to allow discovery of a condition or surveillance of a disease state. Over-the-counter (OTC) tests play a positive role in screening for these binary conditions. They provide immediate testing, allow patients to forego office billing, and ensure patient privacy. The results do not require a differential thought process or an understanding of pre- and post-test probabilities. This type of DTC testing has value because it empowers consumers to monitor specific aspects of their health autonomously.

The Disadvantages of DTC Health Marketing Services

There is a strong national priority focused on containing healthcare costs and improving healthcare quality. Healthcare providers are being asked to be responsible stewards of valuable healthcare resources through strict adherence to evidence based medicine.

The DTC medical marketplace offers low-value medical testing directly to consumers and stands in direct opposition to the mandate for value-based care. Companies are offering saliva, blood, urine and imaging modalities to screen for a host of diseases without the consumer's prior understanding of the pre-test probabilities of the conditions being tested for.

Additionally, genetic testing is being offered despite low to no clinical value. The tests include genetic susceptibility testing for late-onset Alzheimer disease, Parkinson disease, Celiac disease, alpha 1 anti-trypsin deficiency, and hereditary hemochromatosis to name a few. The companies offer no medical advice so patients must go to their physician for interpretation of the information. This approach is fraught with ambiguity. No matter what the context of genetic testing, results fall into three subsets:

- Positive test result, usually providing diagnosis or risk information.
- Negative test result where no genetic variation is identified. This may rule out a condition or suggest reduced risk.
- The gray zone where genetic variants of unknown significance (VUS) are identified. This is known as genetic purgatory.

The current approach to VUS is the passing of a hot potato from the consumer-patient to the doctor and back to the patient who must now live in genetic purgatory. Thus, the private DTC companies avoid accountability for the uncertain medical testing and realize enormous profits from such testing. The physician and the healthcare systems are left to absorb the costs of medical care and retesting resulting from these low-value healthcare services. This is why healthcare policy gurus must affect how these services are allowed to function.

HOW DO DIGITAL AGE PHYSICIANS MEET THEIR FIDUCIARY DUTIES?

Patient access to the information highways and an exponentially increasing array of healthcare information, products, and marketplace DTC testing does not alter the fiduciary duties inherent in the doctor–patient relationship of the physician. While the Internet, social media, DTC laboratory and imaging, and genetic tests surface an assortment of medical concerns, uncertainties, and falsehoods, patients will continue to seek out physicians for advice. The physicians' fiduciary duty remains unchanged: to act in the best interest of the patient.

The approach to this new surfeit of information must be carefully analyzed to determine the best available way to educate the patient, allowing informed medical choice. This educational process must explore the meaning of good and bad testing to allow patient choice that is concordant with their values and preferences.

Physicians must educate patients regarding the low clinical value of much DTC testing for a large segment of the consuming population. Education must include teaching patients that company advertisements tend to entice consumers by appealing to fear of common diseases, such as coronary artery disease, stroke, and cancer. It is a physician's fiduciary duty to teach patients about the limits of DTC testing and to resist the urge to initiate a bulky cascade of unsubstantiated medical care when confronted with DTC testing results of uncertain significance.

The ultimate fiduciary duty is to educate patients so they act in their own best interest. The new characterization of the doctor–patient relationship where patients drive the information highway and consume DTC testing so they are no longer dependent upon physicians for access to medical information and medical services is wrong. Circumstances change but our duty to the patient remains untouched – act in their best interest.

Reprinted with permission, Paterick ZR, Paterick TE. The Physician Fiduciary in the New and Evolving Digital Age—What Young Physicians Need To Know? *Cardio Open A Open J*. 2019; I(1): 1–3

SECTION 6

Physicians, Peer Review, And Legal Conundrums

CHAPTER 29

Peer Review: Practical Aspects and Legal/Ethical Issues Faced By the Medical Staff

Physicians working in hospitals face challenges when it comes to understanding and meeting the medical, legal and ethical subjects outlined in the hospital bylaws. The hospital staff physicians and the hospital administration both aspire for high quality medical care and the assurance of patient safety. Unfortunately when quality concerns surface there can be reasonable differences of opinion as to whether a physician's practice pattern met the accepted threshold of the standard of care. This difference of opinions can lead to conflict that fuels a physician review.

The impediment physicians face is that many of the issues that surface at peer review are veiled in legal concepts for which physicians lack education, training, and familiarity. All physicians working in hospitals would be prudent to become familiar with the hospital bylaws and regulations. The consequences of adverse outcomes when subject to peer review can destroy medical careers.

The peer review process is an important subject for physicians to understand, but one that few physicians understand at a granular level. The difficulty for physicians is that many of the issues presented at peer review are cloaked in legal concepts for which physicians lack education, training, and familiarity. The hospital bylaws and regulations are complex and it requires time and energy to become knowledgeable in their intent and application in the hospital setting.

This chapter explores the roles and duties of the medical staff and the hospital administration in relationship to:

- Peer review.

- The medical staff bylaws and how they facilitate the hospital administration and medical staff in their mission for physicians to practice quality and safe medicine.
- The intricacies of the credentialing and privileging process.
- The prompts for peer review such as reappointment, complaints, and medical errors.
- The process of peer review and role of medical staff leadership versus hospital administration.
- The interaction between the alleged wrong doer physician and the peer review committee.
- The need for legal representation to ensure due process.
- Potential liability for peer review.
- The consequences of peer review actions including sanctions on physician's medical practice, expulsion from the medical staff, and reporting to the state boards and national practitioner data bank.

This conversation is important for all physicians to develop a deep understanding of the peer review process and how it can affect a physician's reputation, professional status, and livelihood.

WHAT ARE THE ROLES AND DUTIES OF THE MEDICAL STAFF AND HOSPITAL ADMINISTRATION IN RELATION TO PEER REVIEW?

The relationship between the medical staff and the hospital administration in connection to peer review is complex. The complexity surfaces because of the variable relationships of hospital-employed versus independent contractor physicians with hospital administration, as well as the emergence of corporate responsibility for quality of care and patient safety. These variable relationships must maintain the trust that an honest and fair peer review process will be available for all medical practitioners. A breakdown in that trust relationship can result in medical staff chaos.

The medical staff and hospital administration must work together to use a peer review process that gauges professional activities and conduct. Professional activities must meet the standard of care and physician behavior must meet the hospital code of conduct. The hospital board expects physicians on the medical staff to better define and monitor processes for physician credentialing, evaluation, peer review and disciplinary actions. Because these are delicate and sensitive issues they can be best addressed by an organized medical staff with the trusting relationship with the hospital administration. Staff physicians need hospital administration to clarify the roles and responsibilities of the President of the medical staff, the Chief of Staff, and the qualified administrative officer. This interplay is crucial in the development of appropriate medical staff and hospital administration relationships and processes.

THE MEDICAL STAFF BYLAWS: OUTLINING EXPECTATIONS OF THE MEDICAL STAFF:

Outlined below are expectations that practitioners should have of each other as members of the medical staff. These expectations reflect current medical staff bylaws, policies and procedures, and organizational policies reflecting the medical staff and hospital administration's values, culture and vision. These expectations provide a guide for the medical staff in selecting measures of practitioner competency.

Patient Care

The medical staff is expected to provide patient care that is compassionate, appropriate, and effective for the promotion of health, prevention of illness, and treatment of disease. The goal is to provide effective patient care that meets or exceeds medical staff standard of care as defined by medical literature review, comparative outcome data, and the results of peer review data. Medical staff members should demonstrate caring and respectful behaviors when interacting with patients and their families and counsel and educate patients and their families.

Medical Knowledge

The medical staff is expected to use evidence-based guidelines when available, as recommended by the appropriate specialty, in selecting the most effective approach to diagnosis and treatment. Physicians must maintain ongoing medical education and board certification and demonstrate superior medical knowledge and technical skills.

Interpersonal and Communication Skills

Medical staff is expected to communicate effectively with other practitioners, caregivers, patients and families to ensure accurate transfer of information through oral and written policies established by hospital policy. Practitioners should request inpatient consultations in a clear succinct manner with the consult and should be practitioner to practitioner in urgent/emergent situations. The medical staff must maintain medical records consistent with the medical staff bylaws, rules, regulations and policies. All medical staff members must work civilly and effectively with all members of the healthcare team.

Professionalism

Practitioners are expected to demonstrate behaviors that reflect a commitment to continuous professional development, ethical practice, an understanding and sensitivity to diversity, and responsible attitude toward patients, family, peers and the public.

Medical staff must act in a professional manner at all times and adhere to the Medical Staff Code of Conduct. There must be a prompt response to all patients needs, participation in emergency call rotations as outlined by the bylaws, rules and regulations, follow ethical principles pertaining to patient information, informed consent and adverse medical and surgical outcomes, and utilize sensitivity and responsiveness to culture, age, gender, and disabilities of patients and staff.

CREDENTIALING AND PRIVILEGING

Credentialing is the process of verifying qualifications to ensure current competence to grant privileges. The term credentialing involves verification of education, training, experience, and licensure to provide services.

The companion piece to credentialing is "privileging," which is the process of authorizing a licensed or certified healthcare practitioner's specific scope of patient care services. Privileging is performed in conjunction with an evaluation of an individual's clinical qualifications and/or performance.

Credentialing and privileging are fundamental duties to the medical staff peer review. These duties are essential to building a trustworthy and competent medical staff. The process can result in differences of opinion as to what privileges will be granted and whether a physician has the credentials to be on the medical staff.

Today it is common practice for hospitals to recruit physicians as employees, this can lead to conflict between private practice physicians and employed physicians resulting in "tribalism" between employed and non-employed hospital staff members, potentially leading to prejudiced evaluations in credentialing and privileges. In jurisdictions recognizing negligent credentialing as a cause of action, the hospital interest in defending itself against these claims may conflict with the medical staff interest in protecting the confidentiality of the peer review processes It is expected for hospitals to initiate a review of physicians' requesting hospital privileges.

This review identifies that physicians have the necessary education and training to perform requested privileges. A second component of credentialing and privileging is review of physician practice pattern to assure she has met the standard of care within the scope of the practitioner's practice. A third component of credentialing and privileging is assurance that the physician has behaved in a manner consistent with the hospital's code of conduct.

THE TRIGGERS FOR PEER REVIEW

Peer review may be instigated for several reasons in United States hospitals. It is expected for hospitals to initiate a peer review of physicians' requesting hospital privileges. A second basis for peer review is allegations that a physician is practicing below the standard of care. A third reason is a physician is acting outside the boundaries of normally accepted hospital behaviors. A fourth reasons for peer review is random selection of cases to improve the overall quality of patient care. Lastly, peer review may be prompted by adverse outcomes to determine root causes for errors, and develop processes to prevent future adverse events.

THE POTENTIAL FOR A SHAM PEER REVIEW

The interplay between the alleged physician wrong doer and the peer review committee, the need for legal representation, due process, potential for liability for peer review, and the consequences of peer review actions; including sanctions on medical practice and expulsion from the medical staff, are best consider by reviewing the Timothy Patrick case.

The personification of fraudulent peer review is identified in the Dr. Timothy Patrick case. Dr. Patrick, a vascular surgeon, sued Columbia Memorial Hospital (CMH) after he was subjected to a deceitful peer review for economic reasons. Patrick had joined a group practice in Astoria, Oregon after several years with the group he elected to decline partnership and pursue his own practice in the same geographic region. His previous colleagues reported Patrick to the hospital executive committee at CMH for peer review asserting "irresponsible behavior" in his medical care of patients. The peer review committee was chaired by a member of the group Patrick left to pursue his own practice. An investigation of the alleged "irresponsible behavior" occurred and the committee voted to terminate Patrick's hospital privileges.

A federal antitrust lawsuit filed by Patrick against the Astoria clinic physicians claiming the defendants partook in a bad faith peer review to quash competition. The United States Supreme Court ruled in favor of Patrick. This ruling by the highest court in the land had an unnerving affect upon physician willingness to participate in peer review. Physicians perceived themselves at magnified legal risk if they participated in a review that ultimately was determined to be a sham. This fear was emanating from the Supreme Court decision awarding Patrick a $2.2 million verdict.

The Patrick decision had a huge negative impact on the necessary and important peer review process. The response to this physician reticence was congressional action introducing Health Care Quality Improvement Act (HCQIA). This act resulted in physician immunity when participating in peer review. This immunity was subject to several factors including:

- That the purported allegations brought to the peer review committee was a furtherance of quality of care issues,
- That there would be a due diligence approach to fact finding,
- And there would be adequate notice and a fair hearing procedure offered to the physician under review.

The introduction of HCQIA transformed the law granting peer review committees and hospitals limited immunity to almost unqualified immunity. This transformative congressional ruling created a situation of grave trepidation for physicians working in a setting of intense marketplace competition where there are attempts by hospitals to stifle competition to have control of the marketplace.

REPORTING TO NATIONAL PRACTITIONER DATA BANK

The National Practitioner Data Bank (NPDB) was created in 1986 under the Health Care Quality Improvement Act of 1986. The NPDB is a repository for reports of medical malpractice payments and certain adverse actions related to healthcare practitioners.

The purpose of the NPDB is an alert system to gather and disclose adverse information about physicians and other healthcare practitioners to restrict their ability to continue their medical practices without people knowing of their previous incompetence or unprofessional actions.

What information is reported to the NPDB? The information reported includes but is not limited to medical malpractice payment, licensure restrictions and clinical/hospital privilege restrictions related to professional competence and conduct, professional society membership actions related to professional competence and conduct, Drug Enforcement Administration (DEA) certification actions and exclusions from participation in Medicare, Medicaid and other federal healthcare programs.

Physicians would be prudent to understand the importance of NPDB reporting requirements because reporting to the NPDN has serious consequences. Even though the NPDB itself does not provide a private cause of action, entities that report practitioners improperly may face lawsuits from reported practitioners. NPDB reports have an impact on practitioner careers and reputations. The impact of a report depends upon the underlying facts and how the report is worded.

Failure to report to the NPDB when required by law has serious consequences. Any malpractice payer that fails to report medical malpractice payments is subject to a civil penalty. Any hospital or other healthcare entity that fails to report adverse actions will have its name published in the Federal Register, and the organization will lose its immunity from liability under Title IV with respect to professional review activities for a period of three years from the date of publication in the Federal Register. Additionally, the Secretary of Health and Human Services (HHS) shall publish a public report that identifies those government agencies that have failed to report information on adverse actions as required.

What actions must be reported to the NPDB? Hospitals and other healthcare entities with formal peer review must report the following: professional review actions based on reasons related to professional competence or conduct adversely affecting clinical privileges for a period longer than 30 days, voluntary surrender of privileges while under, or to avoid, an investigation. "Professional review action" is a peer review action "which is based on the competence or professional conduct of an individual physician (which conduct affects or could affect adversely the health or welfare of a patient or patients)." In addition, hospitals may report clinical privilege actions taken against healthcare practitioners other than physicians if the practitioner's professional competence or conduct could adversely affect the health or welfare of a patient.

CONCLUSION

This "ten thousand foot view" of peer review gives the reader insight into the complex nature of belonging to a medical staff. The potential risks of participating on the medical staff and subject to peer review is self-evident including reputational damage, loss of professional status and livelihood.

Peer review, hearing and appeals procedures, credentialing and privileging, and medical staff bylaws are all critical to fair and equitable treatment of physicians participating on medical staffs. Given the present competitive healthcare landscape it is imperative all physicians take the time to understand the peer review process and to be knowledgeable in concepts that are imbedded in the interchange between the medical staff and the governance of the hospital board.

It is prudent to have legal counsel review the contractual relationship between the medical staff and the hospital executive committee to determine all safeguards are present to ensure a fair and equitable review process. A fair and honest peer review process is in the best interest of all participants on the medical staff and for the patients. It is imperative that physician understand the history of sham reviews as highlighted in the Patrick case.

Physicians must assure all physicians on hospital staffs receive fair and equitable treatment when issues are presented to a peer review committee. Lack of knowledge or understanding of the bylaws and policies is never a defense when subjected to peer review.

CHAPTER 30

Peer Review: The Mandate for Physician Leadership

Physicians working in hospitals face challenges when it comes to understanding and meeting the medical, legal, and ethical subjects outlined in the hospital bylaws. Hospital staff physicians and the hospital administration both aspire for high quality medical care and the assurance of patient safety. Unfortunately, when quality concerns surface, there can be reasonable differences of opinion as to whether a physician's practice pattern met the accepted threshold of the standard of care.

Such differences of opinion can lead to conflict that fuels a physician review. One complication for physicians is that many of the issues that surface at peer reviews are veiled in legal concepts and underpinnings for which physicians lack education, training, and familiarity. It would be prudent for all physicians working in hospitals to become familiar with the hospital bylaws and regulations. Physicians must take a leadership role in assuring fair and equitable peer review.

Physicians are thrust into the world of peer review without the education and training in the legal and ethical principles that are inherent to a fair and trusted peer review process. Physicians must comprehend that the purpose of peer review is to "evaluate professionally a colleague's work." In medicine, colleagues define peer review." An honest and fair peer review process is the staple of an excellent medical staff.

During a peer review, the reviewing physicians must pursue all the relevant facts and determine their veracity. Typical allegations against physicians are practice patterns that do not meet the standard of care or behavioral patterns that do not meet the accepted behavioral standards of the hospital. Medical staff members reviewing a colleague must proceed in a fair and honest manner. A fair and equitable peer review process is essential for a hospital that wants high quality medical care and a safeguard for patient safety.

Organized medicine employs the peer review process as a methodology to gauge professional activities and conduct. Physicians have an ethical and moral responsibility to each other and to patients to assure all hospital practice patterns meet the standard of care. The peer review committee must allow physicians the right to exercise freedom in their medical judgment but ensure that the medical judgment is accepted and consistent with the national standards of care.

Disciplinary hearings where a physician's reputation, professional status, or livelihood is at risk must be objective and fair. To be objective and fair, the hearings must include the following:

- A list of alleged wrongdoings.
- Adequate notice of the right to a hearing.
- The right to defend one's actions.
- Reviewing physicians that have a similar scope of practice as the physician under review.

All reviewing physicians must disclose any conflicts of interest and recuse themselves when conflicted for any reason. The hospital bylaws and administration must ensure safeguards that guarantee all physicians due process when enduring a peer review.

WHY PHYSICIANS NEED TO DEVELOP A DEEP UNDERSTANDING OF THE PEER REVIEW PROCESS

The importance of a fair and equitable peer review process is never so self-evident until a physician is the subject of one. The birth of peer review conceptually started with Ernest Amory Codman. He was an extraordinary surgeon at Massachusetts General Hospital who was ahead of his time. His true passion was the science of quality improvement.

Codman was a surgeon who believed that by prospectively tracking outcomes, we could learn from patient results and advance the field of medicine. He helped develop the concepts integral to present-day morbidity and mortality conferences and started the first national registry in American healthcare.

Given the challenges of medicine today with ever increasing rates of errors and wide variability in quality, many physicians are requesting that Codman's basic tenants be revisited and applied. Codman described patient tracking in a publicly circulated pamphlet in 1914: "Every hospital should monitor every patient it treats long enough to determine whether the treatment has been successful, and then inquire 'if not, why not' with a review to identify root causes of failure with a view to preventing similar failures in the future."

The approach to peer review today had its seeds germinate in the early 1990s when the American College of Surgeons implemented peer review to define the standard of care requirements to be met by medical staff physicians.

The peer review process today includes a peer review committee composed of staff physicians who report to a board of directors. The crucial decision-making authority is the board of directors after an examination of the peer review committee's judgment regarding the charged allegations. As envisioned by Dr. Codman, this peer review process is required by JCAHO for hospital accreditation.

WHAT PROMPTS A PEER REVIEW?

Peer reviews may be instigated in US hospitals for several reasons. It is expected that hospitals will initiate a peer review of physicians requesting hospital privileges to determine whether the physicians have the necessary education and training to perform the requested privileges. A second basis for peer review is the allegation that a physician is practicing below the standard of care. A third reason is that a physician is acting outside the boundaries of normally accepted hospital behavior. A fourth reason for a peer review is the random selection of cases to improve the overall quality of patient care. Lastly, a peer review may be prompted by adverse outcomes to determine the root causes of errors and develop processes to prevent future adverse events.

Across the United States, the lack of a standardized peer review process has allowed varying decisions for similar alleged wrongdoings. This lack of standardization is a major issue that must be confronted by physician leaders.

THE SIGNIFICANCE OF THE PATRICK CASE FOR PEER REVIEW

The personification of a fraudulent peer review is seen in the case of Dr. Timothy Patrick. Dr. Patrick, a vascular surgeon, sued Columbia Memorial Hospital (CMH) after he was subjected to a deceitful peer review for economic reasons. Patrick had joined a group practice in Astoria, Oregon. After several years with the group, he elected to decline partnership and pursue his own practice in the same geographic region. His previous colleagues reported Patrick to the hospital executive committee at CMH for a peer review, asserting "irresponsible behavior" in his medical care of patients. The peer review committee was chaired by a member of the group Patrick left to pursue his own practice. An investigation of the alleged "irresponsible behavior" took place, and the committee voted to terminate Patrick's hospital privileges.

Patrick filed a federal antitrust lawsuit against the Astoria clinic physicians claiming the defendants partook in a bad faith peer review to quash competition. The United States Supreme Court ruled in favor of Patrick. This ruling by the highest court in the land had an unnerving effect upon physicians' willingness to participate in peer reviews. Physicians perceived themselves at a magnified legal risk if they participated in a review that ultimately was determined to be a sham. This fear emanated from the Supreme Court decision awarding Patrick a $2.2 million verdict.

The Patrick decision had a huge negative impact on the necessary and important peer review process. The response to this physician reticence was congressional action introducing the Health Care Quality Improvement Act (HCQIA). This act resulted in physician immunity when participating in peer reviews, subject to several factors: that the purported allegations brought to the peer review committee were a furtherance of quality of care issues; that there would be a due diligence approach to fact finding; and that there would be adequate notice and a fair hearing procedure offered to the physician under review.

The introduction of HCQIA transformed the law granting peer review committees and hospitals limited immunity to almost unqualified immunity. This transformative congressional ruling created a situation of grave trepidation for physicians working in a setting of intense marketplace competition, where attempts are made by hospitals to stifle competition in order to control the marketplace.

Today, sham reviews still occur, and the courts are often viewed as kangaroo courts when considering interference of competition issues. Courts often view hospitals as virtuous entities that are solely interested in quality medical care and patient safety, and they assume that the hospital administration wants to uncover and address all medical errors and safety issues that occur in the hospital so they could be prevented in the future. This suggests a "blind justice," called the "rule of non-review."

This acknowledges the "business judgment rule," implying that the governing board of a private entity, like a hospital, has the right to determine and direct its own internal business and medical affairs. Ernest Codman must be rolling over in his grave! This type of public policy mandates that physician leaders engage in the peer review process to ensure that peer review is honest, fair, and equitable.

THE ESSENCE OF PEER REVIEW

Physicians in the United States accept peer review, but there is some distrust because of a lack of understanding of the legal underpinnings of the peer review process. Health insurance companies have made a huge impact on the peer review process. They are now mandating evidence of quality peer review activity among the doctors in an institution prior to entering into an arrangement with the group of doctors or with the hospital.

The mission statement of the hospital often asserts that the institution aspires to a unified goal of transparency and partnership between the medical staff and the hospital administration to ensure equitable treatment of all disputes arising between a physician and the medical staff. Unfortunately, there are situations where the physician brought into the process and the medical staff has differing opinions about the alleged practice pattern and whether it meets the accepted standard of care. The complexity for physicians is that many issues of a peer review are veiled in legal concepts, in which physicians lack education, training, and familiarity.

The peer review process presents a varied range of issues that warrants legal knowledge and insights. It is imperative to have legal counsel when developing the foundation of the peer review process to assure that ethical, legal, and accreditation principles are developed. Physician leadership must play a critical role in meeting this goal, so that physicians are assured of equity and fairness.

This approach is epitomized in an Arkansas statute that provides that medical staff can, as a matter of law, "engage independent legal counsel to review a professional review action before a final recommendation is made or final action taken." This is particularly important for physicians who are not hospital employees and may represent competition to the employed hospital physicians. All physicians deserve a fair and equitable hearing process and must have the ability to appeal any decisions that impact reputation, professional status, or livelihood.

HEARINGS AND APPEALS

The peer review process quickly identifies the polarity between the physician subject to peer review and the investigative group of physicians. A hearing officer is appointed to preside over the process and offer advice to the hearing committee. The peer review committee's decision can be appealed to the hospital board of directors, which either makes the final decision or makes a recommendation to the peer review committee for the final decision.

It is problematic that hospital attorneys often represent the peer review committee and offer advice. The physician facing allegations may request that the peer review body use counsel not employed by the hospital or from a firm utilized by the hospital. This was highlighted in *Yaqub vs. Salinas Memorial Healthcare System*, in which the court warned that it would strain the due process clause to allow the hospital attorney, who took an active role in assisting the medical executive committee to bring charges against the appellant, to serve as an advisor to the board in the hearing. This type of judicial commentary is advocating for a true due process under the law, and it is crucial for physician leaders to understand this ruling.

CREDENTIALING AND PRIVILEGING

Credentialing and privileging are fundamental duties of a medical staff peer review and are essential to building a trustworthy and competent medical staff. The process can result in differences of opinion as to what privileges will be granted and whether a physician has the credentials to be on the medical staff.

Today it is common practice for hospitals to recruit physicians as employees, which can lead to conflict between private practice physicians and employed physicians resulting in "tribalism" between employed and non-employed hospital staff members and potentially leading to prejudiced evaluations in credentialing and privileges. In jurisdictions recognizing negligent credentialing as a cause of action, the hospital's interest in defending itself against these claims may conflict with the medical staff's interest in protecting the confidentiality of the peer review process.

MEDICAL STAFF BYLAWS

Generally the recognized "majority view" is that medical staff bylaws are interpreted as a contract between the hospital and the medical staff. Even in those jurisdictions where the bylaws are not contractual in nature, differences in opinion between hospital and staff may lead to the need for a process allowing full hearings overseen by impartial judges. Thus, the hospital bylaws must allow active medical staff members to vote on their ability to participate in the elaboration of the rules and regulations impacting physicians, which only the hospital executive committee can act upon.

Therefore, it is incumbent upon the medical staff to hire independent counsel to review medical staff bylaws to ensure that they contain provisions that allow due process and equitable treatment of all staff members and to attain physician membership on the executive committee.

STANDARDIZATION OF PEER REVIEW

The need for standardization of the peer review process is epitomized in the Patrick case, where a sham review required Dr. Patrick to go to the Supreme Court for fairness and equity. Additionally, studies beyond the case example of Patrick have demonstrated that peer reviews are often unreliable measures of quality and have not served the envisioned function of quality improvement. Regulation of peer reviews should result in a two-fold effect: improvement in quality and decreased abuse of the process through sham reviews. National standardization efforts for peer reviews remain challenging, as the process is costly, time intensive, and requires extensive resources. Several models at diverse US hospitals have shown that standardization and structuring of the review process can improve medical care. Another approach is to develop additional protection of the peer review process involving external review to verify that the actions taken are in agreement with JACHO and HCQIA requirements.

CONCLUSION

Peer review, hearing and appeals procedures, credentialing and privileging, and medical staff bylaws are all critical to the fair and equitable treatment of physicians participating on medical staffs. Given the present healthcare landscape, it is imperative that all physicians take the time to understand the peer review process and to become knowledgeable in legal concepts that are imbedded in the interchange between the medical staff and the governance of the hospital board.

It is prudent to have legal counsel review the contractual relationship between the medical staff and the hospital executive committee. A fair and honest peer review process is in the best interest of all participants on the medical staff and of the patients. It is imperative that physician leaders understand the history of sham reviews as highlighted in the Patrick case. Physician leaders must ensure all physicians on hospital staffs receive fair and equitable treatment when issues are presented to a peer review committee.

The intense competition for patients in the medical marketplace and the highly politicized US healthcare system has been of concern to physicians seeking a fair and equitable peer review process. The immunity granted to peer review committees through the HCQIA has the potential to have a devastating effect on a physician's professional status or livelihood. Considering congressional and judicial tolerance of this quandary, substantial and meaningful physician leadership is necessary to remedy the potential deficiencies of the present-day peer review process.

Furthermore, further research is needed to study the peer review process and its outcomes to determine if peer review reforms have altered the prevalence of sham reviews, improved the quality of care, and ensured patient safety.

Reprinted with permission, Zachary Paterick, Timothy E. Paterick, (2019). Peer Review – The Mandate for Physician Leadership, *Hospital Practices and Research*, 4(3); 76-79.

CHAPTER 31

The National Practitioner Data Bank: Requisite Medical-Legal Issues for Physicians

Physicians would be prudent to understand the National Practitioner Data Bank reporting procedures, actions that must be reported to the NPDB, the recent case law reflecting developments in applicable reporting to NPDB, special issues facing the aging physician in light of the Age Discrimination in Employment Act (ADEA) and American with Disabilities Act (ADA), and the evolving peer review and medical staff litigation. This understanding will allow physicians to participate in peer review with a deeper understanding of the medical and legal issues they confront in relationship to hospital privileges and the NPDB. Reports to the NPDB can have a large impact on physician's ability to practice medicine, physician reputation, and physician livelihood.

The National Practitioner Data Bank (NPDB) was established by the Health Care Quality Improvement Act (HCQIA) of 1986, as amended (42 U.S.C. 11101-et. seq.) The HCQIA invokes great authority over physicians to the NPDB. The HCQIA authorizes the NPDB to collect reports of adverse licensure actions against physicians such as revocations, suspensions, reprimands, censures, probation and surrenders; adverse clinical privileges actions against physicians; adverse professional society membership actions against physicians; Drug Enforcement Administration (DEA) certification actions; Medicare/Medicaid exclusions; and medical malpractice payments made for the benefit of any healthcare practitioner.

There is a broad spectrum of organizations that have access to the NPDB data systems including: hospitals, healthcare facilities that have recognized peer review processes and provide healthcare services, and state medical boards. Individual physicians may self-query. Medical malpractice payers, state medical boards, professional societies with formal peer review, and hospitals report information under HCQIA.

This chapter reviews NPDB reporting procedures, an overview of what actions must be reported to the NPDB, some recent case law reflecting developments in applicable reporting to NPDB, special issues facing the aging physician in light of the Age Discrimination in Employment Act (ADEA) and American with Disabilities Act (ADA), and update on peer review and medical staff litigation. Each section is critical for physicians to comprehend as the playing field in medicine as changed dramatically since the introduction of corporate medicine. Playing the game of hospital medicine without knowledge of the game rules is like walking in quick sand.

NATIONAL PRACTITIONER DATA BANK (NPDB) REPORTING

The NPDB is a repository for reports of medical malpractice payments and certain adverse actions related to healthcare practitioners. The purpose of the NPDB is to be an alert system to collect and divulge unfavorable information about physicians to restrict their ability to continue their medical practice without patients knowing of their previous issues of competence or unprofessional actions.

What information is reported to the NPDB? A large swath of data is reportable and is important for physicians to understand. Reportable facts includes medical malpractice payments, licensure restrictions related to professional fitness and conduct, clinical hospital privilege restrictions related to professional competence and conduct, DEA certification actions, and sanctions and exclusions related to participation in Medicare, Medicaid, and other federal healthcare programs are all reported to the NPDB.

Why is it important for physicians to understand NPDB reporting requirements? Because reporting and not reporting to the NPDB can have serious consequences for a physician's career and reputation. The NPDB does not provide a private cause of action, entities that report practitioners improperly may face lawsuits from the reported practitioner for career/reputation damage and/or intentional infliction of emotion distress. The impact of the report depends upon the proximate and contiguous circumstances and the language used in the report. Alternatively, failing to report to the NPDB when required by law may have grave consequences.

The following are examples of when failing to report has serious repercussions:

- Any malpractice payer that does not report medical malpractice payments is subject to civil penalty for each payment not reported.
- Any hospital/healthcare entity that fails to report unfavorable actions will have its name published in the Federal Register and the healthcare entity will lose its immunity from liability under Title 4 with respect to professional review for 3 years.
- Additionally, the secretary of Health and Human Services (HHS) shall publish a public report of the government agencies that have failed to report information as required.

SPECIFICS OF WHAT ACTIONS MUST BE REPORTED TO NPDB

Hospitals and other healthcare bodies with formal peer review must report professional review actions grounded upon "professional review action" that are related to professional competence or conduct negatively affecting clinical privileges for a period of longer than **30 days**, or when physicians relinquish privileges while under, or to circumvent an investigation.

Clinical privileges includes:

- Hospital practice privileges.
- Impact on hospital medical staff membership.
- Impact on hospital network participation.

"Professional review action" is a per-review action that is based upon the competence or professional conduct of an individual physician that could negatively impact the medical care of a patient.

LEGAL REQUIREMENTS AND MECHANICS OF REPORTING PHYSICIANS UNDER APPLICABLE LAW

A Texas court identified that a physician restriction to practice begins at the time a physician cannot practice the full scope of his/her practice.

Walker was a general surgeon holding medical staff privileges at a hospital in Lufkin, Texas. The hospital issued Walker a corrective action plan following a peer review evaluation of his medical care of patients.

The improvement plan mandated that Walker's surgical privileges be restricted until he performed five bowel surgeries with a proctor. The corrective action plan did not specify a time period for the requirements. After 30 days Walker had not completed the five bowel surgeries and the hospital reported him to the NPDB. Walker sued the hospital seeking injunctive relief.

The court held the hospital erred because the corrective action failed to specify a time period. The court concluded "whether a proctoring sanction is reportable should be established by the terms of the sanction at the time it is delivered, and not by whether, in fact, it takes more than 30 days to satisfy the requirement." The revised *NPDB Guidebook* (2018) states, "a restriction begins at the time a physician can not perform the full scope of privileges."

From the NPDB perspective the report to the NPDB should be made if the restriction lasts for a period of time exceeding 30 days irrespective of the number of cases needed in the corrective action. The NPDB clarifies that an agreement not to exercise privileges during an investigation is a restriction of privileges. Any restriction of privileges while under investigation is considered a relinquishment of privileges and must be reported. A practitioner cannot voluntarily agree to restrict privileges to avoid reporting. The 2018 Guidebook states that if a proctor is required for a physician to engage in clinical privileges for more than 30 days it is reportable. Alternatively, if a proctor is not necessary the action should not be reported.

WHEN DOES THE REVIEW PROCESS OF REAPPLICATION BECOME AN INVESTIGATION?

Prior to 2018 it was unclear when the review process for reapplication become an investigation. The 2018 Guidebook answers the question stating this depends on whether" the reappointing hospital had specific concerns" about the applicants competence. The NPDB Guidebook made it clear that follow up questions do not necessarily create an investigation.

Resignation of an applicant prior to a final decision of an applicant's reappointment, where there are specific concerns about the applicant's competence, will be reportable.

AGE DISCRIMINATION IN EMPLOYMENT ACT AND THE AMERICANS WITH DISABILITIES ACT

Approximately 25% of American physicians are 65 years or older and 50% of the U.S. physician force is 50 year or older. There are no laws or rules regulating the competency assessment of aging physicians. Aging has variable effects on people's cognitive and physical fitness capacity. This issue is fraught with complexity because colleagues may be reluctant to question the competence or skill of an aging physician because on long, respected careers and a reputation of a staple in the community.

In the employment context assessing age and health-related competency issues links two sets of laws – disability and age discrimination laws. There are fair employment laws and Age Discrimination in Employment Act (ADEA) attempting to prevent discrimination in employment based upon age. The Americans with Disabilities Act (ADA) attempts to prevent disability discrimination. For decades courts seemed to accept the notion of mandatory retirement ages if they were imbedded in public safety.

There are no case reports in which a court reviewed a healthcare employer's mandatory retirement age. The gestalt is courts would likely reject mandatory retirement age. The trend has been to use screening mechanisms that rely on testing cognitive and physical fitness. The disability discrimination provisions of the ADA strive for case-specific, individualized assessment.

ADA AND ADEA IN THE MEDICAL STAFF CONTEXT

The ADA and ADEA do not apply where a physician is only a member of the medical staff. Hospitals have more autonomy to adopt age and cognitive/fitness for duty examinations in this context, including age-based competency testing. Testing should have a nexus to the nature of the privileges. The testing individual should have a detailed understanding of the physician's practice and the necessary cognitive and physical skills. Examples being: a radiologist needing good visual acuity and a surgeon needing good manual dexterity and physical stamina.

Title 3 of the ADA was found by one court to create a cause of action for a physician that was terminated from a hospital medical staff. The physician was allowed to advance a claim that the hospital improperly denied him staff privileges due to a disability. Dr. Nolan Hetz was disabled by bipolar disorder and sleep apnea. Aurora Medical Center brought a motion to dismiss based upon the argument that Title 3 only applied to the hospital's clients and visitors.

The court found that that the intent of Title 3 ADA does not support such an interpretation, the court held that a physician acting as an independent – contractor may sue a hospital under ADA Title 3 for denial of staff privileges. The court rules that Dr. Hetz was, like a patient, a person using the hospital for personal benefit and the good of the public. The court's take –home point being hospitals should careful to ensure that any fitness-for-duty testing is consistent, job-related and consistent with business necessity.

PEER REVIEW AND MEDICAL STAFF LITIGATION

A cardiologist was summarily suspended by the medical executive committee (MEC) for what the hospital considered substandard care provided to one of the cardiologist's patient. The peer review committee noted four peer review incidents and 10 anonymous reports (MIDAS) involving inadequate care or management as support for the suspension.

The hospital's medical staff bylaws stated that upon suspension a physician is entitled to request an intra-professional conference that is required to occur within a defined period of time. The bylaws also provided that the physician would have the right to "inspect all pertinent and non-privileged information in the hospital's possession prior to the intra-professional conference."

The hospital granted the conference, but the physician alleged they did not give complete access to the records he requested. The hospital only provided four peer review records. The panel recommended that the hospital maintain the summary judgment.

The cardiologist sued for injunctive and declaratory relief. The Licensing Act of Illinois requires hospitals to include certain minimum procedures in their bylaws related to staff privilege decisions. The law includes a right to a fair hearing for administrative summary suspension. The court ruled the cardiologist had a right to inspect all applicable records to the intra-professional conference. The court's take home message was to follow the complete process with issues related to medical staff privileges.

A second case addresses whether a physician has a property interest in medical staff privileges and whether a hospital violates its Bylaws by using a summary suspension on a non- patient care case. Dr. Chang was the Chief Medical Officer (CMO) at the hospital. His medical staff privileges were summarily barred by the hospital. Chang filed a complaint for declaratory and injunctive relief, citing violations of federal and state constitutional due process rights, federal and state law, and hospital bylaws. Chang requested the court to enjoin the hospital from reporting his suspension to the NPDB.

The facts of the case: March 2019 two hospital employees brought claims about Chang to human resources. The allegations were that Dr. Chang had sexually harassed them. The hospital hired an outside attorney to investigate the situation. Dr. Chang was placed on "restrictions and directives" pursuant to medical staff bylaws. The attorney determined that Dr. Chang had engaged in unwelcome sexual activity, including sexual intercourse, toward the employees using coercion and intimidation. After required process, Dr. Chang's medical privileges were summarily suspended.

Critical issues addressed by the court:

- Does Dr. Chang have a property interest in his medical staff privileges that triggers constitutional due process protection? No.
- Did the hospital follow HCQIA due process requirements of a formal hearing before summarily suspending the physician? Yes.
- Does HCQIA require imminent danger to exist before a summary restraint is imposed? No.
- Does sexual harassment of an employee rise to the same level of wrong doing as impairing patient safety? Yes.

The court found:

- The hospital had followed HCQIA's requirements and denied an injunction.
- The suspension was proper and the hospital could report to the NPDB.
- The hospital did not violate hospital bylaws by issuing a summary suspension on a non-patient medical care case.

CONCLUSION

Physicians would be prudent to understand NPDB reporting procedures, what actions must be reported to the NPDB, the case law applicable reporting to NPDB, the special issues facing the aging physician in light of the Age Discrimination in Employment Act (ADEA) and Americans with Disabilities Act (ADA), and the recent evolving peer review and medical staff litigation. This knowledge and understanding will help physicians participate in peer review and will reduce the likelihood of a physician being a subject of NPBD reports.

SECTION 7

The World of Sports and Physician Liability

CHAPTER 32

Medical and Legal Issues in the Cardiovascular Evaluation of Competitive Athletes

Healthy-appearing competitive athletes may harbor unsuspected cardiovascular disease with the potential to cause sudden death. This fact raises issues of physician responsibility in preparticipation screening and eligibility/disqualification decisions. A number of medical-legal cases now represent a framework for screening and eligibility decision-making in high school and college athletes.

Physicians screening competitive athletes should strictly adhere to recommendations from the American Heart Association. Precedent exists for disqualifying athletes with heart disease from competition to prevent unnecessary exposure to risk of injury or death.

By virtue of the court decision in *Larkin v Archdiocese of Cincinnati*, high school students with heart disease have no compelling right to participate in interscholastic sports without medical clearance.

In *Knapp v Northwestern University*, an appellate court ruled that college athletes can be medically disqualified from sports and supported the use of national association medical guidelines by team physicians in formulating eligibility/disqualification decisions. This medical-legal analysis provides guidelines for physicians participating in medical evaluations of competitive athletes by clarifying the standard of care, potential pitfalls, and the evolving liability associated with this clinical practice.

Athletes are considered the healthiest members of our society, and an unexpected death during training or competition is a tragic event with widespread implications. Interest in athletic field deaths has intensified and has become a high-profile and compelling medical event. Such tragedies are always unexpected and counterintuitive, provoking a variety of considerations including implementation of preparticipation screening and disqualification from competitive sports to reduce risk.

Liability issues in screening and management of competitive athletes are of increasing concern to the practicing medical community because some athletes' deaths have triggered disputes in court, holding physicians accountable for alleged grievances. Consequently, a legal framework is evolving related to the alleged failure to properly diagnose, treat, or disqualify individuals from competitive athletics.

CAUSES OF SUDDEN DEATH IN ATHLETES

Sudden death in young athletes largely is due to a variety of clinically unsuspected congenital cardiac abnormalities. In the United States, genetic cardiovascular diseases, including hypertrophic cardiomyopathy (HCM), arrhythmogenic right ventricular cardiomyopathy, Marfan syndrome, and ion channelopathies (e.g., long QT syndrome), account for approximately 40% of sudden deaths in young athletes, with HCM being the single most common cause and accounting for one-third of the cases. Other less-common causes include coronary artery anomalies, myocarditis, aortic valve stenosis, mitral valve prolapse, dilated cardiomyopathy, and premature atherosclerotic coronary artery disease.

Available prevalence data for sudden death in young athletes are limited and may underestimate the magnitude of this public health problem.

Vigorous participation in competitive sports may predispose athletes to sudden collapse by triggering ventricular tachyarrhythmias in the presence of underlying heart disease. Continued training and competition may expose vulnerable athletes to unacceptably high risk for sudden death or disease progression; disqualification from intense sports may be recommended to reduce that risk.

Alternatively, over-diagnoses of cardiac disease may lead to unnecessary restrictions from sports, thereby depriving athletes of considerable psychological and often substantial economic benefits. Diagnostic distinctions between physiological (and benign) athlete's heart and heart disease can often be resolved with noninvasive testing.

PREPARTICIPATION ATHLETIC SCREENING

Preparticipation screening is the systematic medical evaluation of large, general populations of athletes prior to training for the purpose of identifying (or raising suspicion) of cardiovascular abnormalities that could provoke disease progression or sudden death. Identification of these diseases may well prevent or delay some cases of sudden death because of physician-recommended temporary or permanent withdrawal from sports or treatment interventions.

An impediment to implementing preparticipation screening is the large number of young athletes (an estimated 10 million–12 million per year) and the infrequency of sudden death. Furthermore, customary screening practice for U.S. high school and college athletes consists only of performing a personal and family history and a physical examination. The efficacy of this practice has come under scrutiny.

The 1996 American Heart Association consensus panel stipulated that such preparticipation cardiovascular screening is a justifiable clinical practice, but routine noninvasive testing is not recommended due to the low-anticipated yield and associated cost-efficacy considerations. Specific screening recommendations were formulated to target those cardiovascular lesions known to cause youthful sudden death (see Table 1).

MEDICAL-LEGAL ISSUES

The relationship between sports medicine and the law is complex. It evolves from tenuous relationships between physicians, athlete-patients, teams, and institutions.

Athlete–Physician Relationship

Patient-athletes trust their physicians to advise them of the risk for untoward events during competitive sports. Indeed, physicians have a primary obligation to act in the athlete's best medical interest. The law relies on the collective judgment of the medical profession to establish the appropriate nature and scope of medical evaluations to identify cardiovascular abnormalities and other life-threatening conditions in athletes participating in organized sports.

TABLE 1. American Heart Association's 12-Point Recommendations for Preparticipation Screening of High School and College Athletes

Personal Medical History • Exertional chest pain/discomfort • Syncope/near syncope • Excessive exertional and otherwise unexplained dyspnea/fatigue associated with exercise • Prior recognition of heart murmur • Elevated blood pressure
Family Medical History • Premature death (sudden or otherwise) related to heart disease in relatives • Disability from heart disease in close relative younger than 50 years • Specific knowledge of hypertrophic or dilated cardiomyopathy, ion channelopathies such as long QT syndrome, Marfan syndrome, or clinically important arrhythmias
Physical Examination • Heart murmur† • Femoral pulses to exclude aortic coarctation • Physical stigmata of Marfan syndrome • Brachial artery blood pressure (sitting position)

Litigation in the sports arena appears to be increasing and physicians are frequently involved. Lawsuits for medical negligence and malpractice may arise when a breach of the physician's duty has occurred and medical conduct has failed to meet the standard of care, directly causing injury or death.

Lack of judicial resolution in some encounters due to settlement of claims represents an obstacle to establishing a comprehensive medical-legal framework. Nevertheless, measured inferences from such cases can create insights for practicing physicians in avoiding potential liability (See Table 2).

Preparticipation Screening

Case law and statutes are limited in establishing the scope of the physician's role in preparticipation screening. One strategy by which physicians can limit potential liability is strict adherence to the historical stance of the American Heart Association regarding physical screening guidelines.

This principle is underscored by *Izidor v Knight*, in which a community college basketball player sought a sports clearance examination using

TABLE 2. Prudent Recommendations for Physician and Institutional Conduct to Avoid Medical-Legal Encounters in the Evaluation of U.S. High School and College Competitive Athletes

Preparticipation Screening
• Comply with the customary preparticipation screening practice by collecting a comprehensive personal and family medical history and conducting a physical examination in accordance with specific American Heart Association recommendations. • Complete the screening examination and diagnostic assessment before signing the official medical clearance form or allowing formal training and competition to commence, thereby maintaining control over the medical process. • Recognize that when screening raises a suspicion of cardiovascular disease, standard practice requires a specialty consultation with noninvasive testing. • Perform preparticipation screening of college athletes in on-campus healthcare centers, when feasible. • Recognize that the precise patient–physician relationship during standard athlete preparticipation screening is unresolved in legal terms. • When actively engaged in preparticipation screening, attempt to prospectively formulate the scope of their relationship with the patient-athlete to limit risk for medical malpractice, with the aid of legal counsel.
Eligibility/Disqualification Decisions
• Withdraw an athlete from training and competition when the possibility of heart disease surfaces and a specialty consultation with testing is being pursued. • Rely on 2005 Bethesda Conference guidelines when determining whether a detected cardiovascular abnormality justifies temporary or permanent withdrawal from certain sports to reduce the risk of sudden death. • Limit disqualification decisions for cardiovascular disease to athletes in whom the diagnosis is highly probable or definitive. • Be aware of competing interests in volatile situations surrounding eligibility/disqualification decisions, which may insidiously impair a physician's medical judgment. • Resist extrinsic pressures to retain athletic eligibility from the athlete, family members, coaching staff, administrators, alumni, and the public, which may impact the decision-making medical process. • Avoid publicly announcing a medical diagnosis and recommendation in high-profile athletes. • Recognize that disqualification decisions made by team physicians for college sports may be paramount as long as those judgments are consistent with good medical practice to avoid exposing the athlete to unacceptable risks during competition. • Proceed with extreme caution when recommending treatment options for active athletes with established cardiac disease, particularly when alteration of that treatment could reduce its efficacy • Be aware that examining physicians who are not employees of a team or university (and are not a team physician) may be sued for breach of confidentiality should they disclose without authorization medical information about an athlete to the coach, team management, trainer, athletic director, or educational institution

(table continues)

TABLE 2. Prudent Recommendations for Physician and Institutional Conduct to Avoid Medical-Legal Encounters in the Evaluation of U.S. High School and College Competitive Athletes *(continued)*

Eligibility/Disqualification Decisions
• Recognize that signed waivers do not immunize physicians and institutions from liability, and such agreements are generally unenforceable.
• Understand that acting appropriately to disqualify an athlete with cardiovascular disease does not necessarily protect physicians against a lawsuit.
• Recognize that the medical-legal guidelines concerning cardiovascular disease in athletes largely concern high school and college participants and that there is little legal framework for preparticipation screening and disqualification criteria in professional athletes.

a form provided by his institution. A physician assistant noted a heart murmur and two prior syncopal episodes and referred the athlete for echocardiography, which led to a diagnosis of HCM. Unfortunately, the sports authorization clearance form was signed before echocardiography was performed.

Six weeks later, after playing basketball, the athlete died suddenly. The treating physician testified that after the results of the echocardiogram were known, the athlete was notified to withdraw from competitive basketball, but refused to follow this recommendation. Prudent adherence to screening guidelines, taking into account diagnostic findings before providing official medical clearance, would have allowed the physician to control the evaluation process.

In *Ivey v Providence Hospital*, the estate of a student-athlete who died from status asthmaticus after football practice sued Catholic University and a physician for negligence in failing to conduct a proper examination. The estate argued that the physician (unassociated with the university) failed to satisfactorily evaluate the potential consequences of vigorous exercise on his medically uncontrolled pulmonary condition and cardiovascular system. Parties prior to judicial resolution settled the case.

In this case, it would appear that the physician performing the screening examination did not adequately adhere to customary American Heart Association guidelines and satisfactorily evaluate the athlete's fitness to withstand the stress of intercollegiate sports, thereby creating potential liability. Furthermore, it is possible to view Catholic University as negligent for abdicating responsibility for providing a screening process consistent with good medical practice.

By requiring the athletes themselves to seek out and obtain medical clearance outside the college, the process became non-uniform and substandard as well as a circumstance in which obstacles were created for economically compromised student-athletes.

Malpractice liability may arise by improper use of diagnostic tests that would likely disclose a latent cardiac condition during screening. In *Gardner v Holifield*, the mother of a college basketball player alleged that a cardiologist who examined her son as part of preparticipation screening in the student health center misinterpreted the echocardiograms and failed to identify aortic root dilatation, which is a risk factor associated with Marfan syndrome.

The athlete was not withdrawn from basketball and died of aortic dissection six months later. Resolution of the negligence claim was not reached because the court ruled that the health center's physician was protected from liability for negligent medical care by Florida law (under sovereign immunity) afforded employees of public educational institutions.

However, without such unique legal immunity the judgment could well have been physician negligence. In our opinion, the most prudent action would have been for the physician to recommend withdrawal from sports until a comprehensive medical evaluation was completed, and arrange for expert consultation to resolve diagnosis, risks, and treatment options if questions persist.

A lawsuit against a high school football coach, an athletic director, and the school district, *Ramirez v Muroc Joint United School District et al*, also underscores the importance of proper preparticipation medical evaluations. The student-athlete was obese and deconditioned and had no prior experience in competitive sports. He had an abnormal electrocardiogram and a heart murmur that had been known since childhood.

However, the required preparticipation examination was deferred and on the second day of practice he collapsed; the autopsy showed evidence of HCM. It is a reasonable expectation that preparticipation screening before formal athletic participation for this individual would have led to a diagnosis of HCM and disqualification from sports.

Two lawsuits cited with respect to screening involve individual athletes assessed largely in office practice settings with noninvasive testing. This represents a relationship in which physicians have a clear duty of care and primary medical obligation to act in the patient-athlete's best interest.

In contrast, mass population-based preparticipation screening involves a much more limited patient-physician relationship (usually confined to performing a personal and family history and physical examination) in which typically a single physician evaluates a large number of athletes during a short period, often under suboptimal conditions. This circumstance could leave the physicians at uncertain risk for liability when an untimely death due to cardiovascular disease occurs in an athlete previously cleared for competitive sports.

While at present there is insufficient legal precedent directed at the failure to diagnose potentially lethal abnormalities in a large population screening, physicians can try to formulate the scope of their relationship with the patient-athlete in such a way as to limit their liability. Hypothetically, this would require prospectively involving the institution or school district and legal counsel in the development of a proper consent form that addresses the limited scope of the physician's relationship with the patient-athlete.

Concern frequently arises among primary care non-specialists (or non-physician healthcare professionals), who predominantly perform screening of high school athletes, regarding the liability risks associated with such medical evaluations.

Major considerations include (1) difficulty in differentiating innocent from pathological heart murmurs, (2) reliably raising clinical suspicion of potentially lethal cardiovascular lesions that may fall beyond the screening clinician's legitimate expertise, and (3) the dilemma of discerning which patient-athletes are most deserving of expensive noninvasive tests. While there may be no easy answers to these questions, it is clear (as in *Izidor v Knight*) that the recommendation of withdrawal from competition is mandatory when the possibility of heart disease has been raised and a specialty consultation has been pursued.

Alternative strategies, such as volunteer community-based initiatives, have emerged for large-scale screening of high school athletes with collection of a limited personal and family history and a physical examination combined with portable echocardiography to identify cardiac disease (particularly HCM).

Despite benevolent intentions and the potential benefit of such nonprofit initiatives, it would appear that these screening approaches do not fall within the usual scope of the patient-physician relationship, creating uncertain areas of liability.

In professional sports, physicians, often with noninvasive testing, customarily perform preparticipation screening and is generally more comprehensive than the screenings performed in high schools and colleges. However, at present, there is no judicial precedent related to the screening of professional athletes. Professional team physicians are immune from claims of negligence under Worker's Compensation statutes unless intent to harm can be proven.

FAILURE TO DISQUALIFY FROM SPORTS

Identification of cardiovascular abnormalities in athletes often leads to medical-legal controversies regarding eligibility/disqualification decisions. Such a medical decision-making process should be generally conservative and in accord with available guidelines, and should avoid disqualification of athletes without probable or definitive evidence of disease.

National high school and college organizations have not formulated independent standards for excluding participants with heart disease. However, over the past 20 years, the American College of Cardiology's Bethesda Conference expert consensus panels have advanced eligibility and disqualification recommendations for competitive athletes with established cardiovascular abnormalities. The recently updated guidelines[8] from the Bethesda Conference will likely be accepted by physicians and the legal community as the most contemporary consensus in this area. Judicial precedent now provides a role for the Bethesda Conference in resolving legal disputes related to athlete participation. Such national association guidelines have generally been recognized by the courts as substantiation of good medical practice, although not conclusive evidence of the standard of care.

There have been several lawsuits alleging failure to diagnose, treat appropriately, and/or disqualify athletes from competitive sports, thereby providing insights into the potential pitfalls inherent in these medical decisions. In *Gathers v Loyola-Marymount University*, it was alleged that the sudden death of an elite college basketball player (due to inflammatory cardiomyopathy) was caused by negligent reduction of cardioactive medication (i.e., a β-blocker) administered for ventricular tachyarrhythmias to sub-therapeutic doses as a means of continuing and advancing his athletic career.

At that time, Hank Gathers was among the best college players in the country and likely to become a high professional draft selection. Shortly thereafter, he died suddenly during a nationally televised basketball game. Gathers' heirs filed a $32.5-million lawsuit against his physician and the university alleging negligent interference with Gathers' medical care for cardiovascular disease and failure to remove him from college basketball in concert with Bethesda Conference recommendations.

Although the Gathers case was settled prior to judicial resolution, it is likely that a court would have regarded this scenario as malpractice by virtue of a breach of the customary patient-physician relationship and failure to comply with expert consensus recommendations. This case underscores several useful principles: (1) it is appropriate to temporarily disqualify trained athletes with certain cardiovascular abnormalities (e.g., myocarditis) to assess reversibility; (2) be aware of competing interests and extrinsic pressures in volatile situations, which may insidiously impair a physician's medical judgment; and (3) avoid altering treatment strategies to enhance performance. A similar situation arose in *Lillard v State of Oregon*, in which a college basketball player died of a massive stroke after his anticoagulant medication was reduced to a nontherapeutic dosage to enable his athletic career to continue.

Another high-visibility lawsuit involved professional basketball player Reggie Lewis, who fainted during a game. He underwent extensive testing and a panel of cardiologists diagnosed a life-threatening cardiac condition. However, Lewis left the hospital against medical advice and was diagnosed with a benign fainting disorder at a referral center, possibly allowing him to extend his basketball career. He collapsed and died while participating in an informal basketball workout 11 weeks later. The autopsy revealed healed myocarditis (possibly due to adenovirus).

Lewis' widow brought suit against several physicians alleging failure to properly diagnose the heart condition that led to his death. The first trial ended in a hung jury and a second trial ended with a jury decision against negligence. *Harris-Lewis v Mudge* suggests that physicians should proceed cautiously when confronted with athletes who seek medical clearance by soliciting multiple opinions in an effort to influence the final recommendation (i.e., "shopping"). Also evident was the powerful resistance to disqualification on the part of some athletes, particularly in professional sports. This strong desire to remain competitive may exist despite knowledge of a life-threatening condition.

At present, there is no judicial precedent and little to guide disqualification decisions specifically in professional athletes. Furthermore, professional athletes differ from others by virtue of usually being adults (aged ≥21 years), employees of their teams, and involved in sports as a vocation potentially with substantial economic benefit. These factors potentially alter the medical-legal relationship with respect to eligibility when cardiac disease is present.

RESULTING FROM DISQUALIFICATION FROM SPORTS.

Paradoxically, other lawsuits have been brought because physicians restricted individual athletes with heart disease. A unique lawsuit was brought by college basketball player alleging physician negligence for withholding medical clearance to play because of a life-threatening heart condition (i.e., HCM).

In *Penny v Sands*, the plaintiff claimed economic harm to his anticipated professional career by virtue of forced exclusion from intercollegiate basketball. The defendant-cardiologist who diagnosed Penny with HCM recommended against continuing in competitive sports, but Penny ultimately obtained medical clearance from two cardiologists in the United Kingdom. He subsequently collapsed and died while playing in a professional basketball game in England. Although the malpractice suit was voluntarily dismissed after his death, it is unlikely that a court would have awarded Penny's survivors compensation for economic loss after team officials accepted a physician's prudent recommendation that an athlete with established cardiac disease should be disqualified from competitive sports to reduce the risk of sudden death.

Awareness of *Penny v Sands* has periodically raised anxiety and confusion among clinicians by exposing the reality that no practitioner is immune from legal action, as well as conveying a chilling effect to some athlete-physician interactions.

The Americans with Disabilities Act and the Rehabilitation Act were designed to provide disabled people with the opportunity to participate in physical activities that they have the capabilities to perform. The scope of the Americans with Disabilities Act is broad. The Act covers entities that do not receive federal funding, including professional sports teams.

These acts require careful balancing of an impaired athlete's right to participate in sports within his/her physical abilities, physician evaluation of medical risks, and the interest of teams or educational institutions in conducting safe athletic programs. Elements of a cause of action are if the plaintiff (1) has a medical disability that substantially limits a major life activity; (2) is otherwise qualified to participate in competitive sports; and (3) is excluded solely because of discrimination based on a medical disability. Colleges or universities are obligated to abide by these statutes in their relationship with student-athletes, who have used these acts to resist disqualification from competitive sports.

In *Larkin v Archdiocese of Cincinnati*, a federal court held that a high school could exclude an athlete with HCM from its athletic program because students do not have a compelling right to participate in extracurricular activities such as sports without medical clearance. Indeed, Larkin failed to satisfy an Ohio high school athletic association bylaw because cardiologists had judged him to be at an unacceptable risk of sudden death due to heart disease. The court held that the school's medical decision did not violate the Rehabilitation Act, and Larkin was not reinstated into the football program.

In this case, the athlete and his family were willing to waive future claims after complete disclosure of the medical risks of sports competition.

However, the validity and power of such waivers (exculpatory agreements) is unsettled. Physicians and institutions must recognize that a signed waiver does not necessarily provide immunity from liability in the event of an athlete's death. Courts may view these waivers as unenforceable and a violation of public policy for high school and college athletes. Physicians and institutions should seek expert legal advice when confronted by such issues.

In *Knapp v Northwestern University*, a student-athlete who survived a cardiac arrest due to unsuspected cardiovascular disease used the Rehabilitation Act to gain entry into Northwestern's intercollegiate basketball program. As a high school senior he collapsed with ventricular fibrillation during a basketball game, was resuscitated, and received an implantable defibrillator for sudden death prevention. Upon matriculation to Northwestern, the team physician declared Knapp ineligible for the basketball team based on the patient-athlete's medical history, consultation with other cardiology experts, and Bethesda Conference consensus guidelines, concluding that he would be exposed to unacceptable risks during competitive sports.

Knapp sued Northwestern in federal court for violating the Rehabilitation Act, alleging discrimination based on his physical impairment (i.e., the defibrillator). The U.S. District Court judge granted an injunction permitting Knapp full access to the basketball team, but an appellate court reversed that decision, in effect banning Knapp from the team.

The appellate court held that Northwestern had a legal right to establish safe physical qualification standards for its intercollegiate athletes and that sports eligibility is not an inalienable, libertarian right of the athlete. Furthermore, playing college basketball was judged not to be a major life activity.

Such medical decisions regarding eligibility are the proper domain of team physicians and schools as long as the process is based on reliable scientific evidence and expert consensus guidelines (i.e. , Bethesda Conference). Therefore, *Knapp v Northwestern* establishes the legal precedent that college athletes may be medically disqualified from competitive sports to avoid enhanced risk of serious injury or death that cannot otherwise be abolished by the use of medications, long-term monitoring, or the use of protective equipment. Deviations from expert consensus recommendations, which are nevertheless consistent with good medical practice, do not necessarily create physician liability, nor rigidly restrict individual clinical judgment.

Alternatively, compliance with Bethesda Conference recommendations may carry substantial weight and form the basis for a successful defense against allegations of negligence and resolution of future eligibility disputes. In both the *Larkin* and *Knapp* cases the plaintiffs attempted to extend application of the Rehabilitation Act beyond its initial intent, but failed because they would have placed themselves at enhanced risk for serious injury or death.

CONCLUSION

The law requires physicians to use customary skill and care consistent with good medical practice in evaluating an athlete's fitness to participate in sports. The physician's duty is to protect the patient-athlete's well-being while avoiding unnecessary exclusion from competition. The developing medical-legal construct holds that a high school or college may prudently withhold access to competitive sports programs from students with a cardiovascular abnormality to prevent exposure to medically unacceptable risks.

Physicians involved with eligibility decisions in athletes with cardiovascular disease and preparticipation screening may assume some risk of liability. Reducing this liability risk requires an understanding of the evolving judicial framework and compliance with the standard of care and available guidelines, including the American Heart Association's recommendations regarding preparticipation screening and the American College of Cardiology's Bethesda Conference disqualification recommendations.

CHAPTER 33

Preparticipation Cardiovascular Screening of Student-Athletes with Echocardiography: Ethical, Clinical, Economic, and Legal Considerations

The prevention of athletic field, cardiac sudden death is a social imperative. The loss of vibrant and apparently healthy young people is devastating to families and communities. The best approach to screening for the prevention of sudden cardiac death in athletes is a passionately debated topic.

At the center of that debate is the use of echocardiography as a screening tool. When negotiating this issue, it is important to understand both sides of the argument and attempt to meet in the middle with the student-athlete as the winner. This chapter argues in favor of preparticipation, echocardiographic screening after considering ethical, clinical, economic, and legal issues.

Sudden cardiac death (SCD) in a competitive athlete is a tragic event. The sudden death of an athlete shocks the local community. The tragic deaths of many young athletes has led to a social imperative to implement effective means of predicting and preventing sudden death in competitive athletes.

The design and implementation of a proven screening solution remains elusive. To date, large-scale preparticipation screening has been inadequate because it has focused on disease diagnosis and risk factor associations, not on pathophysiologic effectors known to quantify a cardiovascular "risk state." The problem is that disease diagnosis does not quantify risk, and statistical associations do not adequately define cause. Demonstrating a "cause and effect" relationship proves causality.

This chapter explores the ethical, clinical, economic, and legal controversies surrounding echocardiographic screening prior to participation in competitive sport to prevent SCD. These issues are debated by experts on both sides of the issue of whether echocardiographic preparticipation screening has value when viewed from a societal perspective weighing ethical, clinical, economic, and legal considerations.

This exploration will include the ethics of a physician's fiduciary responsibility to the student-athlete, how athletic training prompts remodeling of the anatomy and physiology of the heart to accommodate a state of enhanced cardiovascular performance, how the distinction between adaptive and maladaptive remodeling of the heart requires an understanding of temporally changing myocyte function, how cardiovascular physiologic remodeling associated with athleticism may mimic the features of genetically acquired heart disease, how echocardiography is a cost effective, validated imaging modality that is widely available and capable of simultaneously quantifying variable anatomic and physiologic features of athletes, and how Doppler echocardiography redefines the understanding of normal cardiac remodeling from pre-emergent and overt heart disease.

Additionally, we compare the cost of screening to the dollar value of a statistical life (VSL) saved, and the complex liability issues related to cardiovascular preparticipation screening of student-athletes.

ETHICAL CONSIDERATIONS

Healthy competitive athletes may harbor unsuspected cardiovascular disease with potential to cause SCD. This fact raises the question of physician responsibility in preparticipation screening. The physician–patient (student-athlete) relationship is a member of a special class of legal relationships called *fiduciary relationships*. Through the creation of fiduciary duties, the law recognizes that there are relationships in which the parties inherently have unequal power.

The physician–patient relationship has its foundation on the theory that the physician is learned, skilled, and experienced in those subjects in which the student-athlete has limited insight, such as health. Thus, the student-athlete must place confidence in the professional advice of the physician. The essence of the fiduciary relationship is that the patient's interests must be paramount.

Physicians are familiar with fiduciary duties associated with informed consent to medical treatment. The fiduciary duty extends to all aspects of the physician–patient relationship. Understanding the factors that make the physician–patient relationship a fiduciary one will help physicians recognize potential violations.

The modern athlete is unique to the general population. In competition the athlete tests the cardiovascular system to the limit. The extremes of exertion occur in endurance and strength athletes, exposing the abnormal cardiovascular system to potential for adverse health events and SCD.

Strong ethical argument exists for implementing the highest quality-screening program for student-athletes: the occurrence of athletic SCD during competition is ethically unacceptable if viable approaches to prevent these tragic deaths exist. Reasonable preventive measures to detect previously unrecognized arrhythmias, congenital, or acquired heart disease that may affect the health and longevity of the student-athlete have societal value.

The detection of autosomal-dominant conditions such as hypertrophic cardiomyopathy (HCM), Marfan syndrome, Long QT, and arrhythmogenic right ventricular cardiomyopathy (ARVD) may prevent adverse outcomes in the student-athlete and lead to evaluation of siblings and offspring who have a 50% chance of being affected. The physician's fiduciary responsibility to the student-athlete and a societal imperative to prevent athletic field sudden death ethically mandate the highest level of preparticipation screening.

CARDIAC REMODELING

The athletic heart's structural and functional changes are critical to understand when assessing student-athlete risk during intense competition.

The distinction between adaptive and maladaptive cardiac remodeling is the fundamental challenge in determining individualized risk in athletes.

Classically, an athletic heart is associated with cardiac chamber enlargement, increased left ventricular (LV) mass, and modest root enlargement to accommodate increased physiologic demands. Adaptive morphology and physiology vary considerably among athletes and are affected by each individual athlete's form and intensity of exercise. Cardiovascular remodeling is nonlinear, meaning that any particular feature can fluctuate between normal and abnormal morphology and physiology during the remodeling process. Athletic heart exhibits variable physiologic states.

Intense physical exercise enhances cardiac output 6–8-fold and increases pulmonary oxygen uptake. An athlete's heart rate can vary from <40 beats/minute at rest to >220 beats/minute at peak exertion. The dynamic changes in LV relaxation account for the increased stroke volume and cardiac output at extreme heart rates.

The body's cardiovascular network is a fine-tuned feedback system. The contiguous architecture of the cardiovascular system, including the atria, ventricles and aorta, undergoes continuous remodeling that reflects adaptive and maladaptive changes in both athletic remodeling and disease states.

A disease within a contiguous system, such as hypertension, is referred to as a "continuity disease." Hypertension causes abnormal aortic pressure with negative feedback to the ventricles and subsequently the atria, resulting in remodeling of the adjacent cardiac chambers of the contiguous cardiovascular system.

The distinction between adaptive and maladaptive remodeling requires an understanding of the evolving myocyte changes temporally. The athlete's heart begins with 'hyper-normal' diastolic function and continues to be supernormal to normal while training, whereas the diseased heart evolves along a cascade from early abnormal myocyte dysfunction to myocardial dysfunction. This distinction is highlighted when comparing athletic heart and hypertrophic cardiomyopathy.

In disease states, there is an early transition from normal to abnormal myocyte function, followed by longitudinal myocyte dysfunction manifest as a reduction in early diastolic mitral annular tissue velocity (e'), followed by diastolic strain, strain rate, and twist dysfunction and, ultimately, diminished global systolic strain rate indicating fibrosis and cell death.

Disease processes are rarely a consequence of an abnormality in a single effector. Instead disease is a reflection of multi-feature pathobiology process that interact to yield an emergent disease. The disease process is discernible only by appreciating the conjoined effects of multiple, related components. A cardiovascular system remodels in a similar manner from normal athletic activity and disease related stressors. This explains why a normal athlete can have morphological features that are virtually identical to those in an unrelated disease process. The solution to distinguish normal from abnormal pathophysiologic profiles lies in the tests designed to test causality.

Echocardiography is the most logical means of defining and quantifying physiology and morphology in a single examination. Combining cardiac morphology and physiology is recommended as the most definitive way to classify cardiovascular risk in most athletes.

Echo/Doppler screening is a strategy used in a select population of healthy, asymptomatic individuals to identify pre-emergent disease. Matching pre-emergent disease (without phenotypic expression) "associated" with sudden death through diastolic parameters is the key to differentiating normal from abnormal pathophysiology.

These data are focused on two principal objectives: detecting an imminent life-threatening state at a time when the opportunity for prevention is optimal, and defining the magnitude of imminent risk enlightening physician decision-making and management.

SPECIFIC ECHOCARDIOGRAPHIC FEATURES OF ATHLETIC HEART

The Left Ventricle

The athletic heart typically has increased chamber dimensions and increased LV wall thickness. These findings often mimic the echocardiographic features of diseases affecting the left ventricle.

The unique remodeling of endurance athletes results in eccentric hypertrophy, in which there is increased wall thickness and chamber dilation. Strength-trained athletes display thickening of the LV wall with mild LV dilation, resulting in concentric hypertrophy. Combination athletes typically display a phenotype with overlapping features of endurance and strength-trained athletes. LV eccentric and concentric hypertrophy, without physiologic classification, can be inappropriately misinterpreted as HCM.

Increased LV wall thickness results from chamber pressure, volume overload, or both. The true phenotypic expression is often a combination of pressure and volume overload of the myocardium. Concentric remodeling increases the relative wall thickness without an increase in LV mass. The remodeling of the left ventricle is more eccentric in endurance athletes, but athletes often maintain balanced hypertrophy.

Extreme LV remodeling occurring in some ultra-elite athletes has resulted in LV cavity end diastolic dimensions >60 mm. This magnitude of enlargement is identified in pathologic forms of dilated cardiomyopathy. The severe remodeling may not reverse in all elite athletes with deconditioning; chamber enlargement persists in 20% of retired elite athletes after five years.

LV Diastolic Function

LV diastolic function must be integrated with LV systolic function to comprehensively appraise the athletic heart. Diastolic dysfunction typically precedes systolic dysfunction. Athletic hearts do not accrue diastolic or systolic dysfunction. Trained athletes have enhanced early diastolic LV filling, depicted by increased E-wave velocity and near absence of the A wave, in addition to supernormal medial annular tissue Doppler velocities.

Cardiac diastolic function is a critical factor in distinguishing adaptive remodeling from disease remodeling. This unique ability of diastolic functional parameters to distinguish between health and disease was eloquently shown by abnormal results on tissue Doppler echocardiography in gene mutation positive patients with HCM independent of phenotypic expression.

LV Systolic Function

LV systolic function is consistently in the normal range among highly trained athletes. Elite cyclists may have LV ejection fractions lower than normal. Our experience with highly conditioned, professional basketball players commonly reveals global LV ejection fractions ranging from 45% to 50%, but supernormal tissue Doppler Sm and normal systolic strain and strain rate measurements.

Systolic strain and strain rate imaging of the left ventricle has been used to distinguish maladaptive from physiologic remodeling of the left ventricle. The absence of reductions in global systolic longitudinal strain and strain rate supports the use of strain rate imaging to assess the physiologic increase in wall thickness associated with athletic training.

The effect of endurance training on deformation mechanics, torsion, and the untwisting rate as components of exercise-induced cardiac remodeling in young athletes needs further investigation. LV systolic torsion and peak early diastolic untwisting rate may be important components of exercise-induced cardiac remodeling.

Endurance-trained athletes develop biventricular dilation with enhanced diastolic function, whereas strength-trained athletes develop concentric increases in LV wall thickness with diminished diastolic function. Speckle-tracking echocardiography measures LV systolic and diastolic functions in individuals with structural alterations of the heart from intense physical training. LV untwisting increased with exercise more than LV lengthening or expansion. An exercise-induced increase in LV untwisting rate may enhance early LV diastolic suction, facilitating early LV filling without an increase in left atrial pressure. Patients with HCM have reductions in longitudinal strain and in the untwisting rate in diastole.

The Right Ventricle

Endurance-trained athletes have enlarged RV cavities and increased RV wall thickness compared with sedentary controls. RV enlargement parallels LV enlargement in intensely trained athletes. The RV morphologic features in strength-trained athletes do not significantly vary from those in sedentary controls. The morphologic and functional parameters that appear to distinguish endurance- and strength- trained athletes are RV inflow tract diameter, RV end diastolic area, and tricuspid inflow velocity deceleration time. As expected, in systems that vacillate between normal and abnormal, RV remodeling is heterogeneous across gender, race, and sports discipline.

RV function may be below normal at rest in highly trained athletes, but there is robust RV functional reserve after provocation with exercise, suggesting that the increased RV and right atrial sizes reflect physiologic remodeling rather than maladaptive changes. Thus, RV contractility, strain, and strain rate at rest do not accurately reflect RV function in highly trained athletes, and exercise testing may be essential to assess RV function.

Although differences in RV geometric remodeling is observed in endurance- and strength-trained athletes, few reproducible differences in RV cavity deformation or relaxation exist, suggesting that despite remodeling in athletes, RV systolic and diastolic function remains normal.

The Aorta

The remodeling of the aortic root in highly trained athletes is commonly documented. Increased demand resulting in increased stroke volume often results in a larger aortic conduit. Endurance activity results in high-volume aortic flow with modest systolic blood pressure elevation, and strength training results in normal volume aortic flow with profound elevation of systolic blood pressure.

There is evidence supporting greater aortic root diameter among strength-trained athletes and refuting data showing the largest aortic dimensions in endurance-trained athletes.[57, 58] The best available measurement in the literature on aortic morphology takes into account aortic dimension and body surface area.

The Atria

A remodeled left atrium is normal in the athletic population. Intense athletic training results in increased stroke volume, with subsequent remodeling of all cardiac chambers, including the left and right atria. Left atrial indexed volumes are significantly higher in athletes compared with healthy controls. Doppler tissue imaging is a useful tool to identify improved myocardial diastolic properties in athletes, and speckle-tracking echocardiography elucidates the role of the left atrium in athletic heart remodeling. Left atrial strain and strain rate by two-dimensional speckle tracking are indices of left atrial function that facilitate distinction of physiologic and pathologic remodeling. Left atrial myocardial deformation is significantly impaired in patients with HCM compared with athletes and healthy controls.

SPECIFIC FEATURES OF ACQUIRED HEART DISEASE

Causes of Sudden Cardiac Death

Sudden cardiac death is often due to a quiescent pathophysiologic "trigger" that can become malignant if the "trigger" is disturbed. There are three principal types of triggers: cardiomyopathies, channelopathies, and structural heart disease. The nature of individual and overlapping triggers varies not only by an underlying disease state, but also by pathophysiologic state, genetic determinants, and environmental factors.

People with cardiomyopathies commonly die an arrhythmia death; people with channelopathies may experience arrhythmia death; and people with structural diseases may experience cardiac dysfunction and arrhythmia deaths.

The disease states of sudden cardiac death promote blunted micro- and macro-vascular ischemia and replacement fibrosis, which cause electrical heterogeneity, and induced arrhythmias. The state of a "trigger" can be measured as an aggregate of multiple related features. In athletes a quiescent "trigger" can suddenly transition into a malignant state due to the physiologic stress of exercise. In vulnerable athletes exercise changes LV compliance, rather than LV systolic function. The distinction between a normal and abnormal "trigger" lies in the aggregated pathophysiologic profile of small groups of highly related features of diastolic function (E, A, E/A, e', E/e').

Echocardiographic Cardiac Morphologies Associated with SCD

Cardiomyopathies

Screening for cardiomyopathies is not designed to define a specific disease, but should be focused on the imminent risk of sudden death.

Normal CV function, and alternatively risk, can be effectively and reproducibly measured as a profile of small groups of highly related variables of diastolic function.

This echocardiographic approach has been validated to have a very low incidence of false positive and false negative interpretations. Outliers within a disease module can be appropriately classified. In most circumstances only two to four aggregated diastolic features (e', E/e' ratio, DT, E/A ratio) will suffice to differentiate normal and abnormal.

Asymptomatic diastolic myocyte dysfunction followed by systolic myocyte dysfunction and microvascular ischemia emerge early in the pathophysiologic continuum, while structural (fibrosis) and electrical remodeling (arrhythmogenesis) and symptoms occur later.

The prognostic importance of asymptomatic pre-emergent pathophysiology has only recently been realized. Asymptomatic athletes commonly engage in activities that can accentuate pre-emergent pathophysiology and be acutely detrimental to myocardial function. For screening purposes "cardiomyopathy" can theoretically describe almost any disease affecting the heart in which the heart muscle is structurally abnormal.

Screening should be focused on prognostication of risk, and not detection or characterization of a disease type. The exam requires the acquisition of a small number of data, which define the presence and intensity of emergent cardiac dysfunction. Disease risk is always defined by more than one datum feature.

Hypertrophic cardiomyopathy (HCM) is an exemplary candidate for pathophysiologic screening. HCM rarely has any premonitory symptoms, even under exertion, ECG has a high rate of false positives, ejection fraction (EF) is rarely abnormal, and anatomic remodeling is variable, and typically occurs late in the pathophysiologic cascade. However, associated diastolic dysfunction can be detected and measured early in the HCM cascade, detecting pre-clinical HCM risk.

A screening exam is designed to affirm the existence of abnormal physiologic profile and identify individuals with an abnormal risk profile, independent of morphology. The algebraic summation of a small aggregate of related data (E/A, DT, e', E/e') defines causality, which mirrors the status of an individual's risk state in both a positive and negative direction during serial screening, management, and follow-up. Each cardiomyopathy disease (hypertrophic, restrictive, dilated, ischemic, hypertensive, arrhythmogenic right ventricular, myocarditis, left ventricular non-compaction) has validated pathophysiologic features that can confirm a risk state. Averaged features have a very low incidence of false positives and false negatives results.

Hypertensive Heart Disease

The essential pathophysiologic data used to depict the risk of hypertensive heart disease and "pseudo-HCM" are identical to those of general *cardiomyopathies*. Screening blood pressure and increased LV wall thickness serve only as benchmarks that require physiologic classification as normal compensatory physiology versus emergent heart disease. The overlapping features of normal myocardial remodeling can mimic the features of HCM, hypertensive heart disease, and infiltrative diseases. The goal of screening is to affirm normal and rule out abnormal disease related remodeling.

Ischemic Heart Disease

Although considerable attention is focused on young athletes, the risk of sudden death from coronary artery disease (CAD) is much greater among sports participants > 35 years and is greatest in the fifth decade. The incidence of fatal CAD is reported to be 0.7 per 100,000 people-years for athletes <35 years of age, and 13.7 per 100,000 persons-years for those ≥35 years of age. Ischemic risk represents the cumulative impact of a cascade of pathophysiologic events.

The focus on the late stage features of CAD (ECG abnormalities, angina, wall motion abnormality and infarction) needs to be redirected to the more fundamental underlying pathophysiologic factors (subclinical diastolic and systolic dysfunction) that emerge earlier in the pathophysiologic cascade.

The objective of screening asymptomatic athletes is to disclose imminent pathophysiologic risk (occurrence of an event within 1 year, and not the presence of long-term risk (Framingham Score 10 year risk profile).

Channelopathies

Channelopathies are considered unique and are variably classified as a primary electrical disease. Various forms of electrical cardiomyopathy affect about 1 in 1000 people. Channelopathies are the assumed culprits in cases of undefined sudden death. Interestingly, in recent research subclinical Doppler pathophysiologic changes were identified in nearly 20% of Long QT syndrome patients. These findings prompt speculation that electrical dysfunction (abnormal cardiac repolarization and rhythm) may precipitate macroscopic structural and functional changes detected through diastolic parameters.

Pulmonary Hypertension

Pulmonary artery pressure (PAP) can be estimated in nearly 100% of patients using any one of three simple techniques:

- (1) Systolic *PAP* using the Tricuspid Regurgitant Velocity (TRv) (Normal TRv≤2.8 m/s is considered a reasonable cutoff to define elevated *PAP* in healthy persons;
- (2) Normal *Diastolic PAP* using the end-diastolic Pulmonary Regurgitant Velocity (PRv); (PRv <1.1 m/s is correlated with normal pulmonary pressure; and
- (3) Normal mean PAP using pulmonary flow acceleration time (AcT) >100 ms equates a *mean PAP* < 20-39 mmHg and AcT <75 ms equates to a mean PAP ≥40 mmHg.

Coarctation of the Aorta

Coarctation of the aorta is rare. It should be excluded in every patient with BAV. BAV can be detected and quantified by a simple echo/Doppler signal in the abdominal aorta. In the presence of coarctation the overall aortic velocity is blunted, systolic upstroke is delayed and there is continuous forward flow consistent with a diastolic and systolic gradient and/or collateral flow. Early diastolic reversal of flow is associated with a widely patent aortic arch. Elastic recoil of the ascending aorta causes the low velocity, late-diastolic forward flow seen after the early diastolic reversal.

Anomalous Coronary Artery

An essential component of every athletic screening examination is the visualization of the origin of the proximal coronary arteries, which can be accomplished with transthoracic echocardiography in 70 to over 95% of young athletes. Although the anomalous origin and course of the left or right coronary artery has been reported to be exceedingly rare in young athletes, others have reported that coronary artery anomalies are the second most common association with sudden death in athletes (~17%). The most life-threatening anomaly is left or right coronary artery originating from the contralateral sinus of Valsalva and coursing between the aorta and proximal pulmonary artery.

Aortic Aneurysm

Another component of a screening CV exam is documentation of the anterior-posterior aortic diameter [e.g., leading edge to leading edge, at end-diastole at the level of aortic annulus, sinuses of Valsalva, sinotubular junction, and ascending aorta. An aortic root dimension >40 mm in highly conditioned male athletes and >34 mm in female athletes is uncommon; is unlikely to represent the physiological consequences of exercise training; is most likely an expression of a pathological condition; and mandates size-based surveillance.

There are multiple types of aortic aneurysms, there are three syndromic aortopathies of particular concern in asymptomatic athletes: Marfan syndrome, BAV, and cystic medial necrosis. The presence of any aortic valve regurgitation in a young athlete should alert the examiner to a possible structural abnormality of the aortic valve. The pathophysiology and genetics of these aneurysms are similar and should be recognized as having a life-long enhanced risk of an aortic pathology. Risk of rupture of a non-syndromic aortic aneurysm is expressed as an indexed relative size (i.e., diameter indexed to body surface area).

Valve Disease

Echo/Doppler is a validated approach for evaluating both asymptomatic and symptomatic valvular heart disease. Early echocardiographic screening of valve disease in the general population does not translate into reduced risk of death or cardiovascular events. The objective of preparticipation athletic screening is early detection of imminent risk and not a comprehensive echo anatomic and Doppler hemodynamic exam. A multi-feature diastolic physiologic profile best reflects the magnitude of imminent risk. An athlete with an unremarkable history, normal physiologic profile, and mild anatomic valve disease may be eligible for physician monitored athletic activities.

THE ECONOMICS OF PREPARTICIPATION ECHOCARDIOGRAPHIC SCREENING – IS A COST/BENEFIT ANALYSIS FEASIBLE?

Cost–Benefit Analysis

We must address whether the use of echocardiography, given its potential to identify the majority of causes of SAD, is feasible given the limited resources available for healthcare. The present perception is that screening with echocardiography will yield excessive costs beyond the potential benefits. This is pertinent because we struggle as a society regarding resource allocation. We must compare the cost of screening to the dollar value of a statistical life (VSL) saved.

Cost of Screening

To calculate the cost of a screening echocardiography program in the United States, we assumed universities will buy hand-held echocardiography machines at a cost of roughly $30,000 each, and the cost of evaluation for detected abnormalities will be paid through mandated health insurance required for student-athletes to participate in high school and college sports. There are roughly 400,000 student-athletes at the National Collegiate Athletic Association Division 1, 2, and 3 levels.

- The annual rate of cardiac sudden death is 1:43,000.
- Roughly 10 collegiate sudden athletic deaths occur per year.
- A screening echocardiogram costing $100 per student-athlete would bring the cost of screening to $40 million per year. The screening echocardiogram would include assessment for morphological abnormalities and diastolic physiology.

WHAT IS THE POSITIVE DOLLAR VALUE OF SCREENING?

Methodologies for calculating the VSL or an additional year of statistical life (i.e., value of a statistical life-year [VSLY]) are well substantiated in the literature. Based on these methods, the US Food and Drug

Administration currently uses $7.9 million as its standard/estimated VSL. This number, however, represents the value of a life from birth, rather than from age 18 years (age at time of proposed cardiac screening) to age 78 years (US life expectancy).

To determine a reasonable calculation for VSL through the prevention of SCD, we annualized the US Food and Drug Administration's VSL estimate using a range of discount rates. The discount rates account for the fact that a dollar in the future is worth less than a dollar today; therefore, a dollar's worth of life in the future is worth less than a dollar's worth of life today. Cutler and Richardson reviewed the literature and tested discount rates of zero, 3%, and 6% for VSL calculations, with 3% as the benchmark. At these rates, annualizing $7.9 million over 78 years yields VSLYs of $100,000, $263,000, and $480,000. Using each of these VSLY estimates, one can then calculate the value of each life saved:

$$\textit{Value of Life Saved} = \sum_{t=1}^{T} VSLY/(1+r)^t$$

This assumes a discount rate, r, and saved individual years (T) after the screening. Assuming that screening occurs at age 18 years, T61, and utilizing the discount rates and corresponding VSLY estimates, this calculation yields values of each life saved ranging from $6.1 million to $7.8 million. More specifically, the formula yields a value of $6.1 million assuming a VSLY of $100,000 and a discount rate of zero. It yields a value of $7.3 million assuming a VSLY of $263,000 and a discount rate of 3%. Finally, it yields a value of $7.8 million assuming a VSLY of $480,000 and a discount rate of 6%. Therefore, if screening saves 10 lives, the estimated benefit of screening is $61 million to $78 million. Thus, the cost/ benefit analysis as provided with this prudent and reasonable screening model would favor screening from an economic perspective. The calculus from the lowest common denominator would suggest that screening will benefit society $21 million. This approach of echocardiography screening suggests that universities join forces with the medical community by using their resources to purchase echocardiography machines. This is a reasonable consideration given that athletes are performing for the university, and sports activities add to the overall experience of the entire student body. It is a policy decision that deserves careful scrutiny.

LIABILITY ISSUES SURROUNDING PREPARTICIPATION ECHOCARDIOGRAPHIC SCREENING

Liability Issues

Would a policy recommending echocardiography as a component of preparticipation screening and disqualification expand institutional and physician liability? We know that liability based on negligence requires a physician to act outside of the scope of the standard of care. The utilization of echocardiography in preparticipation screening and disqualification would be within the standard of care and, in fact, would increase the likelihood of detection of the etiologies of SCD and reduce the incidence of SCD through restriction of athletic activity. Thus, the potential liability for missing the diagnosis of a trigger of SCD should necessarily be reduced.

Negligence Law and Duty

Discussion of liability issues invariably begins with the law of negligence. Negligence law provides that there must be a legal duty owed to a student athlete before any discussion of liability can proceed. Courts typically maintain that student athletes have a sufficient programmatic relationship with their educational institution to impose a duty of care on educational institutions and their physicians.

Case Law

Case law suggests that colleges owe all their student-athletes a duty in the scope of their athletic programs to take reasonable precautions against reasonably foreseeable harms. The national trend is to recognize legal duty in the context of programmatic risk.

Although the available case law and statutes limiting the scope of a physician and university's role in preparticipation screening is limited, basic principles of legal responsibility are well established. Physicians must behave in accordance with a professional standard of care that is typically set by customary medical practice. We believe customary medical practice should include preparticipation screening echocardiography.

CONCLUSION

Echocardiographic screening is an emotionally charged debate between experts in the cardiology community. When there is intense negotiation between parties, shared interests are the "elixir of negotiation," the salve that smooths over issues the parties vehemently debate.

The argument for the use of echocardiographic screening prior to athletic participation to prevent SCD is compelling when ethical, clinical, economic and legal issues are carefully considered and meets the shared interest of all involved parties of potentially limiting sudden death on the athletic field.

A paradigm shift of this magnitude will require collaboration amongst educational institution administrators and physicians devoted to screening based upon an in-depth knowledge of adaptive and maladaptive cardiac remodeling.

Reprinted with permission, Paterick, Z.R., Paterick, T.E. Preparticipation Cardiovascular Screening of Student-Athletes with Echocardiography: Ethical, Clinical, Economic, and Legal Considerations. *Curr Cardiol Rep* **21**, 16 (2019). https://doi.org/10.1007/s11886-019-1101-4

www.ingramcontent.com/pod-product-compliance
Lightning Source LLC
LaVergne TN
LVHW052242200926
848481LV00002B/249

* 9 7 8 0 9 8 4 8 3 1 1 3 5 *